COMPARING RELIGIOUS TRADITIONS

Judaism, Christianity, Islam,
Hinduism, and Buddhism on

THE ETHICS OF FAMILY LIFE

What Do We Owe One Another?

Edited by
JACOB NEUSNER
Bard College

With essays by

BRUCE CHILTON
Bard College

BRAD CLOUGH
Bard College

BRIAN K. SMITH
University of California, Riverside

TAMARA SONN
College of William and Mary

WADSWORTH
————————★———————— ™
THOMSON LEARNING

Australia • Canada • Mexico • Singapore • Spain • United Kingdom • United States

Religion Editor: Peter Adams
Assistant Editor: Kara Kindstrom
Editorial Assistant: Mark Andrews
Marketing Manager: Dave Garrison
Print Buyer: Robert King
Permissions Editor: Joohee Lee
Production Service: Matrix Productions

Text Designer: Karen Thomas
Copy Editor: Jan McDearmon
Cover Designer: Bill Stanton
Cover Image: PhotoDisc
Compositor: R&S Book Composition
Cover and Text Printer: Webcom, Limited

Wadsworth/Thomson Learning
10 Davis Drive
Belmont, CA 94002-3098
USA

For more information about our products, contact us:
Thomson Learning Academic
Resource Center
1-800-423-0563
http://www.wadsworth.com

International Headquarters
Thomson Learning
International Division
290 Harbor Drive, 2nd Floor
Stamford, CT 06902-7477
USA

UK/Europe/Middle East/
South Africa
Thomson Learning
Berkshire House
168-173 High Holborn
London WC1V 7AA
United Kingdom

Asia
Thomson Learning
60 Albert Street, #15-01
Albert Complex
Singapore 189969

Canada
Nelson Thomson Learning
1120 Birchmount Road
Toronto, Ontario M1K 5G4
Canada

Library of Congress Cataloging-in-Publication Data
The ethics of family life: what do we owe one another?/edited by Jacob Neusner; with essays by Bruce Chilton . . . [et al.].
    p.   cm.—(Comparing religious traditions)
    ISBN 0-534-53055-9
    1. Religious ethics—Comparative studies. 2. Family—Moral and ethical aspects.
    I. Title: At head of title: Judaism, Christianity, Islam, Hinduism, and Buddhism on the ethics of family life.   II. Neusner, Jacob, [date]   III. Chilton, Bruce.   IV. Series.
BJ1188.E828 2000
291.5′63—dc21   00-040838

This book is printed on acid-free recycled paper.

Contents

‿☙‿

Preface

R eligions not only answer public questions about society, politics, and economics; they also guide individuals in their private lives, as people work
their way through life from birth to death. So to make sense of the world
in which we live, we compare and contrast the choices religions make. To understand the lives people lead, therefore, we study about the religions they pro-
fess and practice together. Here we experiment with what it takes to compare
religions. That is because, in our view, to know only one religion is to understand no religion. Comparison alone affords perspective, a clear picture of the
choices people make and the settings in which they make them. Each religion
forms a coherent whole, the parts of which fit together within a particular rationality. When, as here, we compare the parts of one with the parts of another
religious tradition, we gain perspective on the whole of each of those traditions.
And since we take up what is to all of us a program of familiar human issues—
family, work, and virtue—we deal with what is accessible to us all out of our
life's experiences.

To identify the difficulty of comparing religious traditions, take the social
order first of all. Religions shape economics, politics, and public policy. In economics, the science of the rational disposition of scarce resources, religions variously define what they mean by "scarce resources." Moreover, they form their
own diverse definitions and distinctive conceptions of what we deem "rational,"
as a comparison between Christian and Buddhist philosophy makes clear. But
even where religions concur, the agreement masks difference. Context is everything. Islam and Judaism and Christianity each impose its own prohibition upon

usury. But each draws its own conclusions from that prohibition. When we look closely, we see that the comparison yields mostly contrasts.

So too, in politics each frames a doctrine of how religion relates to the state, that is, to the institutions that legitimately exercise violence. They may concur that the state should realize God's purpose. But they do not form a unified consensus upon the consequences of that conviction. For instance, Hinduism and Buddhism may appear to be in agreement in their uneasiness about the use of force by government, and both dream of a nonviolent state based on moral order. But they do not agree on what these dreams say about actual, less-than-perfect governments.

As to the requirements of the good and the just society formed by the faithful, all three frame a theory of "the mystical body of Christ," or "the Jewish People" (meaning the contemporary continuators of the Israel of which Scripture speaks), or "the ummah" or "community of Islam," a theory rich in implications for the social order. So even where religions appear to resemble one another, they turn out to differ.

The distinctions make a difference not only in intangible ways but to the everyday world, because religion shapes public affairs, not only personal proclivities. We may well form an intense, personal relationship with God. That begins in a private moment of encounter. But commonly, the personal preference spills over into public policy. That is why, when we study about religions, comparing and contrasting their positions on a common program, we deal with facts, not only feelings; culture, not only conscience. In two different traditions originating in India, for example, Hinduism and Buddhism, there is an apparent agreement that the ultimate religious goal consists of freedom or liberation from a world of repeated death and rebirth. But because of different conceptions of the true nature of the self in these two traditions, they have not only conceived of the religious goal differently but have also put forward different religious paths leading to the goal—paths that entail different social, economic, and even political consequences.

Whether religions concur or differ on matters of public policy, how we are to interpret their points of intersection is not always clear. People can say the same thing for different reasons, and they can mean different things by the same statement—and so is the case with religions. For understanding a given chapter in the story a religion tells depends on knowing what came before and what will happen next. Indeed, everything in the end makes sense only in the proper context. Hence, even at points of confluence, how are we to compare and contrast the social, political, and economic conceptions of the great religious traditions, when each body of thought focuses upon distinctive historical experience, a very particular context of public life? Therefore what looks alike—affirmations in common—may upon closer examination prove quite different, and difference may well obscure the meaning of points of concurrence.

That is because the work of comparing religions in their public dimensions involves many complications. When we wish to compare one religion with another, doctrines or practices concerning public life pertain to situations we may find alien or beyond all comprehending. What one religion deems weighty another ignores altogether. Church order preoccupies Christians, but structures that transcend the local circumstance of Judaism do not precipitate equivalent conflict. Judaism precipitates debates on "who is a Jew," or "who, and what, is Israel," meaning, we recall, the holy people of which Scripture speaks. But Catholics do not endlessly debate on who is a Catholic. Religions do not select their issues from a single menu; each frames its system in its own distinctive structure, and a common category formation does not accommodate them all. One may compare it to how they serve dim sum in a Chinese restaurant: different food comes on different carts.

So even if they say the same thing, the shared language does not yield the same consequences. That is why it is difficult for purposes of comparison and contrast to set side by side (to give one example) (1) Christian thinking about Church-state relations with (2) Islamic thinking about the same matter and (3) Judaic doctrines, beginning with the Hebrew Scriptures, about God's stake in holy Israel's public life. Christian doctrines of politics emerge from a long history of Western institutions of church and state and their relationships, and Islamic ones from a quite different history altogether, one of rapid expansion in a remarkably brief period. Judaic doctrines take account of political experiences, such as defeat and political disempowerment, that Islam in its formative age never knew. So if Judaism, Christianity, and Islam concur on valuing peace, as they do, or on assigning to the state responsibilities for the moral ordering of society, as they do, that does not mean they concur on much that matters. Even when religions talk about the same things and come to comparable conclusions, the differences in context make it difficult to find a level plane for the purposes of comparing and contrasting what different traditions say about the same matter. A negative example serves. Buddhist emphasis on monasticism and the rejection of family life prevents us from seeing how much South Asian Buddhists share with Hindus in the ethics of family life.

Given the variables and imponderables that religions draw in their wake, we may wonder whether the work of comparison and contrast in the end demands more than it is worth. Out of despair or sheer incredulity, some may retreat into a latitudinarian tolerance, dismissing religions as all right or all wrong—and who cares? For from such an attitude, all rationality fails. We may incline to give up trying to make sense of the world shaped by religions and the affect upon the world of religion. But these choices prove impractical. Religions make a large difference in their social settings, whether Islam in North Africa, the Middle East, India and Pakistan, and Indonesia and Malaysia; or Christianity in Europe and the Western hemisphere; or Hinduism in India; or Buddhism in Southeastern Asia, China, and Japan; or Judaism on its own in the State of Israel and in the Diaspora—and in its influence upon its continuators, Christianity and Islam. So however tentative our effort to understand the difference religion makes, we cannot desist from trying. For to make sense of the religiously and culturally diverse world in which we live, we need to find generalizations, traits of religion that emerge through the comparison and contrast of religions.

What makes comparison and contrast so urgent? The theory of the matter is simple. These form essential modes of thought when we try to generalize on the basis of a set of cases. If we need to make sense of many things, it is often by looking for what they have in common, the traits of the whole that govern the parts. In the present context, that means to try to generalize about *religion* out of the study of *religions*. Armed with such generalizations, we take up new cases and test them. That is to say, we ask, if I know this set of facts, what else do I know? And we answer that same question, the question of "what else," meaning at its foundation, "so what?"

For example, we may identify rituals important to Judaism and Islam and Buddhism. Can we then say what we mean by "ritual," defining the category out of data that we think belong in that category? Then we know something we may bring to new and unfamiliar data and try to make sense of them. Comparing religious traditions, then, opens the way to generalizing on some cases in quest of understanding about many more cases. Comparison and contrast open the way to answering the question, so what?

That quest for generalization about religion cannot be postponed, because religions—we cannot overstress—form a principal part of public life and culture in many, though not all, of the regions and nations of the world. And that also means, what people think about a given religion will shape the attitudes of nations toward one another. Even now, Western incomprehension of Islam spills over into fear of Muslims. And Islamic thinking about other religions also impedes Muslims' framing a comprehending attitude toward Christian minorities in Muslim countries and Christian, and secular, majorities in Western ones. Public policy in the coming century will encompass religions and our attitudes toward, our opinions of, various religious issues and entities. And because religion makes so vast a difference in so many parts of humanity, tolerance resting on indifference will not suffice. Conflicts loom. People make judgments. We can best confront difference in the benign setting of the academy, before we must face conflicts we cannot understand let alone avoid. To the work of sorting out difference, especially in religions, this labor of comparison and contrast therefore is essential. That means identifying what religions have in common, where they differ, and how to make sense of both. That is the work we undertake in this book and its companions. Where to begin?

We speak of practical things, urgent human questions to which all religions respond in one way or another. We have chosen three points to start with: religious traditions on family life, work, and personal virtue. We flatly claim that family, work, and virtue constitute categories of human existence that are close to universal. They constitute relationships and impose obligations to the others nearby, to the community at large, and to the self. "Family" pertains to relationships between me and those near at hand, "work" between me and those among whom I live, "virtue" between me and myself. Family, community, self—these take the measure of the lives we lead together, matters of public concern, not merely personal predeliction of no practical weight.

Accordingly, the scholars who join together in these pages concur that to study about religion, to seek generalizations that cases yield, one good starting point is to compare and contrast the views of the great religions on urgent and practical issues of everyday life. The reason is that, in our view, certain questions

arise from experiences common to the bulk of humanity. That is why in this
study religions meet on the neutral ground of what happens to every human
being in the course of life.

Take death for example. If we ask Judaism, Islam, Buddhism, Christianity,
and Hinduism to tell us what they have to say about what it means to live in the
knowledge of the end to which life leads us all, the grave, we speak of what all
must address. Not only so, but while diverse religions and cultures variously
frame the issue of that shared experience, all take up precisely the same universal experience of humanity. Here our universal biology overrides our several, diverse cultures. When we speak of existential concerns common to the generality
of humanity, that is what we mean. The case explains what we intend to do
here. But here we choose practical issues of everyday life. That is because all religions take up the task of answering questions common to humanity in general.
What are the universal human issues, the questions of shared and common existence, that we have chosen to take up in our exercise in comparing religious
traditions?

1. Every person, whatever the particularities of circumstance, is born of a
    mother and father. The great world religions we examine here concur that
    special obligations link child to parent and parent to child. If, then, we
    wish to compare Judaism, Christianity, Islam, Hinduism, and Buddhism,
    we find a level plane in the common question: do I owe anything to my
    mother and father, and, if so, what do I owe my mother and my father,
    and what do they owe to me? In all five religions the family forms the
    building block of the social order. How does each define the family and
    the architecture of ethical obligations that family relationships entail?

2. Nearly every person lives in a community that accords to him or her its
    recognition and protection and assigns a position and a worthwhile task to
    participants in its shared life. So we reasonably set side by side the several
    world religions' answers to the question, what do I owe the community of
    which I am a part? For, once again, rising above the differences of context
    and circumstance, the human situation persists: we need guidance on the
    same matter, wherever we live. And that leads us to doctrines of work and
    rest, as religious theories of the social order.

3. Finally, and perhaps of greatest weight, everybody who lives at some point,
    in some way, must answer the question, who am I, and what is the mean-
    ing of my life? The language we have chosen is, what do I owe myself?
    The answers to these questions form a theory of personal virtue. And that
    makes us wonder how religions define the private person and transform
    him or her into the individual embodiment of public policy—as they
    surely do.

In framing these questions, then, we bring to the religious traditions an
agenda of questions that pertain to the private lives of us all, wherever we are
born and raised, whatever the religion we practice (if any). These questions of
human existence, issues of private life, of home and family and the near-at-hand

community—these prove relevant to all humanity, and, we claim, for all humanity in much the same way, in a shared and common context. For we think that birth to a mother and father, life in community, and the search for self-worth together form the great levelers of difference.

What does all this have to do with the comparison and contrast of religions in quest of generalization about religion? In learning from the five world religions described here, we address to them all one and the same question. That common question is uniformly divided up into the same parts, in the same language, for each of the religions examined in sequence. We see these questions as equally relevant, in proportion, in the same way, to all five religions. That is to say, Judaism, Christianity, Islam, Hinduism, and Buddhism all set forth doctrines of (1) family, (2) work, and (3) virtue. These doctrines provide clear and characteristic answers to the questions we have formulated. In other words, we have identified categories that, in our experience as scholars, fit well for the religions that we study, respectively.

Let us now turn to the categories we have chosen. How have we framed the questions? A few words of explanation are in order. In the several chapters, all of us follow a single outline. For the initial volumes of this exercise in comparing religious traditions, here are the outlines that dictate the presentation of each religion.

I. THE ETHICS OF FAMILY LIFE: WHAT DO WE OWE ONE ANOTHER?
   1. Conventional expectation versus this religious tradition: what do husbands and wives owe one another?
   2. What do parents owe their children?
   3. What do children owe their parents?
   4. When the family breaks down: what happens then?
   5. Unconventional families, supernatural families

II. MAKING AN HONEST LIVING: WHAT DO WE OWE THE COMMUNITY?
   1. Why must we work?
   2. How ought we to work? kinds of work to be preferred or avoided
   3. Why must we help others? private gain and public benefit
   4. When work does not work: unemployment, exploitation, and alternatives to proper work
   5. Unconventional work: working for God

III. THE LIFE OF VIRTUE: WHAT DO WE OWE OURSELVES?
   1. Conventional answers versus this religious tradition: who are we really? [conceptions of the person, or, in other words, theological anthropology]
   2. What are the social virtues? [for example, generosity, trust, gratitude]
   3. What is personal virtue? [for example, dignity, self-respect, hope]
   4. How does this religion define character, good and bad?
   5. Beyond the normal virtues: who is the extraordinary person? [for example, the saint]

So much for the common questions addressed to five religious traditions, questions that make possible the comparison and contrast of those traditions.

For all three topical expositions, a single pattern governs. We move from the conventional to the unconventional, and from the system when it works to the system when it breaks down. In each exposition we begin with the conventional issues of ordinary life. This means that through the first three sections we answer the question, what do people ordinarily mean by the matter under discussion, and what are the answers that this religion in everyday terms gives to the question? We then turn at the fourth section to how a given religion deals with failure. At the end, at the fifth section, we ask how a given religion altogether revises the conventional, this-worldly definition. Having laid out an account of matters that is uniform in structure for the religions portrayed here, we leave it to students to draw their own conclusions, frame their own judgments, in discussion beyond the pages of this book.

In the volume on family life, we begin with the family understood in a this-worldly framework, a conventional family, meaning husband, wife, and children, extending outward beyond the nuclear family to grandparents, uncles and aunts, dependents of various kinds, and castes. Then, second, we ask about how this religion deals with the breakdown of the norm, for example, with the family when it breaks down. Finally, we turn from the conventional to the unconventional definition of the same matter, for example, the supernatural family, the family defined in an other-than-this-worldly framework.

When it comes to work, we begin with the ordinary meaning of work, that is, what we do to support our families and ourselves, to earn our keep, and to contribute to the common good. Then we ask about doctrines that deal with the breakdown of the ordinary arrangements for everyday labor. Finally, we take up work in a different, unconventional context.

The same pattern governs the discussion of virtue, by which we mean, how we view ourselves. In this context we take for granted that people ordinarily aspire to think well of themselves, to live lives of virtue. That topic encompasses how this religious tradition defines a human being. Within that broad question are doctrines on public virtues, that is, admirable traits that make for a better society, as well as those on personal ones. The latter characterize individuals and point toward how a given religion defines a truly virtuous person. On the basis of doctrines of virtue we generalize in terms of character: what does this religion admire in the overall quality of a person; what marks a person as basically good or fundamentally evil? And, finally, we turn from the routine to the extraordinary: how does this religion identify the saint, the embodiment of virtue.

So we have undertaken an experiment in comparing religious traditions. Why have we done so? Once more: the payoff comes in the quest for generalizations, in the present instance, how religion shapes the traits of family, work, and virtue. We concentrate on practical questions of comparison, not only because we claim the issues addressed here face nearly all religions and the societies shaped by them, but also because these issues confront all of us as we make our way through life from birth to death. When we compare religions' patterns of belief and behavior, we may or may not cover topics of immediate relevance to our own circumstances. But when we ask about family, work, and virtue, we certainly inquire into what matters in the here and the now. That is the point at which generalization may take place.

For, as we shall see, religions really do concur on some practical matters, and they actually do make the same difference, each in its own context. That does not make them all alike, and it does not validate the ignorant dismissal of difference, "It doesn't matter what you believe as long as you're a good person." Nor does that concurrence permit us to reduce religions to religion, to define a generic religion. What we mean to show is the possibility of generalization, of moving from knowing this fact to explaining other facts, moving from the known to the unknown. That is how we meet our responsibility as academic scholars of religion and how we contribute to others outside of university life as well. All comes down to our sustained response to this simple question: if we know this, what else do we know?

Why the emphasis on practical matters? The academic study of religion maintains that we study about religions and religion and do not advocate the truth of one religion over another, and all of us in these pages affirm that conviction. But no one can imagine that the academic study of religion ought never present us with choices worthy of our consideration, ideas of other men and women that we may make our own. We represent the religions treated here as worthy of the close attention of inquiring minds, in quest, in the end, of insight into the human condition. No other single force in the social order, not politics, not economics, not psychology, not any of the other important elements in making the world what it is—none of them exceeds in power, or in pathos, the force of religion.

The partners in this project express thanks to Wadsworth Publishing Company for adopting the enterprise and guiding it from beginning to end. We benefited, especially, from the oversight and counsel of our editor, Peter Adams. We are also grateful for the helpful comments provided by the reviewers: Leslie Aldritt, Northland College; S. Daniel Breslauer, University of Kansas; Aminah Beverly McCloud, DePaul University; Preston McKever-Floyd, Coastal Carolina University.

The editor thanks the partners in this project for doing the work on time and with panache. He also expresses his personal gratitude to Bard College, for a research grant and for other support for his work as teacher and scholar.

Jacob Neusner
Editor
Bard College

Contributors

Bruce Chilton is Bernard Iddings Bell Professor of Religion at Bard College.

Brad Clough is Assistant Professor of Religion at Bard College.

Jacob Neusner is Research Professor of Religion and Theology at Bard College.

Brian K. Smith is Professor of Religious Studies at the University of California at Riverside.

Tamara Sonn is Kenan Professor of Religious Studies at the College of William and Mary.

1

Judaism

BY JACOB NEUSNER

CONVENTIONAL EXPECTATION VERSUS THIS RELIGIOUS TRADITION: WHAT DO HUSBANDS AND WIVES OWE ONE ANOTHER?

Husbands and wives owe one another loyalty to the common task and reliability in the carrying out of their reciprocal obligations, which are sexual, social, and economic. Their relationship finds its definition, therefore its rules and obligations, in the tasks assigned by the social order to marriage, and that is, childbearing and child raising, on the one side, and the maintenance of the political economy of the holy people, Israel, on the other. The purpose of marriage is to produce the next generation and to support it. Marriage finds its definition in the larger social context that the Torah means to set forth for Israel.

Out of mutual trust and shared achievements—children raised, the household maintained—may emerge emotions of affection and love, and, for one example, sages counsel husbands to afford sexual satisfaction to their wives, saying that if the wife reaches orgasm first, male children—which men are assumed to want—will result. But romantic attitudes do not enjoy a high priority in the value of marriage and the family. The governing language is theological, with the keyword being "holiness." The family is formed when a man betroths a woman and consummates the betrothal, and the word for "betroth" is "sanctify." The relationship of that woman to that man is one of sanctification; she is uniquely his, having consented to consecrate herself to him. God has a heavy stake in what is set apart as sanctified, whether the offering in the Temple on his altar, or the wife in the household in bed. When, as we shall see, the marital relationship breaks down, the same considerations enter in, now through a process of deconsecration of the originally sanctified marital bond. There too, Heaven supervises.

In the polygamous society taken for granted in the classical Judaic sources, to be sure, the husband owes the wife not a counterpart relationship of sexual sanctification but reliable support, material and conjugal, as we shall see. The wife can have sexual relations only with her husband. But with several wives, the husband does not enter into a counterpart status of sanctification to her. When it comes to adultery, however, sages condemn the husband's as much as the wife's. This view is expressed in the context of sages' discussion of the ordeal imposed upon a wife accused of adultery. The pertinent verse of Scripture is "And the man shall be free from iniquity, and the woman shall bear her iniquity" (Numbers 5:31). The passage is interpreted in this way:[1]

> The sense of the foregoing verse of Scripture is that when the man is free of transgression, the water puts his wife to the test, and if the man is not free of transgression, the water does not put his wife to the test.
>
> Bavli-tractate Sotah 5:1 I:1D/28A

That is to say, the ordeal imposed on the wife is null, if to begin with the husband is not free of transgression. It goes without saying that sages also condemn sexual relations for money.

But we should err if we saw the family in classical Judaism through contemporary spectacles. People conventionally think of the nuclear (or extended) family as the primary social unit, distinct from society and autonomous of the political economy that sustains the social order. But in the Torah as set forth by the ancient sages husbands and wives and their children do not form the primary social unit, the building block of society. The household does, and it is not quite the same thing as the family. In the household, the family—husbands and wives and children, the husband's extended family and dependents—finds its defining context. By "the household" in the setting of classical Judaism is meant a coherent social unit, built upon ties of consanguinity and/or dependency, which is also a unit of production, ordinarily meaning agricultural production. Only when we grasp what is at stake in the family, which is the household, shall we understand the specific rules, addressed presently, governing what the husband owes to the wife and the wife to the husband.

The household should be understood in three aspects. First, it marked a unit of production, and the householder was the master of the means of production: it was a farming unit in particular. But, second, the household also delineated a unit of ownership, and the householder became such as the master of a piece of property. Commanding means of production meant, in particular, running a farm. Finally, the household also encompassed an extended family unit of the husband. So to ask about husbands, wives, and children in Judaism, we must find the context in which their mutual obligations take shape, and that means, how husbands, wives, and children work together to support the household.

All relationships within the household, even those that bear the heaviest weight of the structure, between parents and among parents and children, are governed by the needs of the larger social unit, the household itself. That is what defines the smallest whole building block of the social order of Israel, so far as classical Judaism sees matters. The aim of the Torah as sages expound it is to provide for a stable, nurturing relationship between husband and wife. Both parties to the marriage are given a heavy stake in the stability and comfort of the house-

---

[1] All translations are my own, unless otherwise indicated.

hold, and that is why neither party is likely to risk for little reason the material and social benefits of the marriage. Indeed, in a society that made scant provision for the isolated individual, housing being organized by households for example, everyone in the household had good reason to carry out his or her public duties. Households locate themselves in villages or towns, and, within them, in courtyards that themselves debauch onto alleyways, then opening into large public places. So to imagine the family in its social context as Judaism in its classical sources portrays the family, we have to conceive of a world in which mothers, fathers, and children, grandparents, aunts and uncles and cousins, servants (paid a wage in cash or in kind) and slaves (people who sell their work and make their own their master's will) not only share a common residence but also work together in a mostly subsistence farm, part of a barter economy.

It follows that the singularity of the household lies not in its physical let alone genealogical traits, but in its definition of the "family" as a distinct unit of economic production. What made a household into a household was its economic definition of the "family" as a whole and complete unit of production, and the householder—ordinarily male—was the one who controlled that unit of production; that fact made all the difference, and not that all of the household's members were related (that was not the fact at all), nor that all of them lived in a single building distinct from other single buildings, which certainly was not the case. What made the household into a social unit was the economic fact that, among its constituents, all of them both related to one another in some genealogical pattern and also worked within the same economic unit, in a setting distinct from other equivalently autonomous economic units. In the idiom of the Mishnah, the first document of the Oral Torah, they *ate* at the same table, and eating should be understood as an abstraction, not merely as a reference to the fact that people sat down and broke bread together.

The Written Torah (a.k.a. "the Old Testament") does not prepare us for such a picture of society and its building blocks. Ancient Israelite thinkers in Scripture (e.g., the priestly authorship of Leviticus, the prophetic schools that produced Isaiah's and Amos's conceptions) discerned within, and as, "Israel" classes identified by their sacerdotal and genealogical traits and functions, in relationship to other classes; or a mixed multitude of poor and rich. We look in vain in the imagination of the Deuteronomist writers in their several layers for a conception of an "Israel" composed of neatly arranged farms run by landowners, of families made up of households, an Israel with each such household arrayed in its hierarchy, from householder on top, to slave on bottom. But that is how the Oral Torah sees things. Critical to the system of the Mishnah that forms the foundation of classical Judaism is its principal social entity, the village, comprising households, and the progressive model, from the household to village to "all Israel," comprehensively describes whatever of "Israel" the authorship at hand has chosen to describe. The family then is subsumed within the community, its framework defined by the expectation of self-sufficiency, and its governance aimed at justice. Judaism in its classical sources thus focuses upon the society organized in relationship to the control of the means of production—the farm, for the household is always the agricultural unit. That is the context in which we address the situation of the family and the relationships within the family, in particular father and mother to children, and children to parents, husbands to wives and vice versa.

If we cannot define the family apart from its position at the heart of the household, we also should not confuse the household with class status—for example, thinking of the householder as identical with the wealthy. The opposite is suggested on every page of the Mishnah and the Talmuds, in which householders vie with craftsmen for ownership of the leavings of the loom and the chips left behind by the adz. The household, rather, forms an economic and a social classification, defined by function, specifically, its economic function. A poor household was a household, and (in theory; the Mishnah's authorship knows none such in practice) a rich landholding that did not function as a center for a social and economic unit (e.g., an industrial—not a subsistence, family—farm) was not a household. Within the household all local—as distinct from cultic—economic, therefore social, activities and functions were held together. For the unit of production comprised also the unit of social organization, and, of greater import still, the building block of all larger social, now also political, units, with special reference to the village.

In the conception at hand, which sees Israel as made up, on earth, of households and villages, the economic unit also framed the social one, and the two together composed, in conglomerates, the political one, hence a political economy initiated within an economic definition formed out of the elements of production. The law of the Mishnah makes a single cogent statement that the organizing unit of society and politics finds its definition in the irreducible unit of economic production. The Mishnah conceives no other economic unit of production than the household, though it recognizes that such existed; its authorship perceived no other social unit of organization than the household and the conglomeration of households, though that limited vision omitted all reference to substantial parts of the population perceived to be present, such as craftsmen, the unemployed, and the landless. The social foundation of the economy of the Mishnah therefore rested on the household, which in turn formed the foundation of the village, imagined to comprise the community of households, in the charge of small farmers who were free and who owned their land.

How then shall we briefly define the family? The head of the house, or householder, is taken for granted also to be the father of the family around which the household takes shape. In that context we may define the family as the persons that stand to inherit the property of one another or benefit therefrom. Within the villages any Israelite male was assumed to possess the potentiality to become a householder, that is, in context, the master of a domain, a landholder. So in that context, the householder also is the father. What about the mother— can the householder be the mother, not the father? I cannot point to a passage in which it is assumed that a woman is head of a household. But in the law of the Torah women can own land and engage in the economic activities of a household, so the system theoretically could accommodate a woman-householder. In practice, however, a woman is always taken to relate to a man, as her father, then her husband, when he is alive, and, when he is deceased, to her sons or stepsons by her deceased husband. These support her as a widow. It is further taken for granted that when a woman is divorced or widowed, she will remarry within a brief spell, so that the alimony provided in the marriage settlement is meant to tide her over until she does so. Or she reverts to her "father's house," which means that she rejoins the household of her father, if alive; if dead, of her brothers.

With these theoretical remarks in hand, let us turn to the practical statements of the law of the Torah set forth in the Mishnah. These define what the wife owes the husband and the husband the wife. The law focuses, for the wife, on the labor that she owes, and, for the husband, on the restraint he must exercise, the respect for the wife's autonomy he must display. Stated simply: the wife or wives (we deal, in ancient times, with a polygamous society) represent participants in the household, and the wife owes the husband the fruit of her labor. The husband reciprocates by honoring the wife's desires and attitudes and refraining from trying to control and isolate her. The wife's domestic duties encompass these:

> These are the kinds of labor which a woman performs for her husband:
> she (1) grinds flour, (2) bakes bread, (3) does laundry, (4) prepares meals, (5) gives suck to her child, (6) makes the bed, (7) works in wool.
> [If] she brought with her a single slave girl, she does not (1) grind, (2) bake bread, or (3) do laundry.
> [If she brought] two, she does not (4) prepare meals and does not (5) feed her child.
> [If she brought] three, she does not (6) make the bed for him and does not (7) work in wool.
> If she brought four, she sits on a throne.
> R. Eliezer says, "Even if she brought him a hundred slave girls, he forces her to work in wool,
> "for idleness leads to unchastity."
> Rabban Simeon b. Gamaliel says, "Also: He who prohibits his wife by a vow from performing any labor puts her away and pays off her marriage contract. For idleness leads to boredom."
>
> Mishnah-tractate Ketubot 5:5

The wife is a partner with the husband, bearing a particular area of responsibility. She is respected in her work and many depend on her management. The woman of valor of Proverbs 30 is the model here.

The wife, further, is expected to conduct herself in a modest and pious manner, and if she does not do so, the husband may divorce her without paying the alimony that is required in the marriage agreement—a huge incentive for the wife to keep the law:

> And those women go forth without the payment of the marriage contract at all:
> She who transgresses against the law of Moses and Jewish law.
> And what is the law of Moses [which she has transgressed]? [If] (1) she feeds him food which has not been tithed, or (2) has sexual relations with him while she is menstruating, or [if] (3) she does not cut off her dough-offering, or [if] (4) she vows and does not carry out her vow.

And what is the Jewish law? If (1) she goes out with her hair flowing loose, or (2) she spins in the marketplace, or (3) she talks with just anybody,

> Abba Saul says, "Also: if she curses his parents in his presence."
>
> R. Tarfon says, "Also: if she is a loudmouth."
>
> What is a loudmouth? When she talks in her own house, her neighbors can hear her voice.
>
> Mishnah-tractate Ketubot 7:6

The husband, for his part, owes his wives not only the required domestic support for which Scripture provides—food, clothing, conjugal relations—but also an allowance that she may spend as she sees fit:

> He gives her in addition a silver ma'ah [a sixth of a denar] for her needs [per week].
>
> And she eats with him on the Sabbath night [when sexual relations are owing].
>
> And if he does not give her a silver ma'ah for her needs, the fruit of her labor belongs to her. [She may sell what she makes, e.g., spun wool, and use the money ad lib.]
>
> And how much work does she do for him?
>
> The weight of five selas of warp must she spin for him [M. 5:5B7] in Judea (which is ten selas weight in Galilee), or the weight of ten selas of woof in Judah (which are twenty selas in Galilee).
>
> And if she was nursing a child, they take off [the required weight of wool which she must spin as] the fruit of her labor, and they provide more food for her.
>
> Under what circumstances?
>
> In the case of the most poverty-stricken man in Israel.
>
> But in the case of a weightier person, all follows the extent of his capacity [to support his wife].
>
> Mishnah-tractate Ketubot 5:9

What we see in the requirements of husband to wife and wife to husband, then, is heavy emphasis upon shared personal and material obligations. The wife brings to the marriage her dowry, which stands for her share in the father's estate; this reverts to her (hence to her father) in the event of divorce or the husband's demise. So the marriage represents the formation of a partnership based on quite practical considerations. Matters of emotion enter in—but mainly as the husband's responsibility. What we see is very little sentimentality but a great deal of respect and dignity.

What does the husband owe the wife? As to sexual relations, however many wives a husband has, each woman's rights are to be carefully respected; marital rape is forbidden, and a woman who invites sexual relations is highly praised and will produce remarkable children:

> Said R. Ammi bar Abba said R. Assi, "It is forbidden for someone to rape his wife or force his wife to carry out the religious duty (of sexual relations): 'And he that hastes with his feet sins' (Prov. 19:2)."

And said R. Joshua b. Levi, "Whoever rapes his wife will have unworthy children."

Said R. Samuel bar Nahmani said R. Jonathan, "Any man whose wife calls him to sexual relations will have children of the like of which the generation of our lord, Moses, didn't have, as it is said, 'Take you men wise, understanding, and known among your tribes and I will make them rulers over you' (Dt. 1:13); and 'So I took the chiefs of your tribes, wise men and known' (Dt. 1:15)—without reference to 'understanding.' And with reference to Leah, it is written, 'And Leah went out to meet him and said, you must come to me, for I have surely hired you' (Gen. 30:16), and it is written, 'Issachar is a large-boned ass' (Gen. 49:14), and elsewhere, 'And of the children of Issachar, who were men that had understanding of the times' (1 Chr. 12:33)." This was Leah's reward, proving that it is meritorious for a woman to demand sexual relations.

> Bavli-tractate Erubin 10:10:8 II.9/100b

That the perspective is the husband's presents no surprise, the entire system being framed by men. But treating the wife with delicacy and respect brings rewards, and the wife's sexual desires are to be responded to. Correct behavior with women requires modesty and deference:

He who counts out coins into a woman's hand from his own in order to have a chance to stare at her, even if such a one has in hand Torah and good deeds like Moses, our master, will not be quit of the judgment of Gehenna. For it is said, "Hand to hand, he shall not escape from evil" (Prov. 11:21). He shall not escape from the judgment of Gehenna.

> Bavli-tractate Berakhot 9:1 XVII.6, 8/61b

So much for matters of sexual modesty and restraint.

The husband may not abuse the wife, may not try to keep her away from the normal social relations that she should enjoy as an independent personality, and must accord to her all of the rights and dignities of a free woman:

He who prohibits his wife by vow from deriving benefit from him
for a period of thirty days, appoints an agent to provide for her.
[If the effects of the vow are not nullified] for a longer period, he puts her away and pays off her marriage contract.
R. Judah says, "In the case of an Israelite, for [a vow lasting] one month he may continue in the marriage, but for two [or more], he must put her away and pay off her marriage contract.
"But in the case of a priest, for two months he may continue in the marriage, and after three he must put her away and pay off her marriage contract."

> Mishnah-tractate Ketubot 7:1

Since, in the marital negotiations, the husband receives property that, in the event of divorce, he must restore to the wife's father's household, divorce is not undertaken lightly. It involves not only a year of alimony, but also loss of considerable capital or real estate. Hence the husband has a strong incentive not to impose a vow upon the wife that denies her the right to gain benefit from him—eat at his table, share his bed, and the like.

The same considerations strongly discourage the husband from browbeating or otherwise trying to manipulate or control the wife. If he imposes on her a vow not to eat even one sort of fruit or vegetable, he must divorce her, giving her her freedom and losing the capital she has brought into his household:

> He who prohibits his wife by vow from tasting any single kind of produce whatsoever must put her away and pay off her marriage contract.
>   R. Judah says, "In the case of an Israelite, [if the vow is] for one day he may persist in the marriage, but [if it is] for two he must put her away and pay off her marriage contract.
>   "And in the case of a priest, [if it is] for two days he may persist in the marriage, but [if it is] for three he must put her away and pay off her marriage contract."
>
> Mishnah-tractate Ketubot 7:2

The law shows remarkably little patience for the intrusive husband, the controlling husband who would transform his wife into his slave, lacking all freedom of will. The same protection encompasses the wife's right to adorn herself as a beautiful woman; such petty annoyances become very costly:

> He who prohibits his wife by a vow from adorning herself with any single sort of jewelry must put her away and pay off her marriage contract.
>   R. Yosé says, "In the case of poor girls, [if] he has not assigned a time limit [he must divorce them].
>   "But in the case of rich girls, [he may persist in the marriage if he set a time limit] of thirty days."
>
> Mishnah-tractate Ketubot 7:3

The husband must permit the wife to maintain a circle of friends and relationships beyond the limits of the household. The husband may not interfere in the wife's relationships with her father and family; he may not stop her from seeing her relatives:

> He who prohibits his wife by a vow from going home to her father's house—
>   when he [father] is with her in [the same] town,
>   [if it is] for a month, he may persist in the marriage.
>   [If it is] for two, he must put her away and pay off her marriage contract.
>   And when he is in another town, [if the vow is in effect] for one festival season he may persist in the marriage. [But if the vow remains in force] for three, he must put her away and pay off her marriage contract.
>
> Mishnah-tractate Ketubot 7:4

The wife thus has the absolute right to visit her father's household pretty much when her duties permit. Nor may the husband interfere with the wife's normal social intercourse. Here too, if he tries to keep her caged at home and cut off her ties to other people, particularly the society of women, he loses heavily:

> He who prohibits his wife by a vow from going to a house of mourning or to a house of celebration must put her away and pay off her marriage contract,
>> because he locks the door before her.
> But if he claimed that he took such a vow because of some other thing, he is permitted to impose such a vow.

Finally, intimate details of the marriage must be kept private; the woman has a right to her dignity:

> [If he took a vow,] saying to her, (1) "On condition that you say to So-and-so what you said to me," or (2) "what I said to you," or (3) "that you draw water and pour it out onto the ash heap,"
>> he must put her away and pay off her marriage contract.

Mishnah-tractate Ketubot 7:5

In these and other ways, the husband is given a weighty incentive to treat the wife with enormous respect. And, as we have seen, if the woman behaves improperly, not keeping the Torah of Moses, committing adultery, for example, she too loses the assets she has brought to the marriage and the household. The provisions of her marriage settlement are null; the husband keeps the dowry; and she loses everything.

How, then, is the mother-wife-daughter positioned within the household? Along with slaves and minors, women form a classification of Israelites deemed not fully capable of independent will, intentionality, entire responsibility, and action and therefore subject not only to God's will but also to the will of another, the husband or father in the case of the woman, the master in the case of the slave, and the parent in the case of the child, thus Mishnah-tractate Berakhot 3:3: "Women, slaves, and minors are exempt from the recitation of the *Shema* (the Creed, recited morning and night), and from the obligation to wear phylacteries, but are obligated to the recitation of the Prayer, and to post on the doorposts of the house a *mezuzah* (a parchment containing verses of Scripture) and to recite the blessing over the meal." But they do not form part of the community of holy Israel that is obligated to recite blessings publicly, thus Mishnah-tractate Berakhot 7:2: "Women, slaves or minors who ate together with adult Israelite males—they may not invite others to bless on their account."

In a number of specific contexts, moreover, a man and woman are differentiated in the functions that they perform or to which they are obligated. A man imposes a Nazirite vow on his son, and a woman does not impose a Nazirite vow upon her son (Mishnah-tractate Nazir 4:6). A man brings the hair offering for the Nazirite vow of his father, and a woman does not bring a hair offering for the Nazirite vow of her father. The man sells his daughter, and the woman does not sell her daughter, in line with Exodus 21:6. The man arranges for a betrothal of his daughter, and the woman does not arrange for the betrothal of her daughter (Mishnah-tractate Qiddushin 2:1). A man who incurs the death penalty is stoned naked, but a woman is not stoned naked. A man is hanged after being put to death, and a woman is not hanged (Mishnah-tractate Sanhedrin 6:3–4). A man is sold to make restitution for having stolen something, but a woman is not sold to make restitution for having stolen something (Exodus 22:2). The matter is further amplified at Mishnah-tractate Qiddushin 1:7:

> For every commandment concerning the son to which the father is subject—men are liable, and women are exempt.
>
> And for every commandment concerning the father to which the son is subject, men and women are equally liable.
>
> For every positive commandment dependent upon the time [of year], men are liable, and women are exempt.
>
> And for every positive commandment not dependent upon the time, men and women are equally liable.
>
> For every negative commandment, whether dependent upon the time or not dependent upon the time, men and women are equally liable,
>
> except for not marring the corners of the beard, not rounding the corners of the head (Lev. 19:27), and not becoming unclean because of the dead (Lev. 21:1).
>
> Mishnah-tractate Qiddushin 1:7

Women are exempt from religious duties that take her away from responsibilities only she can carry out. She has fixed obligations—for example, to feed her baby. No religious duty pertains that interferes with these obligations. This matter is clarified at Tosefta-tractate Qiddushin 1:10–11:

> *What is a positive commandment dependent upon the time* [of year, for which men are liable and women are exempt (M. Qid. 1:7C)]?
>
> For example, building the *Sukkah,* taking the *lulab,* putting *tefillin.*
>
> What is *a positive commandment not dependent upon the time of year* (M. Qid. 1:7D)?
>
> For example, restoring lost property to its rightful owner, sending forth the bird, building a parapet, and putting on *sisit* (show-fringes).
>
> R. Simeon declares women exempt from the requirement of wearing *sisit,* because it is a positive commandment dependent upon time.
>
> Tosefta-tractate Qiddushin 1:10

> What is *a commandment pertaining to the son concerning the father to which men and women are equally liable* (M. Qid. 1:7B)]?
>
> Giving him food to eat and something to drink and clothing him and covering him and taking him out and bringing him in and washing his face, his hands, and his feet.
>
> All the same are men and women. But the husband has sufficient means to do these things for the child, and the wife does not have sufficient means to do them,
>
> for others have power over her.
>
> Tosefta-tractate Qiddushin 1:11

In a moment, we shall see how the Talmud takes up the issue of what the father owes to the son.

So too, a woman is not obligated to study the Torah or to wear tefillin (phylacteries), so Yerushalmi-tractate Erubin 10:1 I.2: He who is liable to study Torah also is liable to wear *tefillin*. Women, who are not liable to study Torah, also are not liable to wear *tefillin*. We should note that in contemporary Judaism, provision is made for women to study Torah; they are accepted as Reform, Conservative, and Reconstructionist rabbis; Orthodox Judaism in the State of Israel and overseas has founded yeshivot—Talmud study centers—for women. The picture of women as excluded from the active life of the faith has changed dramatically in the past generation.

Nonetheless, it is taken for granted that women are subject to men, daughters to fathers, then wives to husbands; widows are assumed to return to their fathers' households. Marriage is the natural condition of man and woman

> Said R. Hanilai, "Any man who has no wife lives without joy, blessing, goodness: Joy: 'and you shall rejoice, you and your house' (Dt. 14:26). Blessing: 'to cause a blessing to rest on your house' (Ez. 44:30). Goodness: 'it is not good that man should be alone' (Gen. 2:18)."
>
> In the West they say: without Torah and without a wall of refuge. Without Torah: "Is it that I have no help in me and that sound wisdom is driven entirely out of me" (Job 6:13). Without a wall of refuge: "A woman shall form a wall about a man" (Jer. 31:22).
>
> Raba bar Ulla said, "Without peace: 'and you shall know that your tent is in peace, and you shall visit your habitation and shall miss nothing' (Job 5:24)."
>
> He who loves his wife as he loves himself, he who honors her more than he honors himself, he who raises up his sons and daughters in the right path, and he who marries them off close to the time of their puberty—of such a one, Scripture says, "And you shall know that your tabernacle shall be in peace and you shall visit your habitation and you shall not sin" (Job 5:24).
>
> Bavli-tractate Yebamot 6:6 II.19–21

So much for the household as the setting for the relationship of husbands and wives. But what about the larger society of holy Israel, the world in which the Torah affords access to, and knowledge of, God through God's own self-manifestation?

Now, we realize, the supreme religious activity focuses upon Torah-study, ordinarily as a disciple to a master. But by definition a woman cannot become a disciple to a master; she is the wife of her husband and no other social role is open to her. Then how do wives and mothers participate in the merit of Torah-study? It is rarely through active participation in the processes of learning and debate. Women come to listen to the study of the Torah, and bring their children as an act of merit as well:

> When R. Joshua got old, his disciples came to visit him. He said to them, "My sons, what was the new point that you had today in school?"
>
> They said to him, "We are your disciples, and your water [alone] do we drink."
>
> He said to them, "God forbid! it is impossible that there is a generation of sages that is orphaned [and without suitable guidance]. Whose week was it to teach?"

They said to him, "It was the week of R. Eleazar b. Azariah."

He said to them, "And what was the topic of the narrative today?"

They said to him, "It was the passage that begins, 'Assemble the people, the men and the women and the children' (Dt. 31:12)."

He said to them, "And what did he expound in that connection?"

They said to him, "This is how he interpreted it. 'The men come to learn, the women to listen, but why do the children come? It is to provide the occasion for the gaining of a reward for those who bring them.'"

He said to them, "You had a good pearl in your hands, and you wanted to make me lose it! If you had come only to let me hear this one thing, it would have been enough for me."

The Fathers According to Rabbi Nathan XVIII:II.1

What then is the husband's primary obligation to his wives? Apart from the three requirements that Scripture sets forth—food, clothing, conjugal relations—he must bring peace to his household; in the situation of polygamy, that represents a considerable assignment. But even in the nuclear family, the task demands constant effort:

Simeon b. Gamaliel says, "Whoever brings peace to his own household is credited by Scripture as though he brought peace in Israel, for every individual.

"And whoever brings envy and contention into his household is as if he brought envy and contention in Israel.

"For everyone is the monarch in his own household.

"As it is said, *That every man should rule in his own household* (Est. 1:22)."

The Fathers According to Rabbi Nathan XXVIII:III.1

WHAT DO PARENTS OWE THEIR CHILDREN?

A religion that constructs its system through normative rules and that makes its statements by formulating laws ("governing legal rulings") finds no difficulty in answering questions of obligation. An explicit reply to the question at hand is set forth in a simple sentence. The father owes the son a number of specific duties. He must bring him into the covenant of Abraham through circumcision. He must redeem him, if the son is a firstborn and the father is not of the priestly caste, by handing over to a priest five silver coins; he must teach him Torah; he must get him a wife; and he must teach him a trade. In these ways the father provides for the son's religious, personal, and economic future. The matter is handsomely expounded in the Talmud of Babylonia (a.k.a. Bavli), and the passage is accessible. Hence by examining the main points and how they are expounded, we see the way in which Judaism conducts the exposition and amplification of its rules. The initial statement occurs in the Tosefta, the first commentary to the Mishnah, in connection with the passage we have already examined, at Mishnah-tractate Qiddushin 1:7, "For every commandment concerning the son to which the father is subject." That matter is then spelled out in the Tosefta, given here in boldface type. I then indent the systematic amplification of the matter, further indenting secondary comments. The Talmud is bilingual, giving the laws in Hebrew, the analyses in Aramaic. I use italics to signify Aramaic, and regular type for the Hebrew. In this way, as we see how the passage makes its statement, we also enter into the rules of analysis that the Talmud follows and identify what matters to the Talmud in its exposition of any given topic:

> **The father is responsible with respect to his son to circumcise him, to redeem him, to teach him Torah, to marry him off to a woman, and to teach him a trade.**
>
> **And there are those who say, also to teach him to swim.**
>
> **R. Judah says, "Anyone who does not teach his son a trade is as though he trains him to be a gangster"**
>
> [T. Qid. 1:11F–H].

Since the Mishnah and the Tosefta ordinarily state rules without citing passages of the Written Torah to support or sustain those rules, the Talmud systematically identifies the basis in Scripture, the Written Torah, for the rules set forth in the Oral Torah. The Talmud has three questions in mind: how do we know the rule? how do we know what to do if the rule is not kept? and how do we know the responsibility of the individual where society lets him down? Here is a systematic exposition of the answers to those three questions:

> . . . . **To circumcise him:** *How on the basis of Scripture do we know that he must do so?*
>
> *As it is written,* "And Abraham circumcised Isaac, his son" (Gen. 21:4).
>
> *And how do we know that if his father did not circumcise him, the court is liable to circumcise him?*
>
> *As it is written,* "Every male among you shall be circumcised" (Gen. 17:10).
>
> *And how do we know that if the court did not circumcise him, he is liable to circumcise himself?*
>
> *As it is written,* "And the uncircumcised male who will not circumcise the flesh of his foreskin, that soul shall be cut off" (Gen. 17:14).
>
> **To redeem him:** *How on the basis of Scripture do we know that he must do so?*
>
> *As it is written,* "And all the firstborn of man among your sons you shall redeem" (Ex. 13:13).
>
> *And whence do we know that if the father did not redeem him, he is liable to redeem himself?*
>
> *As it is written,* "Nevertheless the firstborn of man you shall surely redeem" (Num. 18:15).
>
> **To teach him Torah:** *How on the basis of Scripture do we know that fact?*
>
> "And you shall teach them to your sons" (Dt. 11:19).
>
> *And that in a case in which his father did not teach him, he is liable to teach himself?*
>
> "And you shall study" (Dt. 5:1).

Now a digression asks a question not required by the original statement: to what extent is so open-ended an obligation as Torah-study obligatory? How much does the father have to do? Sages immediately turn to Scripture for facts, governing precedents, on the basis of which to answer the question:

> To what extent is a man obligated to teach his son Torah?
>
> Said R. Judah said Samuel, "The exemplary case is Zebulun b. Dan, whose grandfather taught him Scripture, Mishnah, Talmud analysis, law and lore."
>
> *An objection was raised:* If he taught him Scripture, he need not teach him Mishnah, and said Raba, "Scripture refers to Torah, as in the case of Zebulun b. Dan, but also not as in the case of Zebulun b. Dan: As in the case of Zebulun b. Dan, whose grandfather taught him, but not as in the case of Zebulun b. Dan, *for in that case involved were lessons in Scripture, Mishnah, Talmud analysis, laws and lore, but here involved is only Scripture alone."*
>
> *And is the grandfather so obligated? And hasn't it been taught on Tannaite authority:* "And you shall teach them to your sons" (Dt. 11:19)—and not to your grandsons. And how am I to interpret, "And you shall make them known to your sons and your sons' sons" (Dt. 4:9)? This lets you know that whoever teaches his son Torah is regarded by Scripture as though he had taught not only him but also his son and his son's son to the end of all generations.
>
> *He made his statement in line with the position of the following Tannaite authority, as has been taught on Tannaite authority:* "And you shall teach them to your sons": I know only that this applies to your sons. How do I know that it applies to your sons' sons? It is said, "And you shall make them known to your sons and your sons' sons." Then why say, "And you shall teach them to your sons"? To teach: Your sons but not your daughters.

Now we return to the original task of expounding the basic rule. Note that the source in Scripture is constantly at issue; the sages of Judaism mean to translate the laws and stories of Scripture into the way of life of the community of Judaism, that is, into rules and regulations for the social order. That is why there is a constant interchange with the revealed Torah of Moses:

> **To marry him off to a woman:**
> *What is the source in Scripture?*
> Because it is said in Scripture, "Take wives for yourselves and produce sons and daughters, and take wives for your sons and give your daughters to husbands" (Jer. 29:6).
> *Well, there's no problem about marrying off a son, the decision is his. But as regards the daughter, does the matter depend on him? [You have to find the husband, too.]*
> *This is the sense of Jeremiah's statement:* "Give her a dowry, clothes, ornaments, so men will come looking for her."
> **And to teach him a trade:**
> *What is the source in Scripture?*
> Said Hezekiah, "Said Scripture, 'See to a livelihood with the wife whom you love' (Qoh. 9:9)."

If this refers literally to a wife, then, just as the father is obligated to find a wife for him, so he is obligated to teach him a trade. If the meaning of "wife" is as a metaphor for Torah, then just as he is obligated to teach him Torah, so he is obligated to teach him a trade.

And there are those who say, also to teach him to swim:

How come?

Because it can save his life.

R. Judah says, "Anyone who does not teach his son a trade trains him to be a gangster":

Can you imagine, to be a gangster?! Rather, is as though he trains him to be a gangster.

And what's at issue here?

At issue here is training him in commerce [Judah rejecting commerce].

Bavli-tractate Qiddushin 1:7 I.2/29A

Here, then, is an explicit answer to the question, what does the father owe the son? I cannot identify any passage in the classical sources of Judaism that specifies what the mother owes the daughter.

But both parents owe their children an honorable example of how to conduct themselves. And they owe the children a heritage of virtue and not of sin, because Scripture is explicit that God visits the iniquity of the fathers upon the children but shows steadfast love for a thousand generations of those who love him and keep his commandments, so Exodus 20:5–6. Sages in the Oral Torah clarify the former matter: God punishes the sons who continue the sins of the father, but not those who repent of the father's sins:

"visiting the iniquity of the fathers upon the children:"

That is when there is no break in the chain, but not when there is a break in the chain.

How so?

In the case of a wicked person, son of a wicked person, son of a wicked person.

When Moses heard this matter, "Moses made haste and bowed his head toward the earth and worshipped" (Ex. 34:8).

He said, "God forbid, there cannot be among all the Israelites a wicked person, son of a wicked person, son of a wicked person."

Might one suppose that, just as the measure of punishment covers four generations, so the measure of goodness covers the same span of four generations?

Scripture says, "to thousands."

If "to thousands," might I understand that the minimum plural of "thousands" is two?

Scripture says, "to a thousand generations" (Dt. 7:9), that is to say, to generations beyond all discover and all counting.

Mekhilta LII:I.8

The question of fairness is implicit: if the father has sinned, what has the son done to merit punishment? The question finds its answer in a revision of the facts of the matter: if the son continues the father's tradition, he will be punished as the father was. This turns matters around.

Not only so, but Scripture assigns yet another obligation to the parents, and that is what they owe to the community in the upbringing of their children. Parents obligate themselves to raise honorable children—and, if they fail, to take action to protect the community from their offspring. That conception is explained, as we shall see, by appeal to two facts of sages' world. The first is, humanity will live beyond the grave, being raised from the dead at the last judgment. Then those who have sinned and atoned for their sin in this life will enter eternal life, as much as those who did not sin at all. Hence death is not the end of everything but a prelude to resurrection. If a sinner or criminal is put to death, that atones for the sin or crime; then the sinner or criminal dies innocent, having paid the penalty for the sin or crime, and so will enjoy life eternal. Sages state matters in so many words in explaining Scripture's rule that "a stubborn and rebellious son, who will not obey the voice of his father or the voice of his mother" is referred to the "elders of the city." The parents then explain to the government, "This our son is stubborn and rebellious, he will not obey our voices, he is a glutton and a drunkard." The son, found guilty, is put to death (Dt. 21:18–21). Why so? The sages explain: A rebellious and incorrigible son is tried on account of [what he may] end up to be. Let him die while yet innocent, and let him not die when he is guilty (Mishnah-tractate Sanhedrin 8:5).

While Scripture assigns the task to the father, as is commonly the case, the sages of the Oral Torah expand the responsibility to encompass the mother as well:

> [If] his father wanted [to put him to judgment as a rebellious and incorrigible son] but his mother did not want to do so,
>
> [if] his father did not want and his mother did want [to put him to judgment],
>
> he is not declared a rebellious and incorrigible son—
>
> until both of them want [to put him to judgment].
>
> R. Judah says, "If his mother was unworthy of his father, he is not declared to be a rebellious and incorrigible son."
>
> Mishnah-tractate Sanhedrin 8:4

Sages further provide so many alibis and exceptions that, in the end, they conclude, no one has ever been tried, convicted, and put to death as a "rebellious and incorrigible son," but it is a matter of theory, worth attention in its own right. And the point they wish to make, which vastly transcends the matter of what parents owe their children, is, as noted just now, to make sure the child remains eligible to stand in judgment and so gain the resurrection out of the grave that is the promise of God to holy Israel:

> A rebellious and incorrigible son is tried on account of [what he may] end up to be.
>
> Let him die while yet innocent, and let him not die when he is guilty.
>
> For when the evil folk die, it is a benefit to them and a benefit to the world.

But [when the] righteous folk [die], it is bad for them and bad for the world.

Wine and sleep for the wicked are a benefit for them and a benefit for the world.

But for the righteous, they are bad for them and bad for the world.

Dispersion for the evil is a benefit for them and a benefit for the world.

But for the righteous, it is bad for them and bad for the world.

Gathering together for the evil is bad for them and bad for the world.

But for the righteous, it is a benefit for them and a benefit for the world.

Tranquility for the evil is bad for them and bad for the world.

But for the righteous, it is a benefit for them and a benefit for the world.

Mishnah-tractate Sanhedrin 8:5

We see, therefore, that the parents bear responsibility for their children now and in the world to come, and that is the main point. Having joined God in the creation of life—for there are three partners with a stake in every person, the mother, the father, and God—the parents owe the children the capacity to earn a living, the model of the life of honor and dignity, and a chance at the ultimate promise of the Torah, which is eternal life and triumph over death.

WHAT DO CHILDREN OWE
THEIR PARENTS?

The Ten Commandments deem honor of father and mother as one of the principles of God's dominion; paying honor to parents represents a primary act of acceptance of God's rule (Exodus 20:12). Virtue encompasses respect for the father and the mother as for God. Then sages take as their task to spell out what honor of parents means. They want concrete actions of respect, support, and obligation: supporting parents with food, drink, and clothing:

"Honor your father and your mother [that your days may be long in the land which the Lord your God gives you]:"

Might I infer that this is with words?

Scripture says, "Honor the Lord with your substance" (Prov. 3:9).

That means, with food, drink, and fresh garments.

That honoring parents is tantamount to honoring God is made explicit. The reason is not difficult to fathom. It is stated explicitly:

Our rabbis have taught on Tannaite authority:

Three form a partnership in the creation of a human being, the Holy One, blessed be He, one's father and one's mother. When someone honors father and mother, said the Holy One, blessed be He, "I credit it to them as though I had lived among them and they honored me."

B. Qiddushin 1:7 II.2/30B–31A

The same view is spelled out: honoring parents is like honoring God, cursing parents is like cursing God:

It is said, "Honor your father and your mother" (Ex. 20:12), and it is further said, "Honor the Lord with your wealth" (Prov. 3:9).

Scripture thereby establishes an analogy between the honor of father and mother and the honor of the Omnipresent.

It is said, "He who curses his father or his mother will certainly die" (Prov. 20:20), and it is said, "Any person who curses his God will bear his sin" (Lev. 24:15).

Scripture thereby establishes an analogy between cursing father and mother and cursing the Omnipresent.

But it is not possible to refer to smiting Heaven [in the way in which one is warned not to hit one's parents].

And that is entirely reasonable, for all three of them are partners [in a human being]

Sifra Qedoshim CXCV:II.2

Why should the parents be given the same honor as God? When we recall that the act of procreation recapitulates God's act of creation, making life, we realize that the parents are possessed of the power of creation and in that aspect are like God. Since the parents compare with God, the honor owing to God extends to the parents:

Rabbi says, "Precious before the One who spoke and brought the world into being is the honor owing to father and mother,

"for he has declared equal the honor owing to them and the honor owing to him, the fear owing to them and the fear owing to him, cursing them and cursing him.

"It is written: 'Honor your father and your mother,' and as a counterpart: 'Honor the Lord with your substance' (Prov. 3:9).

"Scripture thus has declared equal the honor owing to them and the honor owing to him.

"'You shall fear every man his mother and his father' (Lev. 19:3), and, as a counterpart: 'You shall fear the Lord your God' (Dt. 6:13).

"Scripture thus has declared equal the fear owing to them and the fear owing to him.

"'And he who curses his father or his mother shall surely be put to death' (Ex. 21:17), and correspondingly: 'Whoever curses his God' (Lev. 24:15).

"Scripture thus has declared equal the cursing them and cursing him."

Mekhilta Attributed to R. Ishmael LIV:I.1ff.

So much for the matter in principle. What, in real life, is involved in honoring parents? Sages set forth cases to make their point that there is no limit within what is permissible in the Torah. They appealed to the example of a righteous gentile, who gave up great wealth in order not to disturb his father's sleep:

Said R. Judah said Samuel, "They asked R. Eliezer, to what extent is one obligated to honor one's father and one's mother? He said to them, 'Go and observe how a certain gentile has treated his father in Ashkelon, and Dama b. Netinah is his name.'"

On one occasion they wanted to buy from him precious stones for the ephod, in the amount of six hundred thousand (*R. Kahana repeated as the Tannaite version,* eight hundred thousand) but the keys were lying under his father's pillow, and he would not disturb him. Another year the Holy One, blessed be He, gave him his reward, for a red cow was born to him in his corral, and sages of Israel came to him. He said to them, "I know full well of you that if I should demand of you all the money in the world, you will give it to me. But now I ask of you only that sum of money that I lost in honor of my father."

And said R. Hanina, "Now if someone who is not subject to commandments acts in such a way, then if someone who is subject to the commandment acts in such a way, all the more so! For said R. Hanina, 'Greater is he who is commanded and acts on that account than he who is not commanded and acts on that account.'"

Not only so, but honor of parents is relative to the case; there are no fixed rules:

A Tannaite statement of Abimi b. R. Abbahu: There is he who feeds his father pheasant to eat but this drives the son from the world, and there is he who binds his father up to the grinding wheel, and this brings the son into the world to come. [Someone fed the father pheasants but when the father asked how he could afford them, said, "It's none of your business, chew and eat." By contrast, someone was grinding on a mill and the father was summoned for the corvée, so the son said to the father, "You grind for me and I'll go in your place."]

Sages themselves set the example. They were treated with great deference, being holy men, but that did not stop them from accepting the most demeaning tasks for the parents:

R. Tarfon's mother—whenever she wanted to get into bed, he would bend down and let her climb up on his back, and when she wanted to get out, she would step down on him. He went and praised himself in the schoolhouse. They said to him, "So you still haven't got to half the honor that is owing: Has she thrown down a money bag in your presence into the sea, without your answering back to her?"

Sages' theory that honoring parents was honoring God found realization in a specific sage's attitude:

R. Joseph—when he heard the sound of his mother's steps, he said, "Let me arise before the Presence of God, who approaches."

B. Qiddushin 1:7 II.2/30B–31A

The emphasis upon the theological basis for honoring parents reminds us, once more, that Judaism in its classical statement sets forth not random teachings and wise sayings but a system in which each component fits together with all others. That is because the details of the system work in small ways to realize the system's larger message. Truisms about honoring parents turn out to recapitulate the main point, which is, God forms the center of Israel's existence; Israel's task is to know and love God by forming a holy society worthy of God's rule, so that, at the end of days, Israel—meaning all who accept God's self-manifestation in the Torah—will stand in judgment and enter into eternal life. We have come a long way from the requirements of the Israelite household—but only to discover what is at stake in that household, with its union of this-worldly and transcendental tasks and obligations.

WHEN THE FAMILY BREAKS DOWN: WHAT HAPPENS THEN?

If the relationship of the wife to the husband is sanctified, at her assent, through betrothal and consummation of the marriage, how and at whose initiative is that bond of sanctification dissolved—secularized? When the family breaks down, the husband has the power to dissolve the marriage. Then the wife returns to her father's house, with designated portions of her dowry, and supported by alimony for a year. That is the material result of the breakdown of the marriage; the household is left unaffected, except in the specific, material ways involving alimony and the dowry. But how is the original act of sanctification nullified? Our special interest focuses upon the way by which the status, or relationship, of sanctification is removed and how the woman reenters secular status of the unattached woman. Here the foci of sages' interest prove consequential. For man's part in the matter, everything depends upon a document, which on earth properly done, is ratified in Heaven as an act consequential in the sight of God. The media of sanctification involve the willing exchange of money, a writ, or sexual relations with betrothal the intent. The consummation of the union depends, further, on the provision of the marriage contract, which protects the woman in the event of divorce or the husband's death by providing for alimony. In these transactions, the woman's former status is removed by the provision of a document that nullifies the token of betrothal and the relationship that represents, and that brings about the enforcement of the marriage contract and its provisions. So the document at the end—for which Scripture makes provision—completes the document at the outset, of which Scripture knows nothing, but for which the logic of the transaction, matching beginning to end, surely calls.

To understand the answer to the question, how do we deconsecrate what has been sanctified? we have to consider the analogous situation, the sanctification of an animal for the altar of the Temple in Jerusalem, at which point the animal may not be used for any other purpose. When a farmer consecrates an animal for a particular cultic purpose, for example, as a sin-offering, the transaction involves a very specific process. He must identify the particular sin that is to be expiated by the particular animal (or in the case of what is unclear, designate an animal in a way that takes account of his uncertainty as to the sin he has committed). He must then make certain that the officiating priest makes the offering "in the proper name," meaning it must fall into the category of offering that is required and no other; the act of tossing the blood must be performed with the correct, appropriate, particular intentionality. Once the intentionality of the farmer has been realized in the tossing of the blood, what is left of the blood is no longer sacred. It may be used as fertilizer. So the key to the status of sanctification is the intentionality of the farmer, and the moment that intentionality has reached fruition, the status of the sacred falls away from what is no longer required to carry out that intention.

What happens if the farmer's intentionality in sanctifying the beast is not realized? If the farmer does not utilize the animal he has designated, or consecrated, to the altar for his particular sin, he must undertake the appropriate process of disposing of the still-consecrated beast in a manner appropriate to its status and, more to the point, to the purpose that, by his act of will, he has planned to use the beast. When it comes to the transformation of the woman's status, from secular and available to any appropriate Israelite to sacred to a single, specified individual male, the process of sanctification is equally particular, and the result equivalently decisive.

Then what brings about the deconsecration of the woman takes on heavy significance, since Heaven, as much as man and woman, takes a keen interest in the process. The counterpart to the process of the disposition of the beast sanctified to the altar for a given purpose by a designated sacrifier differs at one fundamental point. The man's act of will in consecrating the beast cannot be nullified by a corresponding act of will to deconsecrate it. Scripture is very clear on that point, when it forbids even an act of substitution of one beast for another (Leviticus 27:11). If the man should decide he wishes to offer beast B rather than beast A, beast B is consecrated, but beast A retains its prior status. That is because an additional participant in the transaction has had his say and cannot now be dismissed, and that, of course, is Heaven. Once the beast has been consecrated, therefore, it leaves the status of consecration only with Heaven's assent, that is, by following the procedures that the law deems appropriate.

Heaven has a different relationship to the marriage, and other parties enter in. When the husband determines that he wishes to deconsecrate the wife, he has the power to do so only in such a manner that the wife is fully informed and takes an active role in the transaction, receiving the writ of divorce—initiated solely on the husband's volition to be sure—on terms that she has the power to dictate. The law states eloquently that she must play a fully conscious role in the transaction when it says she may not be asleep when the writ is handed over to her, and she may not be misinformed as to its character. Thus she must know that the document is a writ of divorce; she must be awake; if she sets conditions for the reception of the document, these must be met. In these fundamental ways, then, she accedes to the process of deconsecration, to the secularization of her status within the Israelite household.

Does Heaven take an equivalent role to its engagement in the disposition of the sanctified beast and if so, where and how does that engagement take effect? The answer is, predictably, that Heaven, not only the husband and wife, concerns itself with the change in the woman's status as holy. Where, in the repertoire of the law, does that concern express itself? It is in the valid preparation of the document itself. That document—properly written, properly witnessed, properly handed over—serves to deconsecrate the woman, as surely as the rites of disposition of the consecrated animal not used for its correct purpose deal with the change in status of that beast. So it is the document that is the medium of effecting, or of annulling, the status of consecration. And what gives the document effect?

The answer is in two parts. First, the witnesses who certify the document are the key element in the process; the document is validated by valid witnesses, and lacking valid witnesses, even though it is correctly written and delivered, it has no effect at all. In the end, the particular witnesses attest not only to the facts of what is incised in the writing but also to the specificity of the writing: this man, this woman, this document. Then what is to be said about the witnesses to the preparation of the document, for whom do they stand? Given Heaven's stake in the transaction and the witnesses' status as nonparticipants, we may offer only one answer: the witnesses validate the document and give it effect because they stand as Heaven's surrogates. Israelite males not related to the parties, the witnesses accord cognizance on earth in behalf of Heaven to that change in intentionality and status that the document attests. When the witnesses to the validity of the writ that was written overseas and delivered in the Land of Israel say, "Before us it was written and before us it was signed" (that is, by the witnesses to the document itself), they confirm what is at stake in the entire transaction: Heaven has been informed of the change of intention on the part of the husband, releasing the wife from her status of sanctification to him. So the change in intentionality must be attested on earth in behalf of Heaven. And that which is certified by the witnesses is not only the validity of the writing of the document but the explicit transaction that has brought about the writing: the husband has instructed the scribe to write the writ of divorce, that particular writ of divorce, for his wife, for the named wife and no other woman (even of the same name). When he has done that, pronouncing his intent to nullify the relationship of sanctification that he proffered and the woman accepted, then all else follows.

But Heaven wants something else as well. Not only must the intention be articulated, and explicitly in the transaction at hand and no other, but the document itself must give evidence of counterpart specificity. What makes all the difference? The law specifies irregularities of two classes: first, those that do not fundamentally invalidate the transaction and, second, those that so completely invalidate the transaction that the original status of sanctification retains effect, despite what the husband has said, and despite what the wife has correctly received by way of documentary confirmation of the change of intentionality and therefore status, his and hers, respectively. That represents a most weighty result, with long-term consequences.

What conditions do not nullify the transaction? Confusing the writ of divorce of two couples bearing the same names presents a situation that can be sorted out. If the two writs of divorce are written side by side, so that the signatures have to be assigned to the respective writs, that is a problem that can be solved. The document may be spread over two sheets: if one left over part [of the text of] the writ of divorce and wrote it on the second page, and the witnesses are below, it is valid.

On the other hand, we have two explicit situations that produce the catas-
trophe of a totally invalid exchange, such that the woman remains sanctified to
the husband who has indicated the intention of divorcing her. That is to say, in
two circumstances the husband's intentionality does not register with Heaven:

> If he wrote the writ of divorce dating it according to an era which is not ap-
> plicable, for example, according to the era of the Medes, according to the era
> of the Greeks, according to the building of the Temple, according to the de-
> struction of the Temple, [if] he was in the east and wrote, "In the west," in
> the west and wrote, "In the east," she goes forth from this one [whom she
> married on the strength of the divorce from the former husband] and from
> that one [the first husband]. And she requires a writ of divorce from this one
> and from that one.
>
> Mishnah-tractate Gittin 8:5

> If the scribe wrote a writ of divorce for the man and a quittance [receipt
> given to the husband for her marriage contract payment] for the woman, and
> he erred and gave the writ of divorce to the woman and the quittance to the
> man, and they then exchanged them for one another, and if after a while, lo,
> the writ of divorce turns up in the hand of the man, and the quittance in the
> hand of the woman—she goes forth from this one and from that one.
>
> Mishnah-tractate Gittin 8:8

The two rules produce this question: who has the power to nullify even the effect of the intentionality of the husband? It is the scribe. If he errs in dating the
document, or if he errs and writes down the wrong location of the participant,
then, whatever the husband's intentionality and whatever the wife's (wrong) im-
pression of what has taken place, the writ is null, and the result is as specified,
chaotic. So too if the scribe made a mistake in transmitting the documents that
are to be exchanged, the transaction is null.

Then the question presses: why has the scribe so critical a role in the transaction that he can utterly upset the intentionality of the one and the consequent
conclusion drawn by the other party, husband and wife, respectively? The reason is clear: the law attributes to the scribe a role in the transaction as critical, in
its way, as the role of the husband in commissioning the document and the wife
in receiving it. And what is it that the scribe can do to ruin the transaction? He
can do two things. First, he can commit the unpardonable sin of not delivering
the document to the correct party at the husband's instructions. That is, the husband has told him to deliver the writ of divorce to the wife, but he has given
her the quittance instead. The woman has never validly received the writ. The
scribe must realize and not thwart the husband's intentionality.

But what about the other matter, misdating the document, misidentifying
the parties? Here what has happened is that the writ no longer pertains to those
mentioned in it. The scribe has placed the parties in a different period from that
in which they live, dating them, by reason of the document, in some other time;
or he has placed them in a different locale from the one where they are situated.
He has set forth a document for some others than the ones before him, and he
has given to those before him a spurious time and place. So the law raises yet

again its requirement on the acute localization of the piece of writing: this woman, here and now, her and her alone, this man, here and now, him and him alone. That is to say, the law has underscored the conception, the conviction really, that the moment and act of sanctification are unique, specific, not to be duplicated or replicated in any way or manner. When God oversees this holy relationship, he does not wish it to be confused with any other. That is why, when God is informed of the change of intentionality that has brought about the consecration of the woman to the man, he must be given exact information.

The law before us rests on profound reflection about the character of intentionality and its effects. What the law ascertains encompasses not only the intentionality and will of the husband, not only the conscious, explicit cognizance of the wife, but the facts of the case. Specifically, the law insists that the husband's act of will carries effect only when confirmed by valid action. Intention on its own is null. The full realization of the intention, involving valid provision for all required actions, alone carries effect. Not only so, but a third party, the scribe, intervenes in the realization of the husband's will. That means facts beyond the husband's control and the wife's power to secure a right to supervise and review matters take over—with truly dreadful and permanent results.

So the wife, having acted on the writ invalidated by the scribe's—not her or her husband's—actions or intentionality, emerges as the victim of circumstances quite in contradiction to anybody's will. The upshot is, by the rule of the law, she may not then claim that her intention—in this case, the acquiescence in a successive relationship of consecration—has been thwarted by the actions or errors of a third party and so ought to be honored in the breach. The law rejects that claim. She acted in accord with the rules of intentionality and in good faith—and it makes no difference. And the first husband, with all goodwill, cannot confirm that he intended to divorce the woman, and her actions fully accord with his initiatory intentionality. The law dismisses that allegation as well. Neither bears material consequence in the validation of what is, by reason of the facts of the case, an invalid transaction.

But the scribe possesses no intentionality in the transaction (other than the will we assume motivates his practice of his profession, that is, professionalism). The very role accorded to the scribe, not to the contracting parties, underscores the position of the law. It is that intentionality not confirmed by the correct deeds in the end does not suffice. The scribe's errors stand athwart the realization of the intentionality of the husband and the participation (where possible) of the wife; but the scribe obviously did not intend to make mistakes. So what stands in judgment of intentionality and its effect are the facts of the case: the objective actions taken by third parties. In a legal system that has made a heavy investment in the priority of intentionality and the power of will, the statement made by the law of divorce sounds a much-needed note of warning. Goodwill and proper intentionality do not govern when facts intervene.

What one means to do contradicted by what one has done willy-nilly changes no facts but makes no difference at all. That is because Heaven still insists upon something more than the correct will. It does, in the end, scrutinize actions, and these alone serve not only to confirm, but also to carry out, the will of the principals in any transaction. And, if we refer to the generative myth of the Torah, where to begin with the power of man to form and exercise intentionality is set forth, we find the reason why. The man and the woman enter the excuses that they gave way to the will of another, so their actions should be set aside. But God punishes all the parties to the act of rebellion—the snake, the woman, and the man. Then the lesson at the origin of all things—the power of humanity's will to stand against Heaven's will—finds its complement in its companion: what matters in the end is the deed, not only the intention.

That fact is underscored by another. Death too severs the marital bond. But on the occasion of death no document is involved, no scribe, no act of preparation, delivery, and attestation. The man's will to be confirmed by a deed plays no role whatever. God's will supersedes. Heaven intervenes, without the man's or the woman's consent. So what man accomplishes through a statement of intentionality confirmed by a documentary action, the writ of divorce, Heaven effects through the husband's death. Then the wife gains the right to enter a new consecrated relationship. That fact affords perspective on the deconsecration of the union that man accomplishes. Specifically, the document serves to attest in a tangible manner to the man's intentionality; the correct conditions of receipt of the document attest to the woman's conscious knowledge of what has happened. Neither can they claim not to have known that the relationship has been severed, and Heaven confirms the act of intentionality embodied in the document.

That is not what happens when the husband dies. Here, since Heaven's will is done without man's consent or woman's articulated awareness, the law sees no need for documentary confirmation, in palpable form, of the desacralization of the marital bond. The widow automatically is free to marry some other man. No one ever articulates that fact, which is everywhere taken for granted. But it does represent a choice, the alternative—keeping the widow "sacred" to the deceased until her own death—never presenting itself in either law or narrative as an option worthy of consideration. No writ of severance is involved; God's decisive action suffices. So much for man's power to bring about the deconsecration of the marital bed. What about God's? He has his own stake in the consecration or deconsecration of the conjugal bond, as we shall now see.

UNCONVENTIONAL FAMILIES, SUPERNATURAL FAMILIES

Were we to ignore the larger theological context that guides the sages in their thinking about any particular topic, we should miss the radical revision upon the very definition of family—the element of the household related by blood—that until this point we have accepted. For the Torah revealed by God to Moses and handed on by tradition to the very sages of the Mishnah, Midrash, and Talmuds, radically revises all this-worldly relationships and patterns. The Torah sees the natural world from a supernatural perspective, through God's spectacles, so to speak. Accordingly, when it comes to relationships of children to parents—and by extension, all other relationships—the Torah recasts matters in a radical manner.

Specifically, the Torah creates a supernatural family, which overtakes the this-worldly family and takes priority over it. That is stated in so many words, when the law specifies that the obligations that a disciple owes to his master transcend those that the son owes to his father:

> [If he has to choose between seeking] what he has lost and what his father has lost,
>> his own takes precedence.
>> what he has lost and what his master has lost,
>> his own takes precedence.
>> what his father has lost and what his master has lost,
>> that of his master takes precedence.
>> For his father brought him into this world.
>> But his master, who taught him wisdom, will bring him into the life.
>> But if his father is a sage, that of his father takes precedence.
> [If] his father and his master were carrying heavy burdens, he removes that of his master, and afterward removes that of his father.
> [If] his father and his master were taken captive,
>> he ransoms his master, and afterward he ransoms his father.
> But if his father is a sage, he ransoms his father, and afterward he ransoms his master.

Mishnah-tractate Baba Mesia 2:11

Matters are carried a step further. Holy Israel in its classical law is organized into castes, the highest being the priests, then the Levites, then the Israelites, and so on down. But a disciple of a sage, one in the lowest caste, takes priority over a high priest who has not mastered the Torah. So the family only exemplifies the Torah's deepest ordering of the social relationships of holy Israel, whether in the home or in the public piazza or in the Temple itself:

> Whatever is offered more regularly than its fellow takes precedence over its fellow, and whatever is more holy than its fellow takes precedence over its fellow.
> [If] a bullock of an anointed priest and a bullock of the congregation [M. Hor. 1:5] are standing [awaiting sacrifice]—
>> the bullock of the anointed [high priest] takes precedence over the bullock of the congregation in all rites pertaining to it.
> The man takes precedence over the woman in the matter of the saving of life and in the matter of returning lost property.
> But a woman takes precedence over a man in the matter of [providing] clothing and redemption from captivity.
> When both of them are standing in danger of defilement, the man takes precedence over the woman.
> A priest takes precedence over a Levite, a Levite over an Israelite, an Israelite over a *mamzer* [the genealogically lowest class of person, that is, the child of parents forbidden by the law of the Torah to marry, e.g., a brother

and a sister, or a married woman and someone other than her husband], a *mamzer* over a *Netin* [the descendant of a family of Temple servants], a *Netin* over a proselyte, a proselyte over a freed slave.

Under what circumstances?

When all of them are equivalent.

But if the *mamzer* was a disciple of a sage and a high priest was an *am haares* [a person unlettered in the Torah], the *mamzer* who is a disciple of a sage takes precedence over a high priest who is an *am haares*.

Mishnah-tractate Horayot 3:6–8

Here Judaism delivers its judgment, and I can imagine no clearer way of setting forth the entire message of the system of classical Judaism than this passage, which treats even the holiest officials of the Temple itself as subordinate, in the social order, to Torah-learning. That is why, as a matter of course, family relationships also are subordinated to those relationships with God that Torah-study realizes.

COMMENTARIES

Christianity on Judaism

by BRUCE CHILTON

The place of "holiness" as the core category of marriage, stressed at the outset of the exposition on Judaism, finds resonance within Christianity, but in a way that makes the fundamental distinctiveness of the two religions plain. Within his famous discussion of marriage, Paul insists that believers who are married to spouses who remain unbelievers should maintain the vows of their marriages (1 Corinthians 7:12–16). (If the unbelieving partner separates, however, that is another matter: then the believing brother or sister is not bound by marital vows in Paul's judgment [7:15]). The principle justifying this insistence is that of sanctification: "for the unbelieving husband is sanctified by the wife, and the unbelieving wife is sanctified by the brother" (1 Corinthians 7:14a, b).

This sanctification is proven, to Paul's mind, by the status of children of such parents: "Otherwise your children would be unclean, but as it is, they are holy" (1 Corinthians 7:14c). To this point, the comparison to the evaluation of marriage within Judaism seems close, but then Paul shows what a different direction Christianity was moving in. His closing, rhetorical question demonstrates the extent to which he was developing a notion of what sanctification involves very different from the definition of holiness within the household as the normative agricultural and sacrificial unit (1 Corinthians 7:16):

How do you know, wife, whether you will save your husband? Or: how do you know, husband, whether you will save your wife?

Two features of the Christian construction of faith are brought immediately to the fore in this statement. One concerns marriage, and the other concerns salvation in its relation to sanctification.

First, Paul is here openly instrumental in his treatment of marriage. That is why, elsewhere in the same chapter, he can commend unmarried people to remain so (1 Corinthians 7:25–35, 39–40). In so doing, he has to admit that he knows no teaching attributable to Jesus that backs his position up, as he does in the case of divorce (v. 25). But he is not backward in giving his opinion, as one who enjoys divine compassion (v. 25), and even the Spirit of God (v. 40). The core of his position is spelled out in the middle of his counsel (7:29–31):

> But I declare this, brothers: the time is shortened. So that for the rest, those having wives should be as not having, those who weep as not weeping and those who rejoice as not rejoicing and those buying as not possessing, and those dealing with the world as not taking full advantage. Because the form of this world is passing away.

Marriage is indeed embedded in the world, but the world itself, in Paul's religious vision, is vanishing. In that perspective, he fully agrees with Jesus' teaching regarding marriage and the resurrection.

In that context of eschatological flux, Paul also represents what became a typical feature of Christianity: the redefinition of sanctification in terms of salvation. Baptism, with its endowment with divine Spirit, is the moment at which one is sanctified (1 Corinthians 6:11). Just as one dies to sin and is raised in relation to God (as Christ was), so one's body after baptism serves the aims of sanctification (Romans 6:1–19). This represents an obvious and systemic departure from the understanding that sanctification is determined in relation to the altar in the Temple.

Both sanctification and marriage are reevaluated in Paul's thinking, and in the tradition of Christian theology, because both are seen as contingent. "Salvation" no longer refers, as in its basic meaning, to extrication from a situation of danger, but to the establishment of a new kind of being, consistent with the Spirit of God, and therefore sanctified. That sanctification was understood to be contagious, by means of marriage and any other structure that permitted the Spirit of God to be communicated, but all such structures were seen to be dissolving in the end of time and of reduced importance compared to the vision of God.

Islam on Judaism

by TAMARA SONN

As in Judaism, the purpose of marriage in Islam is to produce and nurture the next generation, a distinctly social mission. Yet Islam also takes into consideration the personal aspects of marriage, describing marriage partners as "garments" for one another, clearly an allusion to the mutual care and kindness the Qur'an calls for between marriage partners. Also like Judaism, Islam construes marriage as a legal contract. But unlike Judaism, Islam does not describe one marriage partner as a source of sanctification for the other partner. In Islam the source of sanctity for all human beings is submission to the will of God. The producing and nurturing of individuals within the family context is described in the revealed sources as pleasing to God, and for that reason it is a source of merit. But each member of the family is directly responsible to God; none serves as an intermediary or source of holiness for any of the others. Nor does the permission of polygyny in Islam, which is given only under certain conditions, compromise a wife's moral equality with her husband. The importance of individuals' moral responsibility is reflected in the purpose of the family in Islam. The family is essential for nurturing life—physically, socially, spiritually. All Muslims are expected to marry, and their responsibilities within marriage are subject to religious guidance. In that sense, in Islam as in Judaism, the family is the basic unit of society. But the function of that unit is not primarily economic, as it is in classical Judaism. It is to establish in microcosm an ordered society whose purpose is to carry out the revealed will of God. Nevertheless, some of the roles within the family are identified in Islam according to economic responsibility. Accordingly, the Qur'an specifies that men generally are responsible for women because of their economic role, although women have responsibilities and rights, too, among which is the right to own and manage private wealth, as in Judaism. A wife's obligation of obedience seems to be stressed more in Islam than in Judaism. The Qur'an specifies punishments for wives who are suspected of disobedience, without specifying what rights may not be limited by her husband. Still, each individual's religious obligations are the same in Islam, and there is no specific prohibition against women studying the law. Similarly, Muslim children, like Jewish children, are expected to obey their parents. But Muslim children are to put no one—even their parents—in the place of God. If a parent demands unlawful or immoral acts, children are to exercise their independent wills, disobeying such demands in preference for the will of God.

Hinduism on Judaism

by Brian K. Smith

Hinduism and Judaism seem to have many things in common when it comes to the specific and legalistic rulings on how individuals should relate to one another within the family. It is clear that both traditions' ancient texts (written, need it be said, almost exclusively by men) delineate a patriarchal ideal in which husbands and fathers are lords over their wives and children (as well as other members of the extended household); in which wives are subordinate to husbands and participate in religious life primarily through their own appointed household duties; in which the generation and proper upbringing of offspring (and especially sons) is a prime desideratum, as well as a duty; in which children are instructed to honor or even worship their parents (honoring parents is "like honoring God" in both traditions); and in which the family functions as a microcosm within a larger social, political, economic, and religious universe maintained by proper relations between superiors and inferiors.

There are, of course, differences in the ways this ideal picture is detailed. In Hinduism, for example, there seems to be an absence of even the few scruples registered in certain Jewish texts regarding the husband's absolute control over the wife. In Hinduism, the widow is much discouraged from remarrying and reverts back not to her "father's house" (as in Judaism) but to the household of her son. Women in Hinduism were traditionally prohibited from even hearing recitation of the sacred Veda, whereas in Judaism women and children could participate in the "supreme religious activity" of the religion by listening to Torah-study. In general, it would seem that divorce within traditional Judaism is a much more complex affair, and proceeds with much more caution, than in traditional Hinduism (much to the detriment of women in the latter case).

But it is also the case that these two religions set forth their instructions on the ethics of family life from within very different overarching contexts. Judaism, it would seem, models the human family in the image of the ideal relationship between God the Father and humankind, his children. While Professor Neusner writes that "the Torah creates a supernatural family, that overtakes the this-worldly family and takes priority over it," it would also seem that this supernat-ural family nevertheless forms the paradigmatic archetype against which the this-worldly family is structured and measured. The emphasis in Judaism is on the "holiness" or "sanctity" of the family and family relations set within the con-text of the holy bond between God and his people. In Hinduism, the emphasis is on *order,* on the maintenance of the proper relations and duties (dharma) within a cosmic-moral universe that is governed at all levels by each thing and being fulfilling an inborn and "natural" task. Families, and indeed the whole order of the universe, are disrupted in Hinduism (even in those very theistic traditions within the religion) not by *disobedience* but when the assigned dharma is ignored or otherwise left unfulfilled.

Buddhism on Judaism

by BRAD CLOUGH

Since classical Buddhist texts, unlike classical Jewish texts, do not typically dis-cuss the family and its household in terms of their economic and social relations with the larger society, but are almost exclusively concerned with internal fam-ily dynamics, one might suppose that these two traditions do not have much in common to say about the ethics of family life. Upon closer examination, how-ever, one finds more similarities than differences.

With respect to marriage, the key governing language in both Judaic and Buddhist tradition is religious language. Just as the word in Judaism for "be-troth" is "sanctify," Buddhism speaks of the husband and wife worshipping one another, and calls marriage *sadāra-brahmacariya* or the "divine life with (one's) wife." Like the *Sigālovāda Sutta,* the Torah prescribes a stable, caring re-lationship between husband and wife, in which equal responsibility is given to both partners, although in the *Sigālovāda Sutta* it appears that it is the husband who must first meet his duties to his wife, before she is obliged to reciprocate in a loving manner. Nevertheless, it was true in ancient India, where Bud-dhism has its foundations, as in ancient Israel, that women were always under-stood in terms of their relations with men: as daughters to fathers, as wives to husbands, and as widows to their sons or the males of their original family.

Still, both traditions defy conventional norms and condemn a husband's adultery as much as a wife's. Furthermore, both Jewish and Buddhist sources see a wife's duty as primarily consisting of household work, and condemn the wife who gossips and neglects her husband. Buddhism appears to give more room for a wife's authority, while Judaism allows more space for a wife's independence. Buddhism, unlike Judaism, does not have any religious commandments that are specific to men and not to women, and women are not exempt or prohibited from any religious activities. However, most expectations concerning religious behavior in Buddhism are not dependent on times of year, and so, as in Judaism, both men and women are subject to positive religious injunctions that are not time specific. As for the husband's duties, both traditions see them as being largely economic, with the husband being the provider of food, clothing, and shelter for his family. In Judaism, the husband is also responsible for bringing peace to the home, whereas in Buddhism, "the mother is the friend in the home," whose emotionally calming and nurturing presence is most important for familial happiness. In both traditions, the husband owes the wife great respect and faithfulness, and any failure by the husband in these respects is viewed as reprehensible.

Both religions agree that among the main parental obligations to children are religious instruction, arranging marriages, and teaching a trade, although in Buddhism, learning religious teachings is less gender specific, at least in terms of textual ideals. Another point in common is the responsibility of *both* parents to be ethical exemplars for children or, to paraphrase the *Sigālovāda Sutta,* to restrain them from doing evil and support them in doing good. In Buddhism, however, the law of karma almost always applies only to the individual who commits an evil act, so there is no possibility of parental sins visiting future generations of a family.

To quote Professor Neusner, both religions expect children to perform "concrete actions of respect, support, and obligation: supporting parents with food, drink, and clothing." Also, in both religions, honoring parents is tantamount to honoring the divine, although honoring God in Judaism is of significantly greater ultimate importance than honoring gods is in Buddhism. In Buddhism, parents are said to be worthy of offerings, which is also said of those figures whom Buddhists hold in the highest esteem—those who devote their whole lives to the pursuit of spiritual liberation.

As for the dissolution of family, classical Buddhist sources do not address divorce, and in most Buddhist societies, divorce is not an option. Therefore, Buddhism is much less concerned with how to properly put an end to a broken family, and almost entirely concerned with ways of mending such a family.

With respect to unconventional and supernatural families, both religions radically redefine the meaning of family to meet with religious concerns that transcend worldly ones. In Judaism, family relationships are ultimately subordinate to a person's relationship with God, and in Buddhism, it is typically held that the conventional family ultimately must be renounced in favor of the family of monastics, or the family of Buddha, in which the concern is the realization of *nirvāṇa* or *bodhi,* that is, liberation from suffering.

SUMMARY

In Judaism the wife owes the husband a household conducted in accord with the laws of Moses and of Israel, the holy people. The husband owes the wife not only support and sexual satisfaction, but also freedom to maintain relationships outside of his control. The wife and husband have carefully differentiated roles in the family and household and work as partners to maintain a stable family. Parents owe their children an upbringing in the Torah, e.g., circumcision; they must get wives for their sons and husbands for their daughters; they must teach the son a trade and the daughter household skills; and provide for their future. Children owe their parents honor, dignity, and respect. When the family breaks down, the husband provides the wife with alimony to support her until she is able to remarry; the wife returns to her father's house, with the dowry that her father contributed to the now-dissolved family-unit. In addition to the natural family of husband, wife, children, and extended relatives, Judaism recognizes the supernatural family. That is formed by the master of Torah and his disciples. The disciples' obligations to serve the master take priority over their obligations, as sons, to serve their fathers.

GLOSSARY

Abodah   labor; also, Temple service, performing the sacrificial cult in the Temple of Jerusalem; also prayer

Abot   "the Fathers," the sayings of the principal authorities of the Oral Torah of Judaism; a tractate attached to the Mishnah, ca. 200 C.E., at about 250 C.E.

Aggadah   lore, narrative, exegesis of Scripture, theology

B.C.E.   before the Common Era = B.C.

Baba Batra   The last gate, a tractate of the Mishnah-Tosefta-Yerushalmi-Bavli that deals with aspects of civil law

Baba Mesia   The Middle Gate, a tractate of the Mishnah-Tosefta-Yerushalmi-Bavli that deals with aspects of civil law, subject to commentary in the Bavli and the Yerushalmi

Baba Qama   The First Gate, a tractate of the Mishnah-Tosefta-Yerushalmi-Bavli that deals with torts and damages

Bavli   the Talmud of Babylonia, ca. 600 C.E., a systematic commentary to thirty-seven of the sixty-three tractates of the Mishnah

Berakhot   "blessings," a tractate of the Mishnah-Tosefta-Yerushalmi-Bavli that deals with the recitation of the Shema, the creed of Judaism ("Hear, Israel, the Lord our God, the Lord is one"), the presentation of the Prayer (the silent supplication, recited standing, consisting on weekdays of eighteen benedictions), and the staying of blessings before and after eating food, and of blessings on special occasions

C.E.   Common Era = A.D.

Denar   a coin, worth six silver ma'ahs

Elijah the prophet   the harbinger of the coming of the Messiah

Erubin   a tractate of the Mishnah that deals with transporting objects on the Sabbath from public to private domain and vice versa; and the provision of a Sabbath boundary, mingling ownership of property within the boundary into a single domain for purpose of Sabbath observance

Fathers According to Rabbi Nathan   a talmud to Abot; provides biographies to the sages whose sayings are mentioned in Abot

Fathers   *see* Abot

Genesis Rabbah   Rabbinic commentary to the book of Genesis, produced ca. 450 C.E., emphasizes the connection between Israel's life as portrayed in Scripture with its situation in real time.

Get   a writ of divorce

Gittin   tractate of the Mishnah-Tosefta-Yerushalmi-Bavli that deals with the writing and delivery of writs of divorce

Hagigah   tractate of the Halakhah of the Mishnah-Tosefta-Yerushalmi-Bavli that deals with the festal offering presented by pilgrims to the Jerusalem Temple during the festival celebrations of Passover, Pentecost, and Tabernacles

Halakhah   law, norms of behavior

Hillel and Shammai   two principal authorities of the Mishnah, flourished around the beginning of the first century C.E.

Horayot   a tractate of the Mishnah-Tosefta-Yerushalmi-Bavli that deals with the consequences of false teaching on the part of Israel's monarch, high priesthood, and court system

Kesherim   people who are honorable and virtue, literally, "kosher-people"

Ketubot   a tractate of the Mishnah that deals with marriage-agreements, guaranteeing support for a wife in the event of death or divorce

Leviticus Rabbah   Commentary to the book of Leviticus, ca. 450 C.E.

Makkot   tractate of the Halakhah of the Mishnah-Tosefta-Yerushalmi-Bavli that deals with sins punished by flogging, with the punishment for manslaughter, and with administering the flogging

Megillah   a tractate of the Mishnah that deals with the festival of Purim, described in the biblical book of Esther; and with the life of synagogues, with special attention to the public declamation of the Torah

Mekhilta attributed to R. Ishmael   Commentary to the book of Exodus, probably of ca. 250–300 C.E.

Mishnah   a six part exposition of the law, divided into sixty-three tractates, or subject-areas, of the Oral Torah revealed by God to Moses at Mount Sinai and formulated and transmitted wholly in memory until formalized in ca. 200 C.E. under the auspices of Judah the Patriarch, the ruler of the Jewish population of Roman Palestine of that period

Nedarim   tractate of the Halakhah of the Mishnah-Tosefta-Yerushalmi-Bavli that deals with taking vows and releasing them

Pesahim   a tractate of the Mishnah that deals with the festival of Passover, with special attention to the prohibition of leaven on that holy day and the sacrifice of the Pascal lamb; and the Passover meal in the home

Pesiqta deRab Kahana   Rabbinic commentary on passages of Scripture highlighted on various Sabbaths and festivals

Qedoshim   "holy"—the lection of the Torah beginning at Lev. 19:2, "You shall be holy, for I the Lord your God am holy." This is followed by the definition of deeds that sanctify their doer, and deeds that profane him.

Qiddushin   a tractate of the Mishnah that deals with betrothals and matters of caste-status, e.g., Israelite, Levite, Priest, and the like

Qonam   a euphemism for "qorban," meaning, "offering," thus a declaration that something is holy as is an offering in the Temple and therefore not available for secular, everyday use

Sanhedrin   tractate of the Halakhah of the Mishnah-Tosefta-Yerushalmi-Bavli that deals with the operation of the courts of justice, both civil and criminal; and with the crimes or sins that are punished by the four media for inflicting the death penalty, respectively

Shabbat   Hebrew word for the Sabbath; the seventh day, a day of rest, commemorating the creation of the world in six days and God's repose on the Seventh; also the name of a tractate of the Mishnah-Tosefta-Yerushalmio-Bavli that deals with the Sabbath, with special attention to refraining from performing servile labor on that day and transporting objects from public to private domain or vice versa

Sifra   Rabbinic commentary to the book of Leviticus, emphasizes that Scripture forms the valid source for the laws of the Mishnah

Song Rabbah   Song of Songs Rabbah, the rabbinic commentary to the book of the Song of Songs; underscores that the love poem embodies God's love for Israel and Israel's love for God

Sotah   tractate of the Mishnah-Tosefta-Yerushalmi-Bavli that deals with the wife accused of adultery, as portrayed at Numbers 5

Taanit   a tractate of the Mishnah-Tosefta-Yerushalmi-Bavli that deals with fasting in times of crisis, and also the delegation of priests of a given village and its activities when it goes up to Jerusalem to conduct the Temple rites

Talmud   a systematic commentary to a tractate of the Mishnah, clarifying the source in Scripture of a law in the Mishnah, the meanings of words and phrases, and the broader implications of a rule; also augmenting the presentation of the law by the Mishnah through a systematic exposition of correlative topics, whether of law or of theology; the whole characterized by contentious analytical argument

Torah   the Five books of Moses, Genesis, Exodus, Leviticus Numbers, Deuteronomy; more generally, God's teaching to Moses at Mount Sinai, written and oral

Tosefta   a compilation of legal rulings that complement those in the Mishnah and are attributed to the same authorities as are cited in the Mishnah, reached closure at ca. 300 C.E.

Tractate   a topical exposition of a category of law (halakhah) in Judaism, with special reference to the Mishnah's, Tosefta's, Yerushalmi's, and Bavli's topical divisions

Yebamot   a tractate of the Mishnah-Tosefta-Yerushalmi-Bavli that deals with the levirate connection between the widow of a childless man and one of his surviving brothers, as defined at Dt. 25:1–5

Yerushalmi   the Talmud of the Land of Israel ("Jerusalem"), produced in ca. 400 C.E. in Galilee by the sages of the Torah, commenting on thirty-nine of the sixty-three tractates of the Mishnah

Yohanan ben Zakkai   the Rabbinic leader who escaped from Jerusalem before it fell to the Romans in the summer of 68 C.E. and who founded the study-circle that preserved knowledge of the Torah after the calamity and that produced the Mishnah and related traditions

Zekhut   unearned, uncoerced grace, bestowed by God in response to unearned acts of self-sacrifice or of other unusual merit that God craves but cannot coerce

DISCUSSION QUESTIONS

1. What are the three aspects of the household in Judaism, and how do contemporary families in America compare in their dimensions? Why do the needs of the household override those of individual members?

2. What are the kinds of labor that a woman performs for her husband, and why are these calibrated to correspond to the labor-force that the woman brings into the household? What are the counterpart obligations of the husband to the wife? Why in a polygamous society are sexual relations explicitly provided for the wife?

3. Why does Judaism deny the husband control over the wife's activities in maintaining autonomous relationships with others?

4. How would a contemporary American definition of what parents owe their children and what children owe their parents compare with that of Classical Judaism? What do you learn about Judaism from the difference? What do you learn about American secular society from the difference?

5. When the family breaks down, what stake does the woman have in the proper provision of a document of divorce? Why does Heaven concern itself with the same matter? What theological theme comes to the fore in the relationship of the husband and the wife?

6. The artificial family of master and disciples expresses a basic value of Classical Judaism: the priority of Torah-learning. What are comparable artificial families in contemporary American society, and what basic values come to expression in them?

 **INFOTRAC**

If you would like additional information related to the material discussed here, you can visit our Web site: http://www.wadsworth.com

2

Christianity

BY BRUCE CHILTON

Christianity insists categorically upon sexuality and family as vital aspects of how the people of God are to live within the Spirit of God. But the structure of these relationships, which Christianity inherited from the Greco-Roman world in which it flourished, was both patriarchal and subject to injustice (from patriarchy itself, as well as from other powerful forces). Christian theology therefore developed a characteristic ambivalence about marriage and family. On the one hand, both were embraced, as offering an opportunity for Jesus' ideal of love to be worked out. On the other hand, the transformation of both marriage and family themselves became a part of the Christian's agenda.

CONVENTIONAL EXPECTATION VERSUS THIS RELIGIOUS TRADITION: WHAT DO HUSBANDS AND WIVES OWE ONE ANOTHER?

The second Christian century was a time of profound ferment within the Church. The definition of Christianity as distinct from Judaism was widely agreed, on the part of Jews and Christians and representatives of the Roman Empire, and that made for a sense of beleaguered cohesion among Christians. Christians could no longer claim the right as Jews not to take part in the, for them, idolatrous worship of the image of Caesar, and that made for a persistent environment of persecution.[1] On the other hand, the definition as being apart from Judaism pressed Christians into the arena of philosophical debate with many other ways of looking at God (Judaism included), a debate that was then very popular.[2] They gave accounts to outsiders and to one another of how their way was the way the one God would have humanity live.

No book was more popular among Christians at this time than *The Shepherd of Hermas*. This work more than any other represents the synthesis of conven-

---

[1]See Bruce Chilton and Jacob Neusner, editors, *Trading Places: The Intersecting Histories of Judaism and Christianity* (Cleveland: Pilgrim Press, 1996), 37–58.

[2]See Bruce Chilton and Jacob Neusner, *The Intellectual Foundations of Christian and Jewish Discourse: The Philosophy of Religious Argument* (London: Routledge, 1997).

tional and religious expectations concerning life in families that early Christianity achieved. Jaroslav Pelikan is representative of scholarship in his description of the apocalypticism of *The Shepherd of Hermas*:[3]

> The author (or authors) of the *Shepherd* used the format of an apocalyptic summons to call the readers to repentance. The vividness of its eschatological language is exceeded only by the decisiveness of its plea. The Lord had not yet returned, and therefore the work of judgment was not yet complete; but it would soon be finished, and then the consummation would come.

As Pelikan points out, his use of the word *apocalyptic* here does not refer to the hard-and-fast distinction between this world and the world to come. Rather, a process started within the world is pointed toward its eschatological completion. In fact, the line of demarcation between the present and the future is less sharply drawn in *The Shepherd* than it is, say, in the Revelation of John in the New Testament (which was written around 100 C.E.).

In the first vision of *The Shepherd* (chapter 1), an angelic Lady appears to Hermas and accuses him of sin (specifically, of impure thoughts about a woman, whom the angelic Lady resembles). Her analysis of the rewards that attend righteousness, and therefore of the punishments that await evil, is succinct:

> For the righteous man has righteous designs. As long as his designs are righteous, his repute stands fast in heaven, and he finds the Lord ready to assist him in all his doings. But they who have evil designs in their hearts bring upon themselves death and captivity, especially those who obtain this world for themselves, and glory in their wealth, and do not lay hold of the good things which are to come.

The apocalyptic perspective of the angelic promise and threat is evident in the wording of the citation. "The good things which are to come" refers to the heavenly treasure that was commonly held by Christians to be stored for them until the day of judgment (1 Peter 1:3–5).

The apocalyptic convictions of *The Shepherd of Hermas* are evident, and amply support the scholarly reading of the document that has become a matter of consensus. But it is equally apparent that there is another sort of conviction at work. Hermas is assured that the righteous person "finds the Lord ready to assist him in all his doings." The promise, in other words, is for support in the present, not only in the final judgment that is to come. Similarly, the fate of the wicked is "death and captivity," and not a purely eschatological threat.

The social setting of *The Shepherd of Hermas* makes the promise and the threat all the more striking. On the basis of earlier materials, "Hermas" finally composed *The Shepherd* around the year 150 C.E., just when intellectuals reached a crescendo in their attacks on Christians. Fronto, tutor of the emperors Antoninus and Marcus Aurelius (and consul under Hadrian), charged that Christians worshipped an ass's head, sacrificed children, and encouraged promiscuity

---

[3] *The Christian Tradition: A History of the Development of Doctrine* (Chicago: University of Chicago Press, 1971), 126.

during worship.[4] Under such circumstances, to imagine oneself as assisted and punished by the Lord takes on a particular meaning.

The righteous person who "finds the Lord ready to assist him in all his doings" discovers support, then, in an environment of persecution, but not so much prosperity that he becomes one of those who "obtain this world for themselves, and glory in their wealth." Just as Christians attempted to walk a fine line between the Roman hostility that would destroy their lives and the accommodation to Rome that would destroy their souls, so Hermas is called to a life of just getting along with divine support. In that position, he is to escape both the wrath of God and death at the hands of Caesar.

The Shepherd of Hermas is often written off as a product of "no great intelligence."[5] That evaluation is framed in intellectual and literary terms, in comparison with the vigorous theology of other Christian works of the second century (such as those of Justin Martyr, Irenaeus, Tertullian, and Clement of Alexandria). But *The Shepherd* should be evaluated within the social function in Rome that it evidently performed, and performed to such good effect that it was actively discussed whether the work belonged within the New Testament. *The Shepherd* elaborates and develops the recommendation for the social posture of disciples that is already evident in the Gospel according to Mark (from the first century).

Mark's ending has long caused perplexity, because the Gospel closes with the women at the tomb, having been told of the resurrection of Jesus, departing in silence, "for they were afraid" (16:8). Longer endings were later added to Mark, to make it accord better with the other Gospels, but the emphatic silence of the women was clearly intended as the final profile of the original work. Such silence is only perplexing, however, when Mark is read outside the context of the recent and vicious persecution that had been instituted by Nero in 64 C.E. Within that setting, Mark is recommending a rational policy: discipleship with a low profile. The women are to know what they know, but not to spread their knowledge abroad.

The position of Christians in Rome by the time of Hermas is less fraught with immediate danger than during the period of Mark's Gospel, but still precarious. Hermas describes himself as a freed slave who had acquired family and property. His own marginal situation, then, is defined as in between the unstable policy of Rome and the absolute requirements of God. The only acceptable position is to be assisted by the Lord in one's living (on the one hand), but (on the other hand) also not to permit even this divine assistance to turn into a love of wealth. The Markan motif of low-profile discipleship becomes in *The Shepherd of Hermas* a complete program of how to realize that aim in a hostile environment (Hermas I.1–II.4):

> He who brought me up sold me to a certain Rhoda at Rome. After many years I knew her very well, and began to love her as a sister. After some time

---

[4]See Jean Daniélou and Henri Marrou, *The Christian Centuries 1,* translated by V. Cronin (New York: McGraw-Hill, 1964), 86–90.

[5]F. L. Cross, *The Early Christian Fathers* (London: Duckworth, 1960), 26.

I saw her bathing in the river Tiber and gave her my hand and helped her out of the river. When I saw her beauty I reflected in my heart and said: "I should be happy if I had a wife of such beauty and manner." This alone I considered, and nothing else, no, not one thing. After some time, while I was going to Cumae, and glorifying the creations of God, for they are great and remarkable and powerful, and as I walked along I became sleepy. And a spirit took me and took me away through some terrain without a path, through which a man could not walk, but the ground was precipitous and broken up by the streams of water. Then I crossed the river, and came to the level ground and knelt down and began to pray to the Lord and to confess my sins. Now while I was praying heaven opened, and I saw that woman whom I had desired greeting me out of heaven and saying: "Hail, Hermas." And I looked at her, and said to her: "Lady, what are you doing here?" and she answered me: "I was taken up to censure your sins to the Lord." I said to her: "Are you now my accusation?" "No," she said, "but listen to the words which I am going to say to you. 'God who dwells in heaven' and created that which is out of that which is not, and 'increased and multiplied it' for the sake of his holy Church, is angry with you because you sinned against me." I answered and said to her: "Did I sin against you? In what way, or when did I say a shameful word to you? Did I not always regard you as a goddess? Did I not always respect you as a sister? Why do you charge me falsely, woman, with these wicked and impure things?" She laughed and said to me: "The desire of wickedness came up in your heart. Or do you not think that it is a wicked deed for a righteous man if a wicked desire come up in his heart? Yes, it is a sin," said she, "and a great one. For the righteous considers righteous things. As long as his designs are righteous his repute stands fast in heaven, and he finds the Lord favorable in his every concern. But they who consider wicked things in their hearts bring upon themselves death and captivity, especially those who obtain this world for themselves, and take pride in their wealth, and do not lay hold of the good things which are to come. Their souls will repent; yet have they no hope, but they have abandoned themselves and their life. But do you pray to God, and 'He shall heal the sins of yourself' and of all your house and of all the saints."

After she had spoken these words heaven was shut, and I was all trembling and grieving. And I was saying to myself: "If this sin is recorded against me, how shall I be saved? Or how shall I propitiate God for my fully formed sins? Or with what words shall I beseech the Lord so that he will be placated for me?" While I was considering and hesitating over these things in my heart I saw before me a white chair of great size made of snow-white wool; and there came a woman, old and clothed in shining garments with a book in her hands, and she sat down alone and greeted me: "Hail, Hermas! And I, grieving and weeping, said: "Hail, Lady!" And she said to me: "Why are you gloomy, Hermas? You who are patient and without bile, who are always laughing, why are you so downcast in appearance and unhappy?" And I said to her: "Because of a most excellent lady, who says that I sinned against her." And she said: "By no means let this thing happen to the servant of God; but for all that, the thought did arise in your heart concerning her. It is such a design as this which brings sin on the servants of God. For it is an evil and mad purpose against a revered spirit and one already approved, if a man desire an evil deed, and especially if it be Hermas the temperate, who abstains from every evil desire and is full of all simplicity and great innocence.

"But it is not for this that God is angry with you, but in order that you should convert your family, which has done wrong against the Lord, and against you, their parents. But you are indulgent, and do not correct your family, but have allowed them to become corrupt. For this reason the Lord is angry with you, but he will heal all the past evils in your family, for because of their sins and wrong you have been corrupted by the things of daily life. But the great mercy of the Lord has had pity on you and on your family, and will make you strong and will establish you in his glory. Only do not be idle, but have courage and strengthen your family. For as the smith, by hammering his work, prevails in the task which he desires, so also the daily righteous word prevails over wickedness. Do not cease, then, correcting your children, for I know that if they repent with all their heart, they will be inscribed in the books of life with the saints." After she had ceased these words she said to me: "Would you like to hear me read aloud?" and I said: "I should like it, Lady." She said to me: "Listen then, and hear the glories of God." I heard great and wonderful things which I have not the strength to remember; for all the words were frightful, such as a man cannot bear. So I remembered the last words, for they were useful to us and gentle: "Lo, 'the God of the powers,' whom I love, by his mighty power, and by his great understanding 'created the world,' and by his glorious counsel surrounded his creation with beauty, and by his mighty word 'fixed heaven and founded the earth upon the waters,' and by his own wisdom and forethought created his holy Church, which he also blessed—Lo, he changes heaven, and the mountains and the hills and the seas, and all things are becoming smooth for his chosen ones, so he might give them the promise which he made with great glory and joy, if they keep the ordinances of God, which they received with great faith."

So, when she had finished reading, and rose from the chair, there came four young men, and took up the chair and went away towards the east. And she called me and touched my chest and said to me; "Did my reading please you?" and I said to her: "Lady, this last part pleases me, but the first part was hard and difficult." And she said to me: "This last part is for the righteous, but the first part was for the nations and the apostates." While she was speaking with me two men appeared, and took her by the arms and they went away towards the east, where the chair had gone. But she went away cheerfully, and as she went said to me, "Courage, Hermas." While I was going to Cumae, at about the same time as the year before, as I walked along I remembered the vision of the previous year, and the spirit again took me up and brought me away to the same place, where I had been the previous year. So when I came to the place, I knelt down and began to pray to the Lord and to glorify his name, because he had thought me worthy, and had made known to me my former sins. But after I rose from prayer I saw before me the elder lady, whom I had seen the year before, walking and reading out from a little book. And she said to me: "Can you take this as a message to God's elect ones?" I said to her: "Lady, I cannot remember so much; but give me the little book to copy." "Take it," she said, "and give it me back." I took it and went away to a certain place in the country, and copied it all, letter by letter, for I could not distinguish the syllables. So when I had finished the letters of the little book it was suddenly taken out of my hand; but I did not see by whom.

But after fifteen days, when I had fasted and besought the Lord greatly, knowledge of the writing was revealed to me. And these things were written: "Your seed, Hermas, have disregarded God, and have blasphemed the Lord, and have betrayed their parents in great wickedness, and they are called the betrayers of parents, and their betrayal has not profited them, but they have added to their sins wanton deeds and evil matings, and so their crimes have been completed. But make these words known to all your children and to your wife, who shall in future be to you as a sister. For she also does not refrain her tongue, with which she does evil; but when she has heard these words she will refrain it, and will obtain mercy. After you have made known these words to them, which the master commanded me to be revealed to you, all the sins which they have formerly committed shall be forgiven them, and they shall be forgiven for all the saints who have sinned up to this day, if they repent with their whole heart, and put aside double-mindedness from their heart. For the master has sworn to his elect by his glory that if there be still sin after this day has been fixed, they shall have no salvation; for repentance for the just has a limit; the days of repentance have been fulfilled for all the saints, but for the nations repentance is open until the last day. You shall speak, then, to the leaders of the Church, that they reform their ways in righteousness, to receive in full the promises with great glory. You, therefore, 'who work righteousness,' must remain steadfast and be not double-minded, that your company may be with the holy angels. Blessed are you, as many as endure the great persecution which is coming, and as many as shall not deny their life. For the Lord has sworn by his son that those who have denied their Christ have been rejected from their life, that is, those who deny him in the days to come. But those who denied him formerly have obtained forgiveness through his great mercy.

"But, Hermas, no longer bear a grudge against your children, nor neglect your sister, that they may be cleansed from their former sins. For they will be corrected with righteous correction, if you bear no grudge against them. The bearing of grudges works death. But you, Hermas, had great troubles of your own because of the transgressions of your family, because you did not pay attention to them. But you neglected them and became entangled in their evil deeds. But you are saved by not 'having broken away from the living God,' and by your simplicity and great temperance. These things have saved you, if you remain in them, and they save all whose deeds are such, and who walk in innocence and simplicity. These shall overcome all wickedness and remain steadfast to eternal life. 'Blessed' are all they 'who do righteousness'; they shall not perish for ever. But you shall say to Maximus: 'Behold, persecution is coming, if it seems good to you deny again.' 'The Lord is near those that turn to him,' as it is written in the Book of Eldad and Modat, who prophesied to the people in the wilderness."

And a revelation was made to me, brethren, while I slept, by a very beautiful young man who said to me, "Who do you think that the elder lady was from whom you received the little book?" I said, "The Sibyl." "You are wrong," he said, "She is not." "Who is she, then?" I said. "The Church," he said. I said to him, "Why then is she old?" "Because," he said, "she was created the first of all things. For this reason is she old; and for her sake was the world established." And afterwards I saw a vision in my house. The elder lady came and asked me if I had already given the book to the elders. I said that I had not given it. "You have done well," she said, "for I have words to add. When, therefore, I have finished all the words they shall be made known by you to all the elect. You shall therefore write two little books and send one to Clement and one to Grapte. Clement then shall send it to the cities abroad, for that is his duty; and Grapte shall exhort the widows and orphans; but in this city you shall read it yourself with the elders who are in charge of the church."

Hermas lays out his chief concern as the problem of sin. Given that, as he is told, the righteous are only as righteous as their intentions, Hermas panics: "If this sin is recorded against me, how shall I be saved?" (*Shepherd* I.2.1). In another vision, the grounds of his fear are only confirmed. A great and old woman appears, seated on a throne of snow-white wool. That description echoes the appearance of God himself in the vision of Daniel 7:9, and Hermas is eventually told that the venerable matron is the Church (*Shepherd* II.4.1). It is she who underscores what Hermas has already learned (*Shepherd* I.2.4):

For it is an evil and mad purpose against a revered spirit and one already approved, if a man desire an evil deed, and especially if it be Hermas the temperate, who abstains from every evil desire and is full of all simplicity and great innocence.

The authority of the Church, then, only reinforces the desperate predicament of all who are like Hermas. Because the issue is one's intentions and desires, not only one's actions, the problem seems here to be set up as impossible to solve. And in that the issue is the lack of complete control over what he thinks, Hermas' predicament seems to be universal.

The Shepherd of Hermas here identifies, with the greatest precision of any extant document from the early Church, how the problem of sin was seen to threaten the integrity of the faith overall. As compared to the social issue of how to conduct oneself as a disciple in an inhospitable environment, the deeper incongruity of being held responsible for whatever one might think and feel was a far more fundamental problem. After all, that concern could feed the response of a dualistic Gnosticism,[6] which would make the nature of one's desire a symptom of whether one was spiritual in one's constitution. A counsel of despair is

---

[6]Discussed in the Christianity chapter of *Making an Honest Living: What Do We Owe the Community?* (volume 2 of this series).

an obvious response to the command to control one's desire. If Hermas must determine his desires in order to be saved, the most rational course might be to admit that he is not saved and cannot be.

The Shepherd of Hermas resolves the dilemma in what the angelic representation of the Church goes on to say. God's anger for evil intents is confirmed, but the grounds of his anger are said to be other than the issue of intents (*Shepherd* I.3.1):

> But it is not for this that God is angry with you, but in order that you should convert your family, which has sinned against the Lord, and against you, their parents.

The answer to the dilemma of human intention is given: it is the mercy of divine restraint. Although God would justly be angered by the failure of good intent among the righteous, he is compassionate enough to provide a remedy. If at least they will see to the nurture of their families, he will not be angry.

The symmetry of God's willingness to accept the nurture of one's family in the place of intentional perfection is simply stated. In the social realm, one can act with greater conscious control than in the purely personal realm (*Shepherd* I.3.2):

> For as the smith, by hammering his work, overcomes the task which he desires, so also the daily righteous word overcomes all wickedness.

The Shepherd comes to a confidence in reasoned behavior, as influenced by the "Word" of God, which corresponds to Clement of Alexandria's much more philosophical theology of Christ, also developed during the second century. Clement's approach was inventive, and a continuation of the identification between Jesus and the Word of God made in the Gospel according to John (1:1–18) and by Justin Martyr (another second-century thinker). Clement insisted that the Word was influential even on one's passions. But Clement's thought, *The Shepherd* shows us, is also representative of popular Christian belief. The "daily righteous word" of God, God's accessibility through reason and speech and deliberate action, was widely understood to "overcome all wickedness," whether in the world or in one's heart.

The family is a vital sphere of Christian action in *The Shepherd of Hermas,* because it is the one place where it is assumed Hermas exerts influence. "The affairs of daily life" in the world are assumed to corrupt families, and Hermas is instructed to correct his own family, especially his children (*Shepherd* I.3.1–2). Later, the same principle will include Hermas' wife within his family, and it will be extended to the Church at large (*Shepherd* II.2).

The placement of the family at the center of action marks a signal development in Christian theology. The position attributed to Jesus in the primitive Church envisaged the renunciation of family for the sake of the Gospel (Matthew 19:27–30; Mark 10:28–31; Luke 18:28–30). That position was modulated within Early Christianity as represented within the New Testament: the relationships of family were portrayed as providing an opportunity for enacting the love one had learned in Christ (1 Peter 2:18–3:7). By the time of *The Shepherd of Hermas,* however, a deeper transformation in the evaluation of family had occurred. It was now the sphere of first recourse in working out one's constitutional inability to offer God the perfection he required. Here, in fact, is the source of the vital concern for family with classical Christianity. It is not merely a "value" or a place of affection: family is where salvation is ordinarily worked out.

The imperative to Christian leaders sums up the ethical perspective on salvation that is developed in *The Shepherd of Hermas* (II.2.7):

> You, therefore, who do righteousness, remain steadfast and do not be double-minded, that your way might be with the angels.

By this point in the book, it has already been shown that an individual cannot avoid being double-minded to some extent: aspects of the imagination simply evade complete control. But one can be dedicated to the rational, deliberate task of nurturing one's family and the family of the Church: that is what God demands by way of repentance.

A remarkable tension has been evident within Christianity from its classical formulations during the course of the second century. On the one hand, family and sexual relations have been viewed as pertaining to a condition of flesh that is to be overcome; on the other hand, such relationships have been held up as the normative field within which salvation is to be worked out.

The Shepherd of Hermas, precisely because it is a relatively unsophisticated document, represents the tension quite clearly (II.2.3):

> But make these words known to all your children and to your wife, who shall in future be to you as a sister. For she does not refrain her tongue, with which she sins; but when she has heard these words she will refrain it, and will obtain mercy.

Sexual relations are blandly put aside, when they are typified as incestuous (relations with a "sister"). By contrast, inappropriate speech is given labored attention. Christianity constructed for itself the image of the perfect woman—obedient, celibate and silent—because it located the struggle for salvation within social and human terms.

Making flesh the vessel of Spirit inevitably meant that the flesh was neither embraced nor denied as it is, but changed. Wives become "sisters" as certainly as people become angelic in the resurrection (Matthew 22:30; Mark 12:25; Luke 20:36). The perspective of Jesus had emphasized that transformation, but without insisting that people in their flesh would become like angels. In its struggle with Gnosticism during the second century, the faith that came to be known as orthodox embraced the flesh as an ultimate concern in a way that had not been the case earlier.

Mention has already been made of 1 Peter 2:18–3:7, as setting out a classic expression within Christianity of the devotion owed within families. What is fascinating about the passage is that it embeds the relationship between wife and husband within its imperatives for living as a servant class within the Roman world:

> House managers, be submitted in all fear to masters, not only to the good and gentle, but even to the crooked. Because this is grace, if on account of God's

conscience someone endures griefs, suffering unjustly. For what sort of credit is it, if you endure being beaten when you sin? But if you endure by suffering when you do good this is grace with God. For to this you were called, because Messiah suffered for your sake, leaving you behind a pattern, so that you might follow along in his footsteps. He did not do sin, neither was deceit found in his mouth; he was reviled and did not revile in return, suffering he did not threaten, but delivered himself over to the one who judges justly. He himself bore our sins in his body on the wood, so that deceasing to sins we might live to righteousness: by whose wound you were cured. Because you were sheep wandering, but now you have returned to the shepherd and overseer of our lives. Similarly wives: be submitted to our own husbands, so that even if some disobey the word, through the conduct of the wives they will be gained without a word, beholding your holy conduct in fear. Whose adornment should not be the exterior: braiding hair and bedecking with gold and wearing garments, but the interior person of the heart by what is incorruptible, a meek and quiet spirit, which before God is precious. For so once the holy wives also, who hoped in God, adorned themselves, submitting to their own husbands, as Sarah obeyed Abraham, calling him lord, whose children you have become, doing good and not fearing any intimidation. Husbands similarly, dwell together by knowledge with the feminine as a weaker vessel, according honor to fellow heirs also of life's grace so that your prayers are not hindered.

Transparently, the imperative of submission here, both within households and within families, is not a simple confirmation of such institutions within the Greco-Roman world. Rather, obedience is here an exemplary act, designed to "gain" those who are involved with one in such relationships.

WHAT DO PARENTS OWE THEIR CHILDREN?

Once families were perceived as an appropriate setting of exemplary obedience within the Church, parental duties were framed in much the same way as the duties of husbands to wives were defined. Within the New Testament, the picture of a household is often invoked in order to set out the Christian imperative within a social nexus; in effect the Church as such became a household. The letter to the Ephesians, attributed to Paul after his death and written around the year 90 C.E., sets out a fine example (Ephesians 6:1–9):

Children, obey your parents in the Lord, for this is just. Honor your father and mother—such is a first commandment with promise—so that it might be well with you and you might be long-lived on the earth. And fathers, do not provoke your children, but nourish them in the Lord's upbringing and admonition. Servants, obey your lords according to flesh as the Messiah, with fear and trembling in sincerity of heart, not by eye-service as pleasing people, but as Messiah's servants doing the will of God from life, serving with good will as to the Lord and not to people, knowing that each one who does anything good will acquire from the Lord, whether slave or free. And lords, do the same to them, abandoning the threat, knowing that their Lord and yours is in heavens, and that there is not respect of persons with him.

As in the passage from 1 Peter, which was written near the same time, the family and the household are rooted in one another, as in the experience of the Greco-Roman church.

What becomes clear in the passage from Ephesians, however, is that obeying "the Lord" in heaven is the conditioning factor in the obedience of any "lords" on earth. As a result, parents and lords are to understand that their own authority is conditional. Earlier, Paul had already applied that assumption, without working it out in detail. He remarked in 2 Corinthians 12:14 that it is parents who are obliged to store up for the benefit of their children, not the reverse. In that case, Paul is comparing himself to the father of the congregation in Corinth, and household relations were in fact to become a model of community relations among churches.

Clear insight into the emergence of the principal institution of leadership within the ancient Church, the episcopate, is afforded by 1 Timothy, a letter composed in Paul's name to the follower named Timothy, whom (according to Acts 16:1–3) Paul associated with his work, having circumcised him first because he was the son of a Jewish mother and a Greek father. The letter is widely and rightly regarded as pseudonymous, along with the other Pastoral Epistles (2 Timothy and Titus). In content, style, and thought, they address the situation of the Church around the year 100 C.E.[7] Acts itself, of course, was written only some ten years earlier, so what the Pastorals and Acts say in aggregate about Paul and Timothy—a half century earlier—in their relationships, intents, and personal backgrounds, must be approached with great caution if one is seeking historical anecdotes. But history in that sense is not our concern here. First Timothy, whatever it may say accurately or inaccurately from the point of view of a critical understanding of Paul and Timothy, is a source of the first importance in coming to understand the emergence of episcopal authority.

By the time of this letter, a sense of the *institution* of being a bishop had become explicit (1 Timothy 3:1):

> The word is reliable, If anyone aspires to episcopate (*episkope*), he desires a good work.

What follows is not an enumeration of duties, however, but a set of qualifications. A bishop is to be of good repute, and that means that corrupt behavior disqualifies one from the office. Addressing the issue of qualification more positively, 1 Timothy insists a bishop should be monogamous, in control of his own

---

[7]A recent and very interesting study seeks to shelter 2 Timothy from that judgment, but the claim for some element of authenticity in the letter does not affect the present consideration; see Jerome Murphy-O'Connor, *Paul: A Critical Life* (Oxford: Clarendon, 1996), 356–359. For a general discussion, see Bruce Chilton, *Beginning New Testament* (London: SPCK, 1986; Grand Rapids, MI: Eerdmans, 1987), 71–73. The work is also published as *Studi Perjanjian Baru Bagi Pemula,* translated by Ny. C. Corputty-Item (Jakarta: Gunung Mulia, 1994).

house (including his children), and mature (1 Timothy 3:2–7). The emphasis upon control of one's household is helpful in inferring the episcopal functions that are in mind.

The importance of the house (*oikos*) in defining the Church, the local congregation, has been increasingly recognized in recent research.[8] Whether we think of Cornelius in Acts 10 or of Aquila and Priscilla in 1 Corinthians 16:19, the identity of a household with Christ, the baptism of entire families and their retainers, must have constituted a significant advance for the movement centered on the risen Jesus within any city or town we might imagine. The emergence of the episcopate within any such locality corresponds to the need to integrate one household church with another. Who better to do that than someone visibly in charge of his own house? As 1 Timothy itself puts the principle, "But if someone does not know how to conduct his own house, how will he care for the church of God?" (1 Timothy 3:5).

Because a household definition of the Church is operative, a bishop must be hospitable, more literally: "a lover of strangers" (*philoxonos;* 1 Timothy 3:2). Hospitality is a virtue especially stressed within the New Testament as the household definition of the Church emerges as paradigmatic. The utility of the household was its solidarity and its focus; what needed to be resisted was its tendency to exclude others. What applied to any given household applied doubly to the attempt to coordinate and integrate one congregation with another within a given city or locale. As we have seen above, and have detailed in regard to the conception of Israel within the Church in *Judaism in the New Testament,*[9] apostolic Christianity after Paul had to confront the crisis of its own success. The emergence of the Synoptic Gospels, catechetical instruments for the preparation of people for baptism, marked a concerted attempt (probably initiated by the circle of Barnabas in Antioch) to provide for the ecumenical practice of differing kinds of apostolic Christianity with different standards of purity.

WHAT DO CHILDREN OWE THEIR PARENTS?

The obedience of children to parents has already been exemplified within the table of duties enumerated for families and households. Moreover, the passage from Ephesians 6 illustrates the embrace of the Scriptures of Israel within the Church, in this case to show the necessity and wisdom of honoring one's parents.

---

[8]See, for example, Abraham J. Malherbe, *Social Aspects of Early Christianity* (Philadelphia: Fortress Press, 1983), 60–91.

[9]*Practices and Beliefs* (by Bruce Chilton and Jacob Neusner; London and New York: Routledge, 1995), pp. 98–128. This theme is also explored in our trilogy, Christianity and Judaism—The Formative Categories. The titles are *Revelation: The Torah and the Bible* (Valley Forge, PA: Trinity Press International, 1995); *The Body of Faith: Israel and the Church* (Valley Forge, PA: Trinity Press International, 1996); *God in the World* (Harrisburg, PA: Trinity Press International, 1997).

But the deeper motivation, as we have already seen, is to use relations in families to work out the imperative to follow Jesus. That is lucidly brought to expression in the statement that precedes the table of duties in Colossians 3:18–4:1 (Colossians 3:17):

> And everything, whatever you do in word or deed, all is in the name of the Lord Jesus: give thanks to God as father through him.

Here, action is motivated by the express desire to imitate Jesus in relation to God.

Because that imperative is linked to the demand that children should obey their parents (Colossians 3:20), it is apparent that the connection between children and Christ was of theological as well as ethical importance within early Christianity. The advice to parents to "nourish them in the Lord's upbringing and admonition" (Ephesians 6:4) may allude to a growing tradition of how Jesus himself was raised.

After all, by the time and place of Luke's Gospel (ca. 90 C.E., in Antioch) a story of Jesus' behavior as a young adolescent had become exemplary (Luke 2:41–52):

> And his parents proceeded annually to Yerushalem on the feast of Pesach. And when he was twelve years old, they went up according to the custom of the feast and they accomplished the days; when they returned, the child Yeshua remained behind in Yerushalem, and his parent did not know it. They reckoned he was in the caravan, and came a day's way, and searched him out among the relatives and acquaintances. They did not find him, and returned to Yerushalem, searching him out. And it happened after three days they found him in the holy place, sitting in the midst of the teachers and hearing them and interrogating them. But all who heard him were beside themselves, at the understanding and his replies. They saw him and were overwhelmed and his mother said to him, Child, why have you acted with us in this way? Look: your father and I are distressed in seeking you! And he said to them, Why was it that you sought me? Did you not know that it is necessary for me to be among those of my father? And they did not understand the utterance that he spoke to them. And he went down with them and came into Nazareth, and he was submitted to them. And his mother kept all the dicta together in her heart. And Yeshua progressed in wisdom and stature and grace, with God and with humanity.

Although this story superficially accords with the imperative to children within the tables of duties that we have already seen, it also manifests an element of tension between what is owed to one's parents and what is owed to God. In the next section of this essay, it will become apparent how severe that tension could become.

At the stage of Luke's Gospel, however, it was simply necessary to balance the devotion of children with that of parents, so that the principle of enacting God's love would be maintained throughout. This is transparently the case in the parable of the prodigal son (Luke 15:11–32):

Yet he said, Some person had two sons. And the younger of them said to the father, Father, give me the appropriate part of the holdings. Yet he apportioned the property to them. After not many days, the younger son gathered everything together and journeyed into a far region, and there—living dissolutely— he squandered his holdings. But when he had spent everything, there came to that region a hard famine, and he himself began to be lacking. And when he proceeded to join with one of the citizens of that region, he even sent him into his fields to tend pigs. And he longed to be satisfied from the carobs which the pigs ate, and no one gave to him. But coming to himself, he stated, How many of my fathers hires exceed in bread, but I perish here in famine! Arisen, I shall proceed to my father, and I will say to him, Father, I sinned against the heaven and before you: I am no longer worthy to be called your son. Make me as one of your hires. He arose and came to his own father. But while he was still far distant, his father saw him and felt for him and ran, fell upon his neck and kissed him. Yet the son said to him, Father, I sinned against the heaven and before you: I am no longer worthy to be called your son. Make me one of your hires. But the father said to his servants, Quickly: bring out the first robe, and clothe him, and give a ring for his hand and sandals for his feet, and bring the fattened calf: slaughter it and let us celebrate by eating. Because he, my son, was dead and revived, was lost and was found. And they began to celebrate.

But the elder son was in a field, and as he approached, coming to the house, he heard music and dancing. He summoned one of the servers and inquired what this might be. Yet he said to him that: Your brother has arrived, and your father sacrificed the fattened calf, because he has obtained him healthy. But he was angry and did not want to enter. Yet his father came out to summon him. He replied and said to his father, Look: I have served you so many years, and I never transgressed your decree, and you never gave me a goat so that I could celebrate with my friends. But when he came, your son who consumed the property with prostitutes, you sacrificed the fattened calf for him. But he said to him, Child, you are always with me, and everything mine is yours. But it is necessary to celebrate and rejoice, because your brother was dead and lives, and was lost and found.

Devotion to parents could be urged in Luke's Gospel and in Early Christianity not as an absolute imperative, but as a response to the extent to which parental love represented the love of God.

WHEN THE FAMILY BREAKS DOWN: WHAT HAPPENS THEN?

There are rather clear indications that Jesus and his family were on strained terms, and the tension between the conventional expectations of families and the demands of revelation has been one of the most dynamic elements of Christianity's social teaching. Within chapter 3 of Mark, for example, we encounter the following scene (Mark 3:31–35):

> And his mother and his brothers come and standing outside, they sent a dele-
> gation to him, calling him. And a crowd sat around him, and they say to him,
> Look, your mother and your brothers and your sisters seek you outside. He
> replied and says, Who is my mother and my brothers? He looks around at
> those sitting in a circle about him, and says, Look: my mother and my broth-
> ers. Whoever does the will of God, he is my brother and sister and mother.

Not a picture of family bliss, and perhaps an echo of the earlier statement (3:21)
that there were those associated with Jesus who tried to prevent him from en-
gaging in exorcism. They said he was "beside himself." Now he says they are
not true family.

The assertion involved in Mark 3:31–35 insists upon an explicit principle:
the bonds of family are to come second to the will of God. It is much more than
an anecdote concerning a particular dispute. There are such anecdotes in the
New Testament, for example in John 7:1–13. In that case, Jesus and his brothers fight over whether he should go to Jerusalem for the feast of tabernacles. He
adamantly refuses their invitation, but then goes to Jerusalem secretly. The cir-
cumstantial quality of the narrative is interesting, but the bold assertion in Mark
3:35 is all the more trenchant by contrast.

It is common in the study of the New Testament to read such statements of
principle as simple assertions of the value of social structures, such as the Church,
above that of the family. And it is true that, within the development of faith that
the New Testament represents, that understanding did emerge. We find it clearly
expressed (in Jesus' name), for example, in the Gospel according to Matthew
(10:34-41):

> Do not presume that I came to put peace on the earth! I did not come to put
> peace—but a sword! Because I came to separate man against his father, and
> daughter against her mother, and a bride against her mother-in-law, and the
> man's enemies will be his house-members! The one who loves father or
> mother more than me is not worthy of me, and the one who loves son or
> daughter more than me is not worthy of me, and whoever does not take his
> cross and follow behind me, is not worthy of me. The one who has found his
> life will forfeit it, and the one who has forfeited his life for my sake will find
> it. The one who receives you receives me, and the one who receives me re-
> ceives the one who delegated me. The one who receives a prophet in the
> name of a prophet will receive a prophet's reward, and the one who receives
> a righteous man in a righteous man's name will receive a righteous man's
> reward.

This is a well-crafted speech, which represents the perspective of the Church
after the resurrection: the picture is for people to follow Jesus in the way of the
cross, and to put the fellowship of those sent in his name—the name of a prophet
and just man—ahead of any other claim upon loyalty.

But prior to what happened to Jesus in Jerusalem, the Church had no real
organization, no comprehensive structure as a replacement of ordinary relationships. So it will not do to imagine Jesus as replacing the family with another

structure of society. The problem with such readings is that the Galilee that was the context of Jesus' movement for most of his life was grounded in the family as the ordinary unit of social life. A village such as Nazareth consisted only of a couple hundred people, and it made its way as an agricultural service community. The pivotal role of the family is summarized by Richard A. Horsley:[10]

> Villages consisted of a smaller or larger number of families or households. As the most fundamental social form in a traditional agrarian society, the household was the basic unit of production and consumption. According to the Israelite ideal (similar to that of other peasantries), each family worked and lived from the produces of its ancestral inheritance of land. Each household produced most of what it consumed and consumed much of what it produced. As indicated by both rabbinic texts and archaeological excavations, within the village settlement each family lived in a "house" of a small room or two (3 × 4 m) opening off of a courtyard shared with one or more other families. In the courtyard they shared use of oven, millstone, and cistern. In the village they shared use of a common winepress and olive press.

Within the setting that the study of the social context of Galilee has permitted us to appreciate clearly for the first time, Jesus' radical rejection of the bonds of family becomes all the more startling.

He was not in the position, for example, of claiming that urban institutions—such as the Temple or a Pharisaic association or the Roman army—superseded the family. Such urban institutions were not a feature of his programmatic activity, and he did not have significant contact with any city with the exception of Jerusalem (and then, his contact brought about his execution). Jesus understood the kingdom of God as a divine power that was in the process of transforming the world as it can be seen and known. Part of the transformation included the dissolution of the ordinary bonds of family, which were widely experienced as a fundamental category of social life.

Jesus' radical challenge of the place of loyalty to family explains another, famous aspect of his message. He insisted upon including women among his followers, and authorizing their participation in the process of learning (Luke 10:38–42):

> As they traveled he entered a certain village; a certain woman named Martha received him. And her sister, called Miriam, sat at the Lord's feet and heard his word. But Martha was distracted with much serving, approached and said, Lord, does it not matter to you that my sister has left me alone to serve? Speak to her, then, so that she comes to my aid! But the Lord answered and said to her, Martha, Martha, you care and worry and fret about many things, but there is need of few—or one! Because Miriam has chosen the good part, which will not be removed from her.

---

[10]Richard A. Horsley, *Archaeology, History, and Society in Galilee: The Social Context of Jesus and the Rabbis* (Valley Forge, PA: Trinity Press International, 1996), 89. For his discussion of Nazareth, see pp. 108–130.

Passages of this kind were cited during the debate in England concerning the ordination of women, and a case to some extent on biblical grounds did prevail.[11] But here, too, one must not presume that Jesus is offering a structure of society (or of Church). Rather, the word of the kingdom is such that it dissolves the usual constraints, including the constraints of family and sexuality, in the brilliance of its vision of God. If God is in the process of transforming the world and us with it—which is Jesus' understanding of the kingdom[12]—then nothing must stand in the way of the transformation.

More than twenty years after Jesus' execution, Paul—in his letter to the Galatians (written around 53 C.E.)—insisted upon a cognate principle (Galatians 3:28):

> There is neither Jew nor Greek, neither slave nor free, neither male nor female, because you are all one in Jesus Christ.

That widening of the principle, to include the removal of ethnic and economic distinctions, as well as of sexual boundaries, has provided Christianity with a strong sense of the autonomy of human conscience, collective and individual, in the ordering of society. That helps to explain the revolutionary developments in the understanding of sexuality and family that have been characteristic of Christian thought.

Such tension is implicit within Jesus' own teaching. Jesus shared the Zecharian vision, that Israel's gathering would draw in those beyond Israel. His development of motifs and language from the book of Zechariah, by means of his statements and his activities, has been well established.[13] But he did not articulate that vision by claiming—in the Pauline manner—that the distinction between Israel and the nations no longer existed. His entire approach was to focus on the assembly of Israel as the hope of all.

Jesus' famous saying about imitating a child (Mark 10:15; Luke 18:17) and entering the kingdom is a promise that is cast as a threat. Behaving like a child is implicitly commended, but the structure of the conditional statement is overtly pointed against a failure to act like a child: "Whoever does not take the kingdom of God as a child will never enter into it." The orientation is toward what one does or does not do: is it as a child acts? The issue is not what one is. That orientation is sometimes obscured, because the later formulation in Matthew (18:3) demands that the community (addressed in the plural) "turn" and become as children. The imagery in Matthew serves the context of conversion and baptism within the Church, more than it reflects the attempt of Jesus (better represented in Mark and Luke) to identify how the kingdom might be entered.

---

[11]Bruce Chilton, "Opening the Book: Biblical Warrants for the Ordination of Women," *The Modern Churchman* 20.1, 2 (1977), 32–35; and "The Gospel of Jesus and the Ministry of Women," *The Modern Churchman* 22.1 (1978–79), 18–21.

[12]See Chilton, *Pure Kingdom: Jesus' Vision of God.* Studying the Historical Jesus 1 (Grand Rapids, MI: Eerdmans; London: SPCK, 1996).

[13]For discussion, see Chilton, *Pure Kingdom.*

Confusion has also been produced by the translation of the Greek term *dekhomai,* which is here rendered "take." English translations since the King James Version have typically used "receive" here. Tonally (especially in English), there is an important difference between simply taking what one wants and receiving what one has been offered. The Greek verb *dekhomai* will bear either meaning, depending upon the context involved.

Relating the saying to another, well-known statement of Jesus makes it quite clear which context Jesus had in mind. He complains in a source of his sayings called "Q" that people call John crazy for abstaining from food and drink, and call Jesus himself a glutton and a drunkard because he eats and drinks with people. People of that kind, he says, are like children in a marketplace, squabbling over whether they should play happy games or sad games (Matthew 11:16–19; Luke 7:31–35). Jesus' perspective upon children was unromantic; he knows they argue, just as he knows they take what they want.

The apparently more polite rendering, "receive the kingdom of God," runs the risk of dissolving the statement into the banality that we should be like well-behaved children. The view has even been championed that "receiving the kingdom of God as a child" means embracing the kingdom as one would a child, rather than taking it as a child takes.[14] Jesus' usage of the metaphor involved comparison with unruly activity, not polite passivity. The Aramaic term he employed was probably *teqeph,* a term that features in another of his sayings (Matthew 11:12–13; Luke 16:16), and that vividly conveys the image of taking, as a child seizes hold of what he wants.

By seizing hold of the kingdom as a child takes something to play with, one can enter the kingdom. Two grounding metaphors, of entering the kingdom and laying hands on it, are here juxtaposed. Indeed, the parable of the grabby child manifests considerable aphoristic skill in relating those two models in a single statement, and in showing how they are related to one another. Making the kingdom one's sole object of interest, the way a child fixes on a toy, a forbidden object, the mother's nose, makes one pure enough to enter the kingdom.

Once the saying was passed on within the tradition of the Gospels, it became natural for the image of a child to be associated with Christian initiation, and even Christian leadership. Mark (10:13–14, 16) and Luke (18:15–16) cast Jesus' aphorism within a story about children being presented to him, while Matthew—as we have seen—employs the language of repentance ("unless you turn and become as children"), in order to speak of the necessary humility of Jesus' baptized followers (18:1–5).

Contextually, Thomas (saying 22) combines both of these later issues (leadership and initiation) in its presentation of the saying. Mary is presented as asking about the disciples in the previous saying, and Jesus replies with an image of children in saying 21. They remove their clothes as an act of witness when they return a field they have inhabited to its actual owners. The import of the material

---

[14]See Bruce Chilton and J. I. H. McDonald, *Jesus and the Ethics of the Kingdom* (Grand Rapids, MI: Eerdmans; London: SPCK, 1987), 80–89.

is that the disciples are compared to children because they lack shame in regard to sexuality, but at the same time they are understanding and know how to protect themselves from the world. Indeed, the image of children is then dropped, to be replaced with a version of the parable of the wise householder who knows how to defend his property (Matthew 24:43; Luke 12:39), and an allusion to the parable of the alert harvester (Mark 4:26–29). Then comes a saying about suckling children entering the kingdom within saying 22 itself, and finally Jesus says that you will enter the kingdom when you are united with your heavenly image, that is, when you are baptized. The combination and development of material is quite obviously both sophisticated and derivative.

Baptism is not the context in Jesus' original saying. Rather, children are the image of the confusing, grabby, unruly way the kingdom is to be greeted. The picture of children in the marketplace, hard at disorderly play, also appears in the book of Zechariah (8:5): their shrieks are signs of God's return to Jerusalem. Jesus evokes that sign in his saying (Matthew 11:16–17; Luke 7:32), just as his language about people coming from east and west to feast in the kingdom (Matthew 8:11; Luke 13:29) is evocative of the Zecharian language of how God is to gather his people (Zechariah 8:7). In Jesus' conception the purity required by the kingdom was a purity of response, of being like children at rough play in grasping at the kingdom.

The supposition is deeply embedded in the teaching directly attributable to Jesus that children are not well behaved, but recalcitrant. And precisely the thoughtless, robust responsiveness of a child is what Jesus commends as a condition for entering the kingdom of God. Beneath the veneer of well-ordered households in the Greco-Roman world, the New Testament attests a conviction that the wisdom of children is to be found in their disobedience.

UNCONVENTIONAL FAMILIES, SUPERNATURAL FAMILIES

Augustine of Hippo (354–430) is a pivotal figure, to some extent because he lived during a time of severe trial for Christianity, in certain ways as severe as the persecution of the time before Constantine. He crafted a synthesis of Christian social teaching in which the demands of the family and the community are balanced in an integral vision of Christian identity, both individual and collective. Once we have appreciated Augustine's contribution, it will be possible for us to approach the modern issue of sexual identity, which has been a particular focus of Christian thought in recent years.

In 410 C.E., Alaric sacked the city of Rome itself. That event was a stunning blow to the empire generally, but it was a double blow to Latin Christianity. First, the pillage occurred while the empire was Christian; two centuries before, Tertullian had argued that idolatry brought about disaster (*Apologeticus* 41.1), and now Christianity could be said to do so. Second, Latin Christianity—especially in North Africa—had been particularly attracted to a millenarian eschatology.

How could one explain that the triumphant end of history, announced by Eusebius and his followers in connection with Constantine's accession to power, seemed to have been reversed by the Goths?

The explanation of that dilemma occupied Augustine in his *City of God,* a tremendous work of twenty-three books, written between 413 and 426. From the outset, he sounds his theme, that the City of God is an eternal city that exists in the midst of the cities of men; those two cities are both mixed and at odds in this world, but they are to be separated by the final judgment (*City of God* 1.1). That essentially simple thesis is sustained through an account of Roman religion and Hellenistic philosophy, including Augustine's critical appreciation of Plato (books 1–10).

In the central section of his work, Augustine sets out his case within a discussion of truly global history, from the story of the creation in Genesis. From the fall of the angels, which Augustine associates with the separation of light and darkness in Genesis 1:4, he speaks of the striving between good and evil. But the distinction between those two is involved with the will of certain angels, not with any intrinsic wickedness (*City of God* 11.33). People, too, are disordered in their desire, rather than in their creation by God (*City of God* 12.8).

The difference between the will God intends for his creatures and the will they actually evince attests the freedom involved in divine creation. But the effect of perverted will, whether angelic or human, is to establish two antithetical regimes (*City of God* 14.28):

> So two loves have constituted two cities—the earthly is formed by love of self even to contempt of God, the heavenly by love of God even to contempt of self. For the one glories in herself, the other in the Lord. The one seeks glory from man; for the other God, the witness of the conscience, is the greatest glory. . . . In the one the lust for power prevails, both in her own rulers and in the nations she subdues; in the other all serve each other in charity, governors by taking thought for all and subjects by obeying.

By book 18, Augustine arrives at his own time, and repeats that the two cities "alike enjoy temporal goods or suffer temporal ills, but differ in faith, in hope, in love, until they be separated by the final judgment and each receive its end, of which there is no end" (*City of God* 18.54).

That commits Augustine to speak of eschatological issues, which he does until the end of the work as a whole. That is not surprising: Christianity's commitment to the creation as God's work inevitably involves the hope of the transcendence of evil. It is in his discussion of eschatology that Augustine frames classic and orthodox responses to some of the most persistent questions of the Christian theology of his time. He adheres to the expectation of the resurrection of the flesh, not simply of the spiritual body (as had been the manner of Origen during the third century). In so doing, he refutes the Manichaean philosophy, which he accepted prior to his conversion to Christianity. In Manichaeanism, named after a Persian teacher of the third century named Mani, light and darkness are two eternal substances that struggle against one another, and they war over the creation they have both participated in making.

As in the case of Gnosticism, on which it was dependent, Manichaeanism counseled a denial of the flesh. By his insistence on the resurrection of the flesh, Augustine revives the strong assertion of the extent of God's embrace of his own creation in the tradition of Latin Christianity.

Because Augustine was committed to an insistence on the resurrection of the flesh, he had to respond to criticism (*City of God* 22.12):

> Some question us very closely, and in their questioning ridicule our belief in the resurrected flesh. They ask whether abortive fetuses will rise again; they quote the words of the Lord: "Truly I say unto you, not a hair of your head shall perish," and then ask whether all will have equal height and strength, or will have different bodily sizes. For if the size of all bodies is to be equal, how will those abortive births (if they, too, are to rise again) have a bodily size that they did not have before? Or, if they are not to rise, since they were not properly born, but discharged, the same question is raised of infants—when they die in infancy, how will they acquire the stature that we now see is lacking? For we will not deny the resurrection of any who are capable of both being born, and of being born again in baptism. Then they ask how that equality is to be accommodated. For if all are to be as large and as tall as the largest and tallest have been here, the problem concerns not only infants, but also the majority of men: from what source will come the portion that was lacking here, if each one is to receive what he had here?

Augustine shows no liking for such questions, but at the same time he clearly indicates that there was disagreement and ferment within the Church of his period in coming to grips with issues of life after death.

For the moment, what is immediately pertinent to our theme is that Augustine is required for the logic of his own argument to confront the particular issue of sexual differences between people. That is just what he does, later in the same passage (*City of God* 22.17):

> Because it is said, "Until we all come to the perfect man, to the measure of the stature of the fullness of Christ," and "Conformed to the image of the son of God," some believe that women will not rise in female sex, but that all will be males, since God made only man from clay, and the woman from the man. But they seem wiser to me who do not doubt that both sexes will rise. For there will be no lust there, which is the cause of shame. For before they sinned they were naked, and the man and the woman were not ashamed. So all defects will be taken away from those bodies, but their nature will be preserved. The female sex is not a defect, but a natural state, which will then be free from intercourse and childbirth. There will be female parts, not suited to their old use, but to a new beauty, and this will not arouse the greed of the beholder, for there will be no greed, but it will inspire praise of the wisdom and goodness of God, who both created what was not, and freed from corruption what he made.

The objection raised to Augustine's position is on the basis of Genesis 2, where the primordial man and woman are made, and he replies by means of the same passage. His assumption, following the line of his *City of God* as a whole, is that the depiction of the fall of humanity as a result of love of self can be reversed to understand how the love of God will transform us.

Part of that transformation, in Augustine's vision, is to include male and female, no longer as instruments of intercourse and childbirth, but as in the image of God, created male and female (Genesis 1:27[15]). Throughout, it is plain that Augustine casts human sexuality as a problem, beset by the corruption of greed (the debased product of self-love). For that reason, writing as a male, he casts the problem as a whole as that of men wanting women for their own use, and he acknowledges his personal difficulty in just that regard (*City of God* 22.22-23). That particular association of females with sexuality is typical of Late Antiquity, and is especially prominent in Gnostic writings, where women's desire to be as creative as men leads them to literally hysterical reproduction (see, for example, *On the Origin of the World* [16]). What is crucial in Augustine's analysis, however, is the simple and revolutionary statement, "The female sex is not a defect, but a natural state." That denies that femininity is to be described as the privation of the masculine, but must rather be seen as engendered by God as part of creation, and not simply for the practicalities of reproduction.

In other words, Augustine imagines gender, which is engendered by God in God's image, as distinct from sexuality, a characteristic of the corrupt state of humanity. In order to do so, he needs to address the interpretation of a famous teaching of Jesus', in which people in the resurrection are compared to angels, neither marrying nor being given in marriage (Matthew 22:30; Mark 12:25; Luke 20:36; and *City of God* 22.18):

> They will be equal to angels in immortality and happiness not in flesh, nor indeed in resurrection, which the angels had no need of, since they could not die. So the Lord said that there would be no marriage in the resurrection, not that there would be no women. And at the time a question was under consideration that he could have settled more quickly and easily by denying the female sex, if he had foreknown that there was to be none. Instead, he proved that there would be when he said: "They will not marry," which is said of women, "nor take wives," which is said of men. So those who either marry husbands or take wives here will be present there, but will not do those things there.

So for Augustine, people are raised with their created, natural gender, and are raised sufficiently recognizably that they are present to one another in the resurrection.

In his adherence to a kind of millenarianism and to the resurrection of the flesh in the Latin creed, Augustine is very much a product of North Africa and Italy, where he was active (chiefly as a teacher of rhetoric) prior to his conversion

---

[15]Cited in *City of God* 16.6.

[16]See the translation by Hans-Gebhard Bethge and Orval S. Wintermute in *The Nag Hammadi Library,* edited by J. M. Robinson (San Francisco: Harper & Row, 1978), 161–179.

and his return to North Africa. But his *City of God* creates the greater frame, primordial and eschatological, within which history becomes a theological discipline. Here, he argues, is more than a lesson in how to avoid war and create order. And here there is certainly more than the superficial enthusiasm that comes of histories written by the winners. Rather, history for Augustine—and from Augustine—is the interplay of those two forces that determine the existence of every society, every person.

The struggle, however, is not ultimately between good and evil, but between the love of God and the love of self. That is the key to Augustine's ceaseless, pastoral ministry, as well as to his remarkably broad intellectual horizon. In every time and in every place, there is the possibility that the City of God will be revealed and embraced; now, in the Church, we at last know its name, and can see the face of that love which would transform us all. Part of that transformation is the insight that female and male are not only sexual roles, but two sides of engendered humanity in the image of God. The family in its present constitution has also been replaced as the field within which God's love is worked out in human terms. Instead, the City of God is understood to be that which offers the possibility in any place of recognizing in one another the sisters and brothers of Christ.

In the period since the end of the Second World War, feminism has been among the most important influences within the development of Christianity. Feminists have revolutionized both the self-understandings of women and men, and the critical appreciation of the sources of Christianity. By way of definition, we consider feminism here as the effort to evaluate femininity within its own terms of reference, and not merely as a function of sexual utility or attraction.

A good description of feminist interpretation as widely practiced is offered in a recent book, a collaborative effort edited by Elisabeth Schüssler Fiorenza and others:[17]

> Rather than focusing only on the women's passages, it generally seeks to analyze writings in their entirety. This method is used in order to assess how much the texts religiously advocate and foster all women's and marginalized men's subordination and exploitation and how much they transgress the kyriarchal boundaries of their time.

The adjective "kyriarchal" is derived from *kurios* in Greek, which means "lord": the concern here is with a lordship of dominance and a dynamic of what Schüssler Fiorenza calls transgression, but which might more naturally be described as liberation:

> Its contributors "search the scriptures" in a double sense. They scrutinize and interrogate the scriptures to uncover their "crimes" of silencing and marginalization. Moreover, most of them also seek to bring to the fore and make au-

---

[17] *Searching the Scriptures 2: A Feminist Commentary* (New York: Crossroad, 1994), 4.

dible again the subjugated voices and suppressed traditions that have left traces in ancient writings.

The assumption in such work is that what has been subjugated and suppressed in the past might instruct us, that it is coherent enough to provide alternatives, and in some sense better alternatives, to the dominant emphasis of the lords of this world and of Christianity.

The emphasis upon the evaluation of documents in their entirety is in fact characteristic of feminist concerns, because context has long been a paradigmatic issue within feminism. Only within her context can one evaluate a person and assess the degrees to which she might be exploited and/or empowered to express who she is. When that insight is applied to texts, the result is to resist the atomizing of passages, which has been characteristic of conventional scholarship. Instead, one tends to seek the meaning of wholes, and of wholes in relation to one another. It is no coincidence that the period of the influence of feminism has also evidenced a greater interest in the social contexts of Christianity.

In the same volume that Schüssler Fiorenza edited, Turid Karlsen Seim analyzes just the passage in Luke's Gospel (10:38–42) that was introduced above. In a sensitive reading, she emphasizes that empowerment or liberation is the emphasis:[18]

> Mary sitting at the Lord's feet and listening to his words is portrayed in the typical position of the pupil (cf. Acts 22:3). This description of a teacher–pupil relationship is an important feature of the text. The role as student in which Mary is positioned goes beyond the normal opportunity for women to hear the word in the context of worship. Moreover, the text alludes to terms that in rabbinic tradition are connected to teaching institutions. It also echoes other sayings about "hearing the word" as the decisive criterion for discipleship directed to both women and men (see Luke 6:46ff; 8:15, 21; 11:28).

But alongside this liberating tendency of the text, Seim also explores what she calls the "passivity and silence" of Mary. After all, she merely listens, and Martha does not even speak to her, but to Jesus. While men who listen "may become public preachers, women are never given any explicit commission to preach."[19]

What increased attention to context has enabled Seim to do is expose the ambivalence of Luke's Gospel in its presentation of women. She also refers to Acts in this regard, which was written as a sequel to follow Luke (Acts 1:1–5), and that strengthens her analysis. But in that regard, there is a connection she does not make that proves interesting. In Acts 6, the apostles are portrayed as refusing "to abandon the word of the Lord and serve tables" (6:2). That is what prompts them to appoint "servants" (*diakonoi*, "deacons"), who administer nourishment to the community while the apostles continue in prayer and the service of the word (Acts 6:1–6).

---

[18] *Searching the Scriptures*, 745–746.

[19] *Searching the Scriptures*, 748.

Seim is helpful in calling attention to the absence of any explicit authorization that Mary should preach, but it is also appropriate to observe the resonance of Mary with the place of the apostles. Her silence is not well characterized as a mere matter of passivity, because she demonstrates the continuing attendance to the word, which even the apostles were sometimes distracted from. Her "good part" is not merely to be like the apostles, but to be better than them in her constant commitment to the word. That creates a tension in Luke–Acts: women are indeed assigned places, and on the whole they are well described as marginalized, but at the same time the positive but partial correspondence between what women do and what fully empowered men do invites a development beyond the text. Beyond the imperative to preach, the charisma of contemplation is intimated. In just that sense, feminist interpretation may legitimately claim to speak of what texts are pointing to more faithfully than other forms of interpretation.

At first sight, the variety of Christian models of gender and familial relationship may seem bewildering. But the models we have considered in fact relate to each other closely. Feminist confidence that gender is contextual, and to be assessed contextually in regard to its repression and liberation, is not based upon an objective standard of truth, but upon conviction. That conviction is that gender is not merely functional or instrumental, whether for reproduction or of pleasure. Rather, gender is understood to be engendered, part of the meaningful configuration of humanity as shaped by God, which includes relationships that become "family" only in the metaphorical sense of which Jesus spoke. In that sense, feminist interpretation develops naturally from the analysis of Augustine.

But Augustine, of course, worked in no vacuum. The bold conviction of *The Shepherd of Hermas* may seem to be rudely expressed as compared to the vast learning and elegant exposition of *City of God,* but those two works share the confidence that how people relate to one another in social terms represents and develops how they relate to God. Whether it is a question of family or of society, how we behave toward our neighbor is the measure of how God engages us (Matthew 25:31–46). And that is true only because the insight of Jesus is taken to be axiomatic: if God is our truest parent, then our relations need continually to be worked out as sisters and brothers.

Sisters and brothers are related throughout life, and beyond life. Their gender, along with many other elements, are naturally a part of them, and yet they relate to one another, not sexually first of all, but as different members of the same family. Christian attitudes toward gender and family, and even Christian definitions of what those are, have varied quite widely. But throughout there is an underlying coherence. Our most powerful and significant relationship is with God, our common parent. That, for every Christian and for all Christians, is the fully engaged relationship from which meaning is generated. We know who we are, become what we are, understand how we are to be, in relation to God. But all that is for the most part understood, not in the abstract realm, but in how we engage with other children of God. Within that family, relationships are engendered in which we find our gender, our truest expression of the natures given us in creation.

COMMENTARIES

Judaism on Christianity

by Jacob Neusner

Judaism bears no ambivalence about marriage and family, regarding the household as the building block of the social order. Indeed, the notion of treating one's wife as one's sister—sexually forbidden—is expressly rejected by the law of Judaism. If one took a vow not to have sexual relations with his wife, he must divorce her in a very brief interval, paying off her marriage settlement and alimony. Jesus is explicit in treating as subordinate the honor owing to parents:

> Do not think that I have come to bring peace on earth; I have not come to bring peace but a sword. For I have come to set a man against his father and a daughter against her mother and a daughter-in-law against her mother-in-law and a man's foes will be those of his own household. He who loves father or mother more than me is not worthy of me; and he who loves son or daughter more than me is not worthy of me.
>
> Matthew 10:34–37

And Jesus calls into question the centrality of the family in the social order, when he says explicitly:

> While he was still speaking to the people, behold, his mother and his brothers stood outside, asking to speak to him. But he replied to the man who told him, "Who is my mother, and who are my brothers?" And stretching out his hand toward his disciples, he said, "Here are my mother and my brothers! For whoever does the will of my Father in heaven is my brother and sister and mother."
>
> Matthew 12:46–50

So at stake is more than parents; it is the wife and children, the home—the entire household, described with such detail in the commandment on the Sabbath: "you or your sons or your daughters, your manservant or your maidservant, or your cattle, or the sojourner who is within your gates." What troubles me deeply, therefore, is that if I follow Jesus, I abandon my home and family, but the Torah has conferred upon me sacred duties to home and family—and community too. Does Jesus not affirm that it is our task to carry out the commandment that God gave even to Adam and Eve: to be fruitful and multiply, to perpetuate life on earth? Matthew does not tell us that he has married or has a family of his own children; and he does tell his disciples to take up the cross and follow him, and yet, fundamental to the kingdom of Heaven that the Torah asks eternal Israel to bring about is the formation of an enduring society in sanctification. The sayings of Jesus rejecting the primacy of family in favor of the supernatural family formed of his disciples (e.g., Mark 3:31–5) strikingly differ from Judaism's position on the same matter. Judaism differs from Christianity in Judaism's fundamental reading of sexuality as natural to the human condition and subject to sanctification, and in its uncompromising affirmation of the family as the building block of the social order.

Islam on Christianity

by TAMARA SONN

Although some Muslim mystics have practiced it, Islam expressly rejects the Christian ideal of celibacy, as is evident in the often repeated tradition: "There is no monkery in Islam." Not only does celibacy inhibit the proliferation of the faithful, but it subverts the sexual urges, considered in Islam to be a gift from God rather than a sign of decadence. Marriage, therefore, is an honorable state, not a last resort for those incapable of celibacy. Nor does Islam present the relationships within the family as a reflection of divine lordship. Wives and children obey husbands and fathers out of respect and with the assumption that the husbands/fathers are moral and wise. Reflecting the Islamic emphasis on moral responsibility and human equality, no one is expected to obey unjust commands, even from a husband or father, for no one can stand in the place of God.

Hinduism on Christianity

by BRIAN K. SMITH

The ambivalence in Christianity regarding the value of sexuality, marriage, family life and its obligations, and ties to the world, on the one hand, and those of renunciation, celibacy, an other-worldly orientation, and the exclusivistic and absolute demands to put one's own life in the service of Christ and salvation on the other—this ambivalence is simultaneously foreign and familiar to debates and tensions within Hinduism.

In the mainstream Hindu tradition, renunciation of the family (*before the appropriate time*) for whatever reason is regarded as abhorrent. The tradition expects one to marry (at the right time, to the right person), have and raise children, make an honest and good living and succeed in the world to the best of one's ability (within the context of one's appointed caste profession), and, in sum, to carry out one's appointed worldly duties *as religious duties*. Hinduism, in its dominant form, draws no distinction between religious obligations and family or social obligations; the tension within Christianity between what's owed to one's spouse or parents or children and what's owed to God would ordinarily be inconceivable in Hinduism. Conversely, the metaphorization and inclusive extension of the notion of "family" in Christianity to refer to the Church, to all believers, of whatever sort ("There is neither Jew nor Greek, neither slave nor free, neither male nor female, because you are all one in Jesus Christ"), is equally opposed to traditional Hindu sensitivities, organized, as they were, around the particularities and differences of a caste-oriented, hierarchical society.

On the other hand, Hinduism too has recognized for millennia that the demands of worldly life, important though they are, are ultimately not conducive to salvation from this world. An ascetic and world-renunciatory strain has heavily influenced, and in some cases challenged, the this-worldly orientation of caste

Hinduism. The conflict between the demands of dharma or this-worldly duty, and those of *moksha* or liberation from the world of karma and rebirth, is potentially as troublesome as the comparable dichotomy in Christianity. While it appears that Christianity has, at least in some instances, attempted to solve the problem by infusing renunciatory values into family life (and to some extent this can be seen in Hinduism as well), in the mainstream tradition of Hinduism the strategy was to separate the two conflicting demands into separate and distinct "stages of life." The individualistic renunciatory quest is, ordinarily, to follow the completion of worldly, social, and family duties within the ideal structure of the ancient Hindu texts.

With the rise of some of the more radical devotional sects of Hinduism, however, the individual's religious desire for other-worldly goals (including union with the deity) has sometimes superseded the strictures of bourgeois Hinduism. In these cases, the strain between God and Mammon, between family life and its demands and the religious life, are evident in Hinduism as well as in Christianity.

Buddhism on Christianity

by BRAD CLOUGH

Just as Buddhism sees family life in the home as a place where the four "sublime states" (*brahma-vihāra*) of loving-kindness, compassion, sympathetic joy, and equanimity can be cultivated, so Christianity sees family life as an opportunity for working out Jesus' ideal of love.

Like the writing of Christianity's *Shepherd of Hermas,* the composition of the *Sigālovāda Sutta* can be dated to a period when Buddhists, although they did not face as great a threat of persecution as Christians did, were wary of being perceived of as a further challenge to the dominant society and its religious beliefs and practices, which it had already challenged on many fronts. Thus, in both texts we find a synthesis of conventional and religious values with respect to the ethics of family life.

As for specific injunctions found commonly in these two religions, both call upon parents to be vigilant in guiding a child away from evil and toward good. However, in Buddhism, the law of karma dictates that one is ethically responsible and will suffer only for one's own individual intentions and actions. In *Shepherd of Hermas,* it is clear that Hermas' future fate—his salvation or punishment from God—also depends on the conduct of his family, which he has a responsibility to convert. So, in Christianity, the consequences involved in a parent's guiding his family in religious ways are larger.

Both religions urge children to honor and never disobey their parents. But in this matter of children's reciprocal care for their parents, in neither religion is it merely a matter of obligation. In Christianity, it is a way of enacting God's love, and in Buddhism, it is a way of manifesting the compassion that is an integral part of realizing one's inherent potential to become enlightened (*buddha*). Fascinatingly, both religions impart these lessons through a parable about a prodigal son, found in Christianity in the Gospel of Luke, and in Buddhism in the fourth chapter of the Lotus Sutra.

We also find both religions, in their early phases, constructing ideal images of the submissive wife who is an obedient, mild, and soft-spoken partner to her husband. It seems, though, that in Christianity we hear less about what a husband owes his wife. In any case, in the contemporary cases of both religions, feminist thinkers are working to revolutionize how gender is understood, although Christian feminists have done more work in this regard by this point in time.

A noteworthy point of contrast is that whereas the later Christian Church moves away from Jesus' vision of leaving the family behind for the sake of the gospel, later Buddhism does not move nearly as far away from the Buddha's insistence upon the need to go forth from the householder's life, into a renunciatory way of life, although it certainly allows for a rich and rewarding religious life for those laypersons who remain living the family life.

Ultimately, we find in both religions a significant tension between obligations to one's family and obligations to higher religious callings. In Christianity, Jesus says that those who do the will of God are one's true brothers and sisters, and in Buddhism, the true sons and daughters of Buddha are those who devote themselves fully to the spiritual paths that lead to complete liberative insight and selfless compassion for others.

SUMMARY

"Family values" became practically synonymous with Christianity within conservative discourse in America during the late twentieth century. Historically, however, the Church only discovered the central place of familial relationships during the second century, in the midst of its ongoing experience of oppression and persecution within the Roman Empire. Even then, families were felt to be important as a field in which salvation could be worked out, not in any independent or absolute terms. The commendation of these relations was always qualified by the knowledge that Jesus had strongly relativized (and even denied) the significance of his relations with his own parents, brothers, sisters, and kin. Although Early Christianity softened much of Jesus' radicalism, it never forgot the underlying principle that domesticity was of only limited use, even as the extended households of the Hellenistic world became an effective vehicle of Christian extension and growth. Theological assessments, as different superficially as St. Augustine's and contemporary feminism's, have articulated the fundamental tension between acknowledging family and sexual relations as basic, and calling for their comprehensive transformation.

GLOSSARY

Apostle   derived from the Greek *apostolos,* meaning "delegate," which in turn reflects the Judaic custom of the *shaliach,* a person one could send to represent oneself in a personal or business transaction. Jesus sent out such delegates during his life to act as he did, preaching the kingdom of God and healing, but apostles were also delegated when he was experienced as raised from the dead. Some of them (most notably, Paul) had not been among Jesus' disciples during his ministry.

Constantine emperor who issued an edict tolerating Christianity in 313 C.E. and went on to make the once persecuted faith into the de facto religion of the Roman Empire. He actively promoted the unity of the Church, convening the Council of Nicea in 325 C.E. in order to do so, on the grounds that a united empire demanded a united religion. He presided at that Council, which eventually produced the Nicene Creed that is still in use in the Eucharistic worship of most Christians.

Creation how Christianity designates the universe as a whole. That is, it is God's own handiwork, in no sense any sort of pre-existing matter that he just happened to work with. God made all things *ex nihilo,* from nothing, and therefore the world around us reflects the divine glory. Creation is also an ongoing project, so that the transformation of the world as we know it follows naturally from the Christian apprehension of the perceptible, physical universe.

Household churches emerged from the end of the first century as a primary setting of Christianity. The house (*domus* in Latin) of the Hellenistic world accommodated an extensive group of family, relatives, and servants, so that converting the head of the household gave Christians a place to gather, some protection from official and popular suspicion, and the resources needed to propagate the movement until Constantine's policies provided imperial support for churches.

Q short for *Quelle,* the German word for "source." It refers to the collection of Jesus' sayings, perhaps gathered systematically from around the year 35 C.E., which is incorporated in the Gospels according to Matthew and Luke. Whether "Q" was ever a written document remains unknown, but it reflects the teaching of Jesus in the way a rabbi might have drawn his wisdom together into a mishnah.

Zechariah the prophetic book, which in its final chapter depicts an eschatological feast of Tabernacles (Sukkoth) when all the peoples of the earth would gather for sacrifice in Jerusalem. Part of the vision is that no merchandising would occur at that sacred moment, and Zechariah 14 seems to be a key to what Jesus did in the Temple to inflame priestly opinion against him, and ultimately to assure his condemnation by Pontius Pilate.

DISCUSSION QUESTIONS

1. Overall, how would you assess the importance of the *Shepherd of Hermas* as a source for understanding Early Christianity?

2. By what means did Christianity adjust to Roman policies during the first and second centuries?

3. Describe the attitude toward women as it evolved during the period between *The Shepherd* and Augustine, with particular reference to how it was influenced by principal theological themes of Early Christianity.

4. How did the Pastoral Epistles, Luke, and Acts articulate the structures of order and discipline that should govern churches and families?

5. Compare Paul, Augustine, and Elisabeth Schüssler Fiorenza as interpreters of Jesus' attitude toward life in families and toward sexual relationships.

6. Are there principles within Christianity which you would describe as enduring in the evaluation of how families are to be considered?

 **INFOTRAC**

If you would like additional information related to the material discussed here, you can visit our Web site: http://www.wadsworth.com

3

Islam

BY TAMARA SONN

CONVENTIONAL EXPECTATION VERSUS THIS RELIGIOUS TRADITION: WHAT DO HUSBANDS AND WIVES OWE ONE ANOTHER?

Marriage is a contract in Islam, not a sacrament but a solemn agreement that must be properly recited aloud and witnessed. Law pertaining to the details of the contract is extensive and detailed; its general components include the following: While parents often participate in the selection of suitable mates and negotiating the terms of the agreement, the intended spouses are not to be married against their wills and they must approve the terms of the agreement. The contract is technically initiated by the bride or her representative, specifying that she offers herself in marriage in return for something of economic value. As the Qur'an says, "And for the benefit you receive from them, give them their wages, as fixed, and there shall be no sin for you in anything you mutually agree upon after establishing [the dower]" (4:25). The amount specified is to be given to the bride, not to her family, and it is for her own use; she is not required to use or spend it for anyone else's benefit. Accordingly, it allows the wife a degree of economic independence, a kind of security in the event of unforeseen need. The dower may either be specified in the contract or not. It may consist of virtually anything of value: money, material, property, business shares, and so on. Other conditions may also be specified. The various schools of Islamic law have different opinions on the extent to which the wife may specify conditions of marriage, but most authorities in Sunni Islam (the vast majority of Muslims, roughly 85 percent) agree that she may specify that she has the right to divorce under certain conditions. If the dower is not specified in the contract, it must be specified at a later time, such as at consummation of the marriage. Payment of the dower may also be deferred, in full or in part. The time of deferment must be specified either in terms of time (e.g., six months) or an event (e.g., divorce). Marriages may be concluded between people provided they are not already related through relationships such as maternity, paternity, fraternity, sorority, being niece/aunt or nephew/uncle, wet-nurse, or "in-law" relationships.

The legalistic nature of the marriage contract itself should not mask the fact that marriage is the most highly respected social institution in Islam. It is the fundamental human relationship, one that all Muslims are expected to engage in: "Marry the unmarried among you and your male and female slaves who are righteous . . ." (24:32). Marriage not only provides the basic unit of society, but it is the locus of expression of overall Islamic values. And in Islam, all values begin with God. That God is involved in all human relationships is a fundamental principle of Islam:

> Do you not see that God knows everything in the heavens and the earth? There is no secret gathering of three but that God is their fourth, nor of five but that He is their sixth, nor of less than these or more but that He is with them wherever they be. (58:7)

God—or more specifically, the revealed will of God, to which people must submit in order to be called *muslim* (in Arabic, one who submits [to the will of God])—is to be the focus of all human activity, including interpersonal relationships:

> If your fathers, your sons, your brothers, your spouses, your clans, the wealth which you have acquired, the trade whose decline you fear and your houses with which you are so pleased—if all these things are dearer to you than God, his messenger, and struggling in his cause, then wait until God brings down His judgement; God guides not an unrighteous people. (9:24)

All our lives and activity are to be dedicated to God, therefore, and one of the ways we express our submission to God's will is through our treatment of other people. Islam teaches that all people are equal in the sight of God, and the social order should reflect that equality. That means, on the one hand, that no one's command should take precedence over that of God. To obey someone who commands you to do something that God has forbidden amounts to putting that person in the place of God. In Islam, this is called "associating" or "giving partners" to God (*shirk*). It is the most serious sin in Islam because failure to recognize the supremacy of God effectively removes one from the source of divine guidance. Even excessive fear of another person, the kind of fear that would prevent someone from doing what God commands or allow someone to do something forbidden, is a kind of *shirk*. No one should be treated as less valuable or worthy of compassion than anyone else:

> Do you see the one who makes a mockery of religion? That is the person who mistreats orphans and does not work to feed the poor. Woe to those who pray and yet are neglectful of their prayers, those who pray for show and do not contribute to the welfare of the needy. (107:2–7)

Overall, therefore, believers are told to "establish justice" through fair dealings, generosity, and mercy, that is, to recreate in society the equality all share in the eyes of God:

> You who believe, do not let one group of men ridicule another who may be better than they, nor let women [ridicule other] women who may be better

than they. And do not slander one another or call each other names. . . . O people, we have created you from a male and a female and made you into nations and tribes that you may come to know one another. Indeed, the noblest among you in the sight of God is the one who is most morally upright. God is all knowing indeed. (49:12–14)

This ethic of justice and compassion is believed to result from true belief and it is supposed to characterize all human relationships, marriage included. Marriages are supposed to be based on love and tenderness:

And among His signs is that He created you from dust; then you are people scattered about. And among His signs is that he created for you, among yourselves, spouses so that you may find peace in them, and He put love and mercy between you. In that are signs for those who think. (30:21–22)

Spouses are to comfort and protect one another. Muslim men are told that "[wives] are garments unto you and you are garments to them" (2:188). Even a husband who does not have a perfect relationship with his wife is told to look for the good in her: "Live with [your wives] in kindness and if you dislike them, it may be that you are disliking someone in whom God has put a great deal of goodness" (4:20).

Furthermore, as noted, the Qur'an specifies that wives are to be allowed a degree of economic independence. The prevalent practice of giving a dower (gift or financial settlement) to the bride's family, interpreted by many as the mere purchasing of a woman, was replaced by the Qur'an's requirement that the gift be given to the bride herself for her own use. In addition, whatever inheritance a woman brings to the marriage remains her personal property to do with as she will. "Men shall have a share of what they have earned and women a share of what they have earned" (4:33). This right of women to own and dispose of property was upheld in the formulation of Islamic laws based on the Qur'an, and is considered a reflection of Islam's belief in overall human equality.

But belief in human equality in Islam coexists with belief in different roles for different people. The Qur'an thus recognizes distinctions in the roles of spouses: "And [for women] there are rights similar to those [of men] rightly over them, but men are one degree higher" (2:229). Similarly, "Men are responsible for women because God has favored some over others and because they spend of their wealth. So virtuous women are obedient and guard the secrets with God's protection" (4:35). The Qur'an elsewhere states that women and men are protectors of one another: "And believing men and believing women are protectors of one another. They enjoin good and forbid evil and observe prayer, give charity, and obey God and his messenger" (9:71). As a result, there is dispute among contemporary interpreters concerning whether the superior authority of husbands mentioned in Sura 4 of the Qur'an is inherent to the husband as a man or simply a function of the role of breadwinner. The former position is expressed by Lois Lamya al-Faruqi (d. 1986), a scholar of Islamic arts:

Contrary to the goals of the Women's Liberation movement, the Qur'an calls for a society which assigns the ultimate leadership and decision-making role in the family to men. . . . The family . . . has need for someone to carry the burden of ultimate responsibility for the whole. The Qur'an has assigned this role to the most senior male member of the family. It is this patriarchal assignment of power and responsibility which is meant by such expressions as ["but men are one degree higher"] (2:229) and ["men are in charge of women"] (4:35). Contrary to misrepresentations by the Qur'an's enemies, these passages do not mean the subjugation of women to men in a gender-based dictatorship. Such an interpretation shows a blatant disregard of the Qur'an's repeated calls for the equality of the sexes and for its command to show respect and kindness to women. The passages in question point instead to a means for avoiding internal dissension and indecision for the benefit of all family members. They advocate for a patriarchal society.[1]

Islamic modernist Fazlur Rahman (d. 1988) sees things differently. He believes that the responsibility for major decisions in the family rests with whomever bears the brunt of the economic responsibility.

It is certain that, in general, the Qur'an envisages division of labor and a difference in functions (although there is nothing in the Qur'an against women earning wealth and being economically self-sufficient; indeed, the Prophet's first wife owned a business and the Qur'an recognizes the full and independent economic personality of a wife or a daughter). The question is whether the verse quoted is a statement of inherent inequality. We are told that "Men are in charge of women because God has given some humans excellence over others and because men have the liability of expenditure [on women]" [4:35]. This shows that men have a functional, not inherent, superiority over women, for they are charged with earning money and spending it on women. . . . If a woman becomes economically self-sufficient, say by inheritance or earning wealth, and contributes to the household expenditure, the male's superiority would to that extent be reduced, since *as a human,* he has no superiority over his wife.[2]

In other words, as in most religions, there is a range of opinions concerning the question of women's roles in the Muslim family. Are they always to be subservient to their husbands, or is that secondary position a result only of their lower education and earning power? As women become more educated and economically independent, is it natural that they participate in making major decisions affecting the family? Should families be organized on the basis of cooperation rather than hierarchy? Or should wives remain advisors and caregivers to husbands, who are deemed inherently better equipped or destined by God to play the role of decision makers and breadwinners? Despite the range of opinions on these issues, Muslims agree that, whatever the financial situation, males

---

[1]Lamya Lois al-Faruqi, *Women in a Qur'anic Society.* http://www.al-islam.org/al-tawhid/women-society.htm. Section 5, "A Patriarchal Family Organization."

[2]Fazlur Rahman, *Major Themes of the Qur'an* (Minneapolis and Chicago: Bibliotheca Islamica, 1980), 49.

and females are equal before God. The Qur'an repeatedly addresses this issue. For example:

> Indeed who surrender to God, male and female,
> those who believe, male and female,
> those who obey, male and female,
> those who are truthful, male and female,
> those who are patient, male and female,
> those who are humble, male and female,
> those who give charity, male and female,
> those who fast, male and female,
> those who are chaste, male and female,
> those who remember God often, male and female—
> God has prepared for them forgiveness and great reward. (33:35)

This ultimate or moral equality ideally finds expression in a marriage relationship in which both partners flourish.

Nevertheless, as noted above, the Qur'an requires obedience of wives to husbands, according to the verse cited above: "Men are responsible for women because God has favored some over others and because they spend of their wealth. So virtuous women are obedient and guard the secrets with God's protection" (4:35). It is assumed that wives are in charge of running the household properly, but the classical legal codes further stipulate, in accordance with this verse, that women are expected to leave home only with the approval of their husbands. The legal codes also specify that women must have sex with their husbands when their husbands want it, based on the Qur'anic verse: "Your wives are as a fertile ground for you; so approach your fertile ground when and how you want . . ." (2:224). The various schools of law disagree on other details of obedience. However, they agree—based again on verse 4:35—that there are specific measures the husband may take to discipline disobedient wives: "And those on whose part you fear disobedience, warn them and leave them alone in their beds, and discipline them."[3] The law codes further agree that a disobedient wife is not entitled to maintenance.[4]

Husbands are also expected to have sex with their wives on a regular basis, and to do so with gentleness and kindness, although there are no legal penalties

---

[3]The last verb in this sentence, adhuribuhunna, is interpreted by some as "strike them." Thus: "And those you fear may be rebellious admonish; banish them to their couches, and beat them." See A. J. Arberry, The Koran Interpreted, 7th ed. (New York: Macmillan, 1976), 105–106. However, modern commentators who accept this interpretation maintain that such a beating may only be symbolic, carried out with nothing bigger than a toothpick or toothbrush, and never about the face. Interestingly, this is similar to the medieval English law according to which wives were not to be beaten with anything thicker than the husband's thumb—which gives us the phrase "rule of thumb."

[4]"The schools [of Islamic law] concur that a disobedient wife (al-nashizah) is not entitled to maintenance. But they differ regarding the extent of disobedience which causes the maintenance to subside." Laleh Bakhtiar, translator and editor, Encyclopedia of Islamic Law: A Compendium of the Major Schools (Chicago: ABC International Group, 1996), 477ff.

for failure to do so. The law does require, however, that males maintain the children and the mothers of their children: "And the man to whom the child belongs shall be responsible for their [the mother's] food and clothing equitably" (2:234). When Islamic law was formulated, it extended the required maintenance to include shelter as well as food and clothing, in accordance with another verse in the Qur'an: "Lodge them in the houses where you dwell according to your means. . . . Let him with abundance spend of his abundance, and let him whose means are slight spend out of what God has given him" (66:7–8).

In addition, husbands are required to provide for wives through inheritance: "And those of you who die and leave behind wives shall bequeath to their wives provision for a year without being turned out" (2:241). As codified in law, the wife actually receives inheritance determined according to shares that vary according to the number and sex of the survivors. The wife receives one-quarter of the husband's estate if there are no other descendants, and one-eighth if there are. Husbands also inherit from their wives, receiving one-half of the estate, unless there are other descendants, in which case he receives one-quarter of it. This apparent discrepancy in the shares to which husbands and wives are entitled reflects the patriarchal context in which the Qur'an was revealed; males receive greater shares because they are assumed in general to be financially responsible for women. Again, whether inherent or functional, husbands' responsibility for the family and wives' responsibility to obey are enjoined by the Qur'an and supported in oral traditions (hadith) and the legal system based upon these two sources.

Similarly, Islamic law reflects the husbands' responsibility and wives' submissiveness in rules concerning the religion of marriage partners. It is assumed that religion is prerequisite to a successful marriage in Islam. Therefore, the Qur'an requires that believers marry from among believers:

> Do not marry idolatrous women until they become believers; a believing slave is better than an idolatrous woman, though she may be pleasing you. And do not marry [believing women] to idolaters until they become believers; a believing slave is better than an idolater, though he may be pleasing to you. (2:222)

By "idolatrous" is meant those who do not believe in or worship the one God. Because Judaism and Christianity do recognize the one God, the Qur'an recognizes Judaism and Christianity as religions based on true revelation from the one God (al-ilah, "the god," or "Allah"). Jews and Christians are called "people of the book," meaning the book of true revelation, even though it is believed that Jewish and Christian Scriptures have not been preserved and interpreted entirely correctly. Still, Jews and Christians have been exposed to true revelation and, insofar as they believe in the one God and do not interfere in Islamic practice, they may be considered "believers" in Qur'anic language.[5] Therefore, when Islamic

---

[5]The designation of Jews and Christians as believers became a contentious issue in the development of Islamic law and practice, and today it is common to hear them referred to as heretics or even unbelievers. Nevertheless, the Qur'an is clear in its designation of Jews and Christians as having access to true revelation. Although it observes that many of these

law was codified it allowed men to marry Jewish and Christian women. Muslim women, however, are allowed to marry only Muslim men. This is because, as noted, wives are expected to obey their husbands. Since non-Muslim husbands may call upon their wives to do something not in accord with Islamic teaching, such a marriage could result in great stress upon the wife. Furthermore, it is assumed that the purpose of marriage is to procreate and, as in most religions, it is a major duty to bring up children in the family faith. Requiring that women marry Muslim men precludes their having to choose between Islam and the religion of their husbands when educating their children.

One of the most controversial aspects of Islam is its permission for polygyny. Multiple spouses (polygamy) has never been allowed in Islam; women are to be strictly monogamous. Just as in early Judaism, however, Islam allows men to marry more than one wife. In Islam, they are allowed up to four wives at a time, based on the following verse from the Qur'an:

> If you fear that you cannot do justice to orphans, then marry from among women such as you like, two, three, or four. But if you fear you will not be fair, then one or what your right hands possess [i.e., a slave]; that is the closest to fairness. (4:4)

This permission for polygyny is given in the historical context of a society with many widows and orphans. Like other societies at the time, the Arab society in which the Qur'an was revealed was organized in extended families. That kind of society establishes what we now call a social "safety net" in which people in need are cared for by relatives. If children lose their parents through disease or war, for example, they are taken in by uncles and aunts and treated as other family members are. However, at the time of Prophet Muhammad, society was changing and the tribal system was not working as effectively as it had previously. The Qur'an frequently refers to the existence of orphans who were not being properly cared for. It criticizes people for misappropriating the property of orphans and ignoring their rights: "And they ask you about the orphans. Say [that] promotion of their welfare is good. And if you intermix with them, they are your brothers. And God knows the corrupt from the righteous" (2:221). In fact, the verse just preceding the permission to marry up to four wives states: "And give to the orphans their property and do not exchange bad for good, and do not take their property with your own. Indeed, that is a grave sin" (4:3). The reference to fairness among wives is amplified in the same chapter: "You will not be able to keep balance between women, no matter how much you want to do so. So do not turn totally toward one and leave the other suspended" (4:130).

"people of the book" have ignored or misinterpreted their Scriptures and gone astray, the Qur'an acknowledges that there are righteous people among them. See, for example:

> And if the people of the book had believed, it would have been better for them indeed. Some of them are believers, but most of them are disobedient. . . . They are not alike. Among the people of the book there is a faction who are steadfast; they recite the word of God in the night and bow [to God]. They believe in God and the Last day and enjoin good and forbid evil, and compete with one another in good works. And these are the righteous. (3:111–115)

Some modern interpreters take this amplification as a virtual prohibition of polygyny, but that is not how it was interpreted in the legal codes. There the permission for more than one wife is accepted, and the verse's cautionary statements are interpreted simply as a recommendation for equivalent levels of maintenance for all wives, provided they are obedient. In either case, it seems clear that permission for multiple wives was both limited to situations in which the women would not otherwise have been supported and conditional upon the ability to treat multiple wives equally. This has led to significant debate in the contemporary world about the status of polygyny. As Fazlur Rahman summarizes:

> The traditionalist interpretation was that the permission [for polygyny] has legal force while the demand for justice, though important, is left to the conscience of the husband (although traditional Islamic law gave women the right to seek remedy or divorce in case of gross injustice or cruelty). . . . Muslim modernists, on the other hand, tend to give primacy to the demand for justice plus the declaration of the impossibility of justice [to more than one wife], and say that permission for [polygyny] was meant to be only temporary and for a restricted purpose.[6]

In any case, the incidence of polygyny has decreased in the modern world with increased development, urbanization, and education. Although most Muslim countries still allow polygyny, the ideal of monogamy as established by the Qur'an remains. Overall, Muslims agree that Qur'anic teaching allows for changing circumstances and practices. The Qur'an establishes ultimate principles and values that must be the standard by which particular practices are measured. As noted, in the Islamic worldview, the purpose of human existence is to do the will of God, creating a social order that reflects the equality and dignity all human beings share in the eyes of their creator. To the extent that a practice fosters the well-being of society, it is Islamic. If a practice results in suffering or oppression, it cannot be considered to be in accordance with Islamic principles. In this context, the debate over the legitimacy of polygyny in the modern Muslim world continues.

WHAT DO PARENTS OWE
THEIR CHILDREN?

As with spouses, relationships in families must be based primarily on submission (*islam*), above all, to the will of God. To stress the point, the Qur'an cites the story of Noah and his wayward son:

> And it was revealed to Noah, "None of your people will believe except those who have already believed; so do not grieve about what they have been doing. And build an ark under our eyes and our revelation. And do not ask

---

[6]Fazlur Rahman, *Major Themes of the Qur'an*, 47–48.

me about the wrongdoers. They will be drowned." And he made the ark and
every time the elders of his people came by, they made fun of him. He said,
"If you make fun of us, we will make fun of you accordingly. Then you will
know who will be punished and disgraced." Until when our command came
and the fountains burst forth, we said, "Get in it two of every kind, male and
female, and your family except him against whom the word has already been
spoken, and whoever believes." And only a few believed. And he said, "Get
on. In the name of God will be its course and where it will come to rest. My
lord is indeed the most forgiving, merciful." So it moved with them among
waves like mountains, and Noah called to his son who was standing aside,
"Get on with us, my son, and do not be with the unbelievers." He answered,
"I will soon go to a mountain that will protect me from the water." He said,
"There is no shelter this day from the command of God except those to
whom he shows mercy." And the wave came between them and he was
among the drowned. (11:37–44)

Thus, there is no hope even for one's children if they disobey God. But assuming that children are obedient and virtuous, at least attempting to follow their religious training, parents are required to maintain, protect, and guide them,
showing tenderness and mercy. Indeed, as in most religions, the family is the basic
unit of Islamic society. Therefore, the Qur'an articulates principles designed to
establish the family on a firm footing. The maintenance incumbent upon husbands for wives, as noted above, also applies to children: "And the man to whom
the child belongs shall be responsible for their [the mother's] food and clothing
equitably" (2:234). And as above, maintenance consists of food, clothing, and
shelter in accordance with the level of the man's wealth. Mothers are also required
to care for their children. The Qur'an even stipulates that they must nurse for two
years, if possible (2:234). The scripture does allow that this is not meant to be a
burden and that a substitute may be found if the parents agree on it.

Beyond mere physical maintenance, parents are responsible for social nurturing of their children. This begins at birth, whereupon a religious authority or
male relative whispers the Islamic call to prayer in the baby's ears. The next thing
the baby hears is the recitation of the opening chapter of the Qur'an (the
"Fatiha"), to initiate the child's religious training. Another important aspect of
the child's early dedication to Islam is her or his naming. According to oral tradition, certain names are very pleasing to God, such as "Servant of God" ('Abd
Allah, i.e., Abdullah) or servant of any of the other names of God, such as al-
Rahman ("the Merciful," thus Abdulrahman), al-Karim ("the Noble," thus Ab-
dulkarim), or al-Jabbar ("the Almighty," thus Abduljabbar). Other popular
names are those of the Prophet himself—in fact, the name Muhammad is the
most common name in the world—and the names of other important figures in
Islamic history, such as the Prophet's cousin and son-in-law 'Ali, and his close
companions such as 'Umar (Omar) and 'Uthman (Usman, Osman, or Othman).
Names of the Prophet's mother and wives are popular for girls. On the seventh
day after the child's birth, it is customary to celebrate the birth of a child by
giving thanks, often in the form of sacrificing an animal or giving a party. In

accordance with the Qur'an's emphasis on the value of women, this custom is followed for both boys and girls (although traditionally the offering to celebrate the birth of a boy is greater than that celebrating the birth of a girl, a custom that is changing with time).

The child's religious training continues with the teaching of prayers and verses from the Qur'an, such as "b'ism Allah al-Rahman al-Rahim" (in the name of God, the Merciful, the Benevolent). This phrase begins the chapters of the Qur'an and its recitation is customary preceding any important announcement or undertaking, as a way of dedicating it to God. Training continues with the child's being taught to read, again from the Qur'an. It is a traditional and highly respected goal, especially for boys, to memorize the entire Qur'an. For boys who accomplish this goal, a great celebration is common.

Circumcision, although nowhere mentioned in the Qur'an, is considered obligatory for boys. Sometimes it is performed after the boy is able to recite the entire Qur'an, although the age of circumcision varies from region to region and, with education and class, from infancy to puberty. Like the birth itself, it is an occasion for great celebration, marking one as a true Muslim. Whereas in Judaism, circumcision is considered a mark of dedication to the covenant between God and his people, in Islam circumcision is generally associated with purity. This aspect of it is particularly emphasized in those cultures that practice female circumcision, or as it is known by its many opponents, female genital mutilation (FGM). This practice is followed by people primarily in sub-Saharan Africa, whether Muslim, Christian, or otherwise. It is not widely practiced in Islam, and certainly not in the majority of the Muslim world. But in those areas where it is practiced, Muslims believe it is required by their religion, just as do Christians who practice it. Most Muslims consider it permissible but not required, while others consider it to be recommended but not required. Nowadays, many people have taken a firm stand that FGM is not only not required by Islam but, given its cruelty, highly questionable rationale (many believe that a woman is grotesque before the procedure, and that without it will not be able to control sexual desire or may perhaps develop male genitalia), and non-Islamic origins, it is against Islamic principles. There have been efforts to legislate against the practice, although they have been largely unsuccessful. In any case, as education and economic development increase, the practice is becoming less common.

Concerning inheritance, not only does Islamic law stipulate that parents are responsible for each other and for their children, but it specifies that daughters (as well as other females) must be included in inheritance shares:

> For men there is a share of what parents and near relatives leave, and for women there is a share of what parents and near relatives leave, whether it is a little or a lot, a fixed share. And when relatives and orphans and the poor are present at the division, give them from it and speak to them judicious words. And let those who fear, if they leave behind them their own weak children, for them, fear God and say the appropriate word. . . . God commands you concerning your children: A male shall have as much as the share of two females, but if there are females [only], more than two, then they get two thirds of what is left, and if there is one, she shall have the half. (4:8–12)

Again, the disproportion between females' and males' shares is a reflection of the historical context in which the Qur'an was revealed. Daughters were expected to marry and be supported by their husbands. Sons, on the other hand, were expected to marry and support not only their nuclear families but their extended families as well. As noted above, many believe this model is prescriptive, meaning that men should always be the breadwinners while women should be caregivers, but reformers believe that in a changed economy, males and females may share financial responsibility for the family and that, therefore, their inheritance shares should be equal.

Basic rules of inheritance are extremely detailed in Islamic law, beginning with the requirements established by the Qur'an, and extending those required inheritances to include grandchildren and other relatives. Portions of the estate (⅔, ½, ⅓, ¼, ⅙, ⅛) are bequeathed according to fixed rules. For example, if a single daughter or sister is the sole survivor, as in the Qur'anic verse, she receives half the estate, and two or more daughters surviving in the absence of sons receive two-thirds of the estate. A single son receives one-sixth; two or more full brothers receive one-third of the estate, and so on. The system is designed to ensure responsible parenting; children are not to be brought into the world and left without nurturing and support. So important is the law on proper support for family members that it allows bequests to others besides family members only once all debts are paid and all designated family members are taken care of. Even then, only up to one-third of the estate may be disposed of in this way.

It is interesting that the Qur'an pays special attention to daughters. This is because among the reforms it seeks to implement is elevation in the status of women. In the days of "ignorance" (al-jahiliyya) before the revelation of the Qur'an, the status of women in the Arabian peninsula was very low indeed. Historical evidence indicates that wives were bought and sold, and even inherited. Widows and orphans were particularly at risk, as mentioned above, and frequently marginalized economically. Marriage was generally the only sort of refuge, and polygyny was unlimited. The Qur'an characterizes this denigration of women as unjust and chastises those who feel disappointment upon the birth of a daughter:

> When one of them is given the good news of [the birth of] a girl, his face darkens as he suppresses his unhappiness. He hides from people because of the evil the good news meant to him [and wonders] whether to keep her in disgrace or push her into the earth. Indeed, evil is what they judge. (16:59–60; cf. 43:18)

It utterly forbids female infanticide, a practice apparently common in the society to which the Qur'an was revealed. The Qur'an warns of a time "when the girl buried alive will be asked for what sin she was killed?" (81:9–10).

Daughters, therefore, no less than sons, are to be cherished and respected. Yet, as in the husband-wife relationship, males are responsible for female family members. In accordance with the verse mentioned above—"Men have responsibility for women"—fathers and other male family members are considered the guardians or protectors of women. This includes, beyond mere maintenance, responsibility for the choice of a daughter's marriage partner. Girls are not to be forced to marry people against their will, but the Qur'an clearly assumes males' responsibility for ultimate decisions in marriage in that it addresses only males on this issue. We saw above, for example, in the stipulations concerning marriage-able partners, that men were told not to marry off their daughters to idolatrous men. Thus, in practice, the ultimate responsibility for a woman's first marriage lies with her father or, in case the father is deceased, the next closest male relative.

It should be noted that laws of inheritance do not apply to illegitimate children. Islamic law is very careful in determining the lack of legitimacy. For one thing, it requires four eyewitnesses to give evidence that illicit sexual intercourse has taken place, virtually prohibiting the successful proof of willing sex between unmarried people. This is in accordance with the Qur'anic requirement: "And those who accuse chaste women, and then do not bring four witnesses, whip them with eighty lashes and never accept any testimony of theirs, for they are the transgressors" (24:5). Therefore, in the case of married women, it is very difficult to prove a child has been fathered by someone other than a woman's husband. Besides that, Islamic law allows for the legitimacy of a child issuing from intercourse "by mistake." This can happen if two people thought they were married (but it turns out that their contract was somehow invalid), if they did not know that they were not allowed to have intercourse (i.e., that they did not have the intention of committing a prohibited act), or if one is coerced, insane, drunk, or asleep. A child born from any such act is considered legitimate, with the right to be supported by its father like any other legitimate child. Children born of a willfully illicit liaison are not entitled to inherit from the parents.

WHAT DO CHILDREN OWE
THEIR PARENTS?

As noted, the Qur'an articulates the importance of strong family relationships. It stresses in particular the importance of respect and kindness on the part of children toward parents. When recounting the failures of earlier generations to submit to the will of God, it highlights the failure to behave with "kindness to parents and to relatives and orphans and the poor" (2:84). Believers are enjoined to "worship God and do not associate anything with him, and be kind to parents and relatives and orphans and the needy and neighbors who are relatives and neighbors who are strangers and companions and travelers and slaves" (4:37). This kindness is to last throughout their lives:

> Your Lord requires that you worship none but him and kindness toward parents. If one of them or both of them become old with you, never say to them any word of disgust or reproach but address them with respectful words. (17:24)

Children are to show not only respect but also gratitude toward parents: "And we have required people concerning parents—mothers bear you in great weakness and nurse you for two years—'Give thanks to me and to your parents. To me you will return'" (31:15). Elsewhere:

And we require people to be good to their parents. Your mother bears you in
pain and gives birth in pain. And the bearing and nursing takes thirty months
until when you attain adulthood and reach forty years of age; say, "My Lord,
allow me to be grateful for your blessings which you have given me and my
parents, and that I may do good works to please you. And make my offspring
virtuous for me." (46:16)

People who respond this way are described as the righteous, those who will
dwell in paradise. They are, in fact, *muslim,* as the Qur'an uses the term.

Children are even required to bequeath property to surviving parents according to the fixed share system mentioned above:

And parents shall each have a sixth of the inheritance if [the deceased] has a
child, but if he has no child and his parents are his heirs, then his mother gets a
third, and if he has brothers and sisters, then his mother gets one sixth [of what
is left] after any bequests he may have made and debts [have been paid]. You do
not know which of your fathers and your children is nearer to you in benefit
[so this] fixing [of shares] is from God. Indeed, God is all knowing, wise. (4:12)

However, even with such strong emphasis on children's care and concern for
parents, the Qur'an says that parents who try to lead children astray or who do
evil must not be obeyed or emulated: "We have certainly admonished people to
be good to parents, but should they exert pressure upon you to associate others
with Me [in things] of which you have no knowledge, then do not obey them"
(29:8). Again:

O Believers, establish justice, being witnesses for God, even if the evidence
goes against yourselves or against your parents or relatives and regardless of
whether the witness is rich or poor. Under all circumstances God has priority
for you. (4:135)

Yet even in cases in which children cannot obey wayward parents, they are
called upon to be respectful and kind to parents, doing what they can for them
short of obeying. For example, readers are reminded of the story of Abraham
saying to his father, "Azar, do you take idols for gods? Indeed, I see you and your
people in obvious error. And so we showed Abraham the kingdom of heavens
and earth, and so he would be certain" (6:75–76). Elsewhere, Abraham says to
his father:

"O my father, why do you worship what does not hear, see or help you? O
my father, knowledge has come to me that has not come to you, so follow
me and I will guide you to an even path. O my father, do not serve Satan,
the rebel against the merciful one. O my father, I am afraid that a punishment
from the merciful one will take hold of you, as a friend of Satan." And he answered, "Do you turn away from my gods, Abraham? If you do not stop, I
will punish you, so leave me alone." And [Abraham] said, "Peace to you. I
will ask forgiveness of my Lord for you. He is merciful to me. And I will stay
away from you and from what you call upon that is not God, and I will pray
to my Lord; let my prayers to my Lord not be disappointed." (19:43–49)

In another mention of this episode, the Qur'an stresses that even this wayward father was treated with tenderness: "And Abraham's asking forgiveness for his father was only because of a promise he had made to him, but when it became clear to him that he was an enemy of God, he separated himself from him. Indeed, Abraham was kind and patient" (9:114). Similarly:

> There is a good model for you in Abraham and those with him, when they said to their people, "We are free of you and what you worship that is not God. We do not believe with you. Animosity and hatred have begun between us and you forever until you believe in God alone, except for Abraham's saying to his father, "I will ask forgiveness for you, but I have no power over God in favor of you. Our Lord, in you we put our trust and to you we turn and to you is the return." (60:5)

Except in such extreme cases, children are to obey their parents. Children are also expected to support their parents in their old age. This is because most schools of law have extended the requirement that the father support the mother and children as long as they are dependent upon them to the reciprocal case of elderly parents being dependent upon children for support.

WHEN THE FAMILY BREAKS DOWN: WHAT HAPPENS THEN?

According to a popular hadith report, there is nothing more pleasing to God than freeing a slave and nothing more displeasing to God than divorce. Because of the importance placed on the family in Islam, divorce is strongly discouraged. Yet, as noted, marriage is not sacramental; it is a contract between people with legal, not spiritual, force. Thus, despite the Qur'an's strong stand on the positive relations that should exist between spouses, it is realistic in acknowledging that people quarrel and sometimes find it impossible to live with one another in peace. It therefore allows divorce and stipulates conditions for it. In fact, an entire chapter is devoted to divorce, carefully outlining the major issues involved:

> In the name of God, the most gracious and merciful.
> O Prophet, when you divorce women, divorce them for a specified period and observe the period and fear God. Do not send them out from their houses, and they should not leave except if they commit a serious misdeed. These are the limits established by God and whoever goes beyond the limits of God wrongs himself. You do not know, maybe after that God will settle the matter.
> When they have reached their prescribed period, keep them with honor or part with them with honor, and call two just witnesses from among yourselves and bear witness for God. Whoever believes in God and the last day should be warned by this, and God will make a way out for whoever fears God.
> And God will provide for him where he does not expect it. And whoever puts trust in God, He will suffice for him. Truly God will achieve his purpose. God has appointed a [proper] measure for everything.
> And for your women who have lost hope of further menstruation, if you are in doubt, their prescribed period will be three months, as for those who

have not yet begun to menstruate. And the prescribed period for those who are pregnant is when they have delivered their burden. And God will provide for whoever fears God.

That is God's command which he has revealed to you. And God will acquit the evil deeds and give a good reward to whoever fears God.

House them in the homes where you live, according to your means, and do not bother them in such a way as to cause them trouble. And if they are pregnant, support them until they deliver their burden. If they nurse for you, pay them and discuss together with dignity, but if you find difficulty with each other, then have another nurse.

The man of means should spend out of his abundance, and the man of lesser means should spend out of what God has given him. God does not ask anyone more than he has provided. God will indeed bring ease after hardship.

How many cities turned against the command of its Lord and his messengers, and we held it accountable and punished it severely.

So it felt the consequences of its action and its end was destruction.

God has prepared for them a terrible punishment, so fear God, people of understanding who believe. God has revealed a reminder.

A messenger who recounts the clear signs of God to you so believers may do good deeds from dark until light. Whoever believes in God and does good deeds will enter paradise, flowing with rivers, and live there forever. God has indeed provided well for him.

God is the creator of the seven heavens and made earth like them. The command is revealed there so you may know that God is all-powerful and all-knowing. (Sura 65)

Divorce is very simple to obtain in Islamic law; it simply requires the husband's decree (although Shi'i law requires two witnesses and that the decree be articulated in a specific form). Nevertheless, there are two important issues in the Qur'an's discussion of divorce. Divorce is to be preceded by trial separation, during which arbitration is to occur and support of some kind is to be provided. Regarding trial separation, the Qur'an says that this may occur twice before a final divorce: "Divorce is lawful twice; after that either you should keep [your wife] in kindness or send [her] free in kindness" (2:230). Accordingly, initial (or revocable) divorces may be rescinded during the specified waiting period, provided the marriage has been consummated. The waiting period—established to determine whether or not the woman is pregnant, so as to be able to ascertain paternity—was set at three menstrual cycles, based on another verse:

And divorced women shall wait by themselves for three periods and it is not allowed for them to hide what God has created in their wombs if they believe in God and the Last Day; and their husbands have the greater right to take them back during that period, provided they desire reconciliation. (2:229)[7]

---

[7]The waiting period (*'iddah*) after a husband's death is four months and ten days, according to the following Qur'anic verse: "And those of you who die and leave wives behind, they shall wait concerning themselves four months and ten [days]" (2:235).

During this period, the wife is entitled to maintenance and is subject to obedience. It is also a time when reconciliation can occur, as the Qur'an encourages:
"And if you fear a rift between them then appoint an arbiter from his family and
an arbiter from her family. If they want reconciliation, God will establish it between them. Indeed, God is all knowing and aware" (4:36). Later in the same
chapter, in fact, the Qur'an emphasizes that "reconciliation is best" (4:129). If
after two such episodes the couple still cannot get along, irrevocable divorce is
pronounced and the couple may not remarry until the woman has married and
divorced another man. The Qur'an says,

> If he divorces her [again, after the first two revocable divorces], then she is
> not lawful for him until she marries another husband, and if he divorces her,
> then it is no sin for them to return to each other, if they are sure they can ob-
> serve the rules of God. (2:231)

In cases of irrevocable divorce, return of the dower may not be demanded
and any dower deferred until divorce must be paid, as the Qur'an specifies repeatedly. For example, "And if you want to replace one wife with another and
you have already given one of them a large amount of wealth, do not take anything away from it" (4:21). This rule, however, applies only for obedient wives:
"And it is not lawful for you that you take anything of what you have given them
unless both fear that they cannot observe the rules of God" (2:229). The dower,
therefore, not only provides for a degree of economic independence for women,
it also provides for support in the case of divorce, and it can even allow the wife
to initiate divorce. Although generally in Islamic law divorce is initiated by the
husband, provision is made for the wife to effectively pay her husband to divorce
her irrevocably—by giving back the dower—according to the Qur'anic verse:
"And if you fear that they cannot observe the rules of God, then it is no sin for
either in what she gives to get her freedom. These are the rules of God, so do
not disobey them and whoever disobeys the rule of God are wrongdoers"
(2:230). The various schools of Islamic law incorporated this provision for "divorce for consideration" into law, allowing the amount in question to be whatever is agreed upon by the spouses.[8]

Despite such special provisions, husbands are responsible for wives, even in
divorce before consummation of the marriage. The Qur'an says:

> It is no sin if you divorce women before you have touched them and have
> not fixed a dower, but provide for them, the rich man according to his means
> and the poor man according to his. . . . And if you divorce them before you
> have touched them but have fixed the dower, then pay half of it unless they
> or [their guardians] remit, but that you should pay is nearer to righteousness.
> (2:237–8)

---

[8]Technically, in Sunni law, "divorce for consideration" may also be initiated by someone
other than the wife, even a stranger. Provided the husband agrees and the terms are met,
the wife need not agree or even know about it until it is completed. See Laleh Bakhtiar,
translator and editor, *Encyclopedia of Islamic Law: A Compendium of the Major Schools*,
512–513. This is, however, a legal provision that is rarely invoked.

These provisions were included in Islamic legal codes, stipulating that if divorce occurs before consummation and before specification of the dower, the divorced wife shall receive a gift. If the divorce occurs after payment of the dower, the divorced woman is required to return half of it. Similarly, the Qur'an requires that divorced wives should be provided for: "And for divorced women [there should be] provision according to justice—an obligation on those who are righteous" (2:242).

Although efforts at reconciliation are encouraged, if they fail then final divorce results. If there are children, provided the child was born within the first six months of marriage (considered to be the minimum gestation period), paternity is assumed to be certain and, custody ultimately goes to the father. This means that the mother is allowed to care for the child when she or he is young, provided she is sane, trustworthy, and honorable, does not remarry, and allows the father access to the children. But at a certain age, custody goes to the father. Some schools of law require that the mother be Muslim in order to take custody of the children, but not all. The age at which custody reverts to the father varies in the opinions of the schools of law, from age two to puberty for boys and from age seven to the time of marriage for girls. If the mother remarries or moves away from the father, custody of young children usually goes to the grandparents until the specified age.

UNCONVENTIONAL FAMILIES, SUPERNATURAL FAMILIES

Islamic law allows for two kinds of marriage considered unconventional by Western standards. One is known as "temporary marriage" (*mutah*). It is based on the Qur'anic verse quoted above ("And for what you receive from them, give them their due, as fixed, and there shall be no sin for you in anything you mutually agree upon once it is fixed" 4:25). Included in the things possible to stipulate is the duration of the contract. While Sunni law accepts that this kind of marriage (based on a contract specifying a limited time frame) was once acceptable in Islam, the schools of law agree that it is no longer legitimate. In general, Sunni contract law does not allow inclusion of provisions that weaken the contract, and it is believed that stipulation of a marriage for a limited time weakens the marriage bond. Shi'i law, however, accepts marriages based on contracts stipulating a limit to the length of the marriage as still valid. Accordingly, temporary marriage may be contracted, provided the specified witness and verbal articulation are present and the dower is determined. Children born in this type of marriage have exactly the same rights as children in other Islamic marriages. However, the wife in a temporary marriage is not entitled to maintenance or inheritance from the husband, unless arrangements for these are agreed upon by the husband in the contract. Once the contract's time is up, the former wife is treated as a divorcée, with a necessary waiting period before she is eligible for remarriage.

Another type of unconventional marriage possible in Islamic law is similar to what we call in the modern West a "commuter marriage," that is, a marriage in which the partners do not live together. The typical "commuter marriage" results from the fact that one of the spouses has to be away from home for work. But in Islam, a marriage contract can specify that they do not live together permanently. According to some schools of law, it is possible to stipulate in the marriage contract that the husband will allow the wife to remain in her own home, even in another city, for the duration of their marriage. Although the majority of Sunni schools do not consider this stipulation valid, it is one that has come up in the modern era wherein economic conditions are such that spouses may live in different cities for the sake of their jobs, just as in the West. In such marriages, all other standard duties and responsibilities of both spouses remain according to Islamic laws.

In accordance with the laws of maintenance and inheritance described above, single-parent households are possible in Islam. In the case of divorce, the wife will have custody of small children, who will then go to the father at the specified ages. In case of the death of one of the spouses, the other would take over custody, although the extended family is expected to participate.

However, given the extreme care Islam takes in specifying the division of labor and balance of duties between husbands and wives, single-parent families are not encouraged. In fact, some laws prevent the establishment of unconventional families. For example, Islamic law does not allow for the legal adoption of children as we do it in the West. This is according to the Qur'an, which says:

> God has not made two hearts in a man's chest and has not made your wives into your mothers when you separate from them saying, "Be as my mother's back." That is your own saying, the words of your mouths, but God speaks the truth and guides the way. Call them after their fathers. That is more just with God. (33:4–5)

Taking in an abandoned child, an orphan, or one whose parentage is not known does not establish legal adoption, that is, to make the child an heir or disqualify her or him as marriageable. It is, however, considered an honorable act of generosity, and such guardians are advised by the Qur'an to treat these children equitably.

No other forms of family life are permissible in Islam. As in Judaism and Christianity, homosexuality is forbidden, as is "living together" between marriageable males and females. Sexual relations outside those permitted in Islamic law are punishable in a variety of ways, depending upon the degree of responsibility of the partners, and in today's world only a few countries carry out the strict religiously mandated punishments for illicit sexual relations, such as whipping. In any case, only free, sane adults in full possession of their senses at the time the act was committed are subject to the ultimate punishment, stoning. Nevertheless, the severity of the punishments draws attention to the importance Islam places on solid and responsible family relations.

COMMENTARIES

Judaism on Islam

by JACOB NEUSNER

Judaism concurs with Islam that the transaction involves a contract as well. The marriage agreement, Ketubah, is recited at the wedding rite and is witnessed. As in Islam, it is a document that is enforceable in a court of law. The wife is promised upkeep during the marriage, and alimony should the marriage end in divorce or the husband's death. The property that she brings to the marriage is protected and, in the case of multiple wives, her property is assigned to her children, not those of the same husband and one of the other co-wives.

But the language of Judaism is sanctification: the sanctification of a particular woman for a particular man. And that conception merges the language of acquisition with the language of sanctification. A householder buys a cow; in acquiring it, he does not sanctify it. Unless he means to offer it on the altar in Jerusalem, a person who utilizes the same cow (e.g., milks it or uses it for ploughing) does not offend God. The issue of sanctification does not enter the transaction. But a householder who acquires a woman thereby consecrates the woman as his wife. Another person who utilizes the same woman (e.g., has sexual relations with her and produces children by her) enormously outrages God (not to mention the husband). The category, sanctification and its opposite, applies. Yet in both instances the result is acquiring title to, rights over, the cow or the woman. Indeed, slaves, movables, and real estate prove analogous to the betrothal of a woman. The transaction by which a householder acquires a wife, slave, movables, or real estate forms the genus, the language and categories and action-symbols proving constant.

But when it comes to the woman, an enormous point of difference renders the woman an active participant in the transfer of title. As in Islam, she has to consent, and when she does, her status as person, not merely as property, changes; and the change is called sanctification. So the opening exposition of the Halakhah serves to establish the genus—money, writ, usucaption for the slave; money, writ, act of sexual relations (comparable to usucaption) for the woman. These are compared and contrasted and firmly situated in a single classification: things that are acquired by the householder through a common repertoire of procedures of transfer of title from owner to owner.

Islamic and Judaic law concur on many points. Both take for granted that both parties to a marriage belong to the faith. But while Islamic law permits Muslim men to marry non-Muslim women, Judaic law makes no such distinction. Status as to belonging to Israel, the holy people brought into being at Sinai, descends through the mother, so an Israelite man married to a gentile woman cannot produce Israelite children. In this regard, Islamic law is guided by a different metaphor from the one that governs in the case of Judaism. Islamic and Judaic law concur on a man's making multiple marriages (polygyny). Jews living in Christian countries from 1000 C.E. ceased to practice polygyny, but those living in Muslim countries continued to do so into the twentieth century. Islamic and Judaic law further concur on the primary responsibility of raising children in the faith, and they deem the task to be incurred at birth. Judaism concurs with Islam that daughters may inherit, but that is only when there are no sons. The basic points of intersection between Judaism and Islam should not obscure the fundamental difference in Judaism's governing metaphor for marriage, drawn as it is from the language of sanctification and sacrifice.

Christianity on Islam

by BRUCE CHILTON

There is a curious feature about this generally clear exposition, which—within the terms of reference of Christianity—requires investigation. It opens with the contention, later repeated, that marriage in Islam is not "a sacrament," or even sacramental. The contrast is made with a solemn agreement or contract. Implicitly, this comparison is with Catholic Christianity, where marriage does feature as one of seven enumerated sacraments. But quite apart from issues of enumeration and definition, a sacramental evaluation of marital vows among Christians is and has always been widespread.

The curiosity is nonetheless that, having denied that marriage is a sacrament within Islam, the exposition goes on in substance to define it precisely as such. The chapter spells out the detailed nature of the contract involved and the promises and obligations that attach, and proceeds explicitly to associate marriage with the "signs" God has given. Within Christian tradition, a sacrament is an outward and visible sign of an inward and spiritual grace. Particularly, the term *sacramentum* in Latin refers to joining oneself by oath to a contract, and that agreement then includes divine participation. In the Gospel according to John, Jesus is asked for a sign comparable to the manna that was provided to Israel in the wilderness, and he replies (John 6:32):

> Amen, Amen, I say to you: Moses did not give you the bread from heaven,
> but my father gives you the true bread from heaven.

When asked for that bread, Jesus replies in a long, poetic discourse that he himself is the bread of life, available to those who come to him in the celebration of Eucharist and providing them with eternal life (John 6:34–58).

Without spelling out any sacramental dogma, John's Gospel here gives us the coordinates of sacramental thinking within primitive Christianity and its successors. What makes a sacrament more than a human oath is that it is an effectual sign of divine power. In the case of John 6, the believer who binds himself to the sign of Jesus himself in the Eucharist's bread and wine is granted eternal life. That paradigm of human intention combined with divine power is regularly deployed whenever the language of sacrament is used in Christian theology.

That brings us back to the question of what is being denied when marriage in Islam is said not to be sacramental. The stated purpose is to stress the contractual definition of marriage, much as in the emphasis on payment of dower. But there is a deeper question here. In the Pauline take on marriage (discussed in Christianity's response to the exposition on Judaism), believers may save and sanctify unbelievers, while the prohibition of unions with idolaters in Islam is explicit. The contrast, of course, is not simply an opposition, in that Christianity and Judaism do not fall under the category of a idolatry. Moreover, the Qur'an is not dealing in 2:222 with preexisting marriages, as Paul is in 1 Corinthians 7. But having said that, a difference in emphasis is notable. That difference turns on how fundamental obedience is taken to be.

Obedience in the Qur'an is as pivotal as it is in Christianity's *Shepherd of Hermas,* as may be seen in the story of Noah and his wayward son (Qur'an 11:37–44). But in Islam it seems even more vital. Hence (for example) marriage with idolaters is excluded, responsibility for a woman's first marriage lies with her father (or next closest male relative), and the fixed-share system applies to bequests from children to parents. Within the history of Christianity, many comparable arrangements have prevailed, but they cannot claim the same degree of elemental warrant that they have in Islam. Likewise, although homosexuality and cohabitation outside of marriage have been prohibited by Christian societies in many eras, neither is prohibited categorically within its Scriptures, which is why considerable controversy today prevails over such matters, not only within churches, but within societies historically shaped by Christian teaching.

The distinctively Christian perspective on all its sacraments, marriage included, is that they have the capacity to transform and influence those who take part in them beyond their capacity to understand precisely what is going on or to be fully and consciously obedient to that process as a whole.

Hinduism on Islam

by Brian K. Smith

One of the striking differences between traditional Hinduism and Islam on this issue stems from the latter's practice of giving the wife a measure of economic independence within the family. Following the Qur'an's dictates, the establishment in Islam of the institution of the husband providing his bride with a dower, which is hers and hers alone, can be sharply contrasted with the institution of the dowry in Hinduism. The latter requires the bride's family to offer the groom payment (in whatever form) for marrying the woman; the dowry has been and continues to be a major expectation and the potential source of much abuse and misery for women (and their families) in India.

These two opposing practices entail very different ideological and practical ramifications. In Islam, the economic independence of women is not only situated within an ideological framework where, theoretically at least, men and women are regarded as equals in the sight of God, but also practically the institution of the dower allows women within a marriage (and in the event of divorce) a degree of freedom quite unknown to the portrait of the wife and widow painted in the ancient Hindu texts. The notion that men and women are "equal" (in the sight of God or otherwise) is absent in traditional Hinduism, just as is the notion that human beings born into different castes are "equal." While the actual treatment of women in traditional Islam may not conform to modern expectations, the fact that religiously Islam insists on such equality contrasts it, in general, with the emphasis on religiously ordained inequality—between the genders and between castes—within Hinduism.

The framework in which Islam discusses the ethics of family life is one guided, first and foremost, by the notion that "All our lives and activity are to be dedicated to God" and "one of the ways we express our submission to God's will is through our treatment of other people." Compassion and ethical treatment of others, from family members to utter strangers, is by no means absent in Hinduism; in fact, such virtues are stressed. But in most forms of Hinduism, such ethical behavior is not so much regarded as the manifestation of one's "submission" to a deity but rather as both the proper and intelligent way to live a life: proper, because it is mandated in the texts on dharma or one's duty to others; intelligent, because of the laws of karma (which teach that you shall "reap what you sow").

Buddhism on Islam

by Brad Clough

Buddhism, unlike Islam, has rarely endeavored to extend its values outside of its own religious communities to larger societies in the form of law, and so in Buddhism we find less specific and detailed discussions of certain aspects of family life, such as marriage, inheritance, and divorce, which have legal ramifications.

Nevertheless, the Qur'an's statement that God does not guide and brings down his judgment upon those who hold family dearer than God, sounds similar to statements in the Pāli canon which say that even one's dearest family members cannot do what the Dharma can do. The only difference here is that Islam is highly theistic (those who submit to the will of God are Muslims) and Buddhism subscribes to a highly qualified form of theism, in which divine realms and beings are of secondary importance at best, in comparison with the primary importance of the Buddha's teachings (those who take refuge in the Buddha, Dharma, and Sangha are Buddhists).

So, while God is involved in all human relationships in Islam, it is the Dharma that dictates how people relate to one another in Buddhism. In terms of how family members should treat one another, both religions place a premium on generosity, faithfulness, and mercy. Buddhism has placed the responsibility of creating a loving and peaceful home mostly in the hands of the mother, whereas in Islam that responsibility seems to fall equally on both parents. As for economic responsibility, there is a slight but significant difference between the two religions, in that in Buddhism the husband is expected to be the provider and the wife the protector of wealth, while in Islam the wife is actually owed some portion of the husband's wealth upon marriage and his death. As Professor Sonn points out, this has afforded Muslim women a degree of economic independence that women in other religions usually have not enjoyed, especially in premodern times. In Buddhism, the wives are given a greater role in family decisions, which in Islam typically fall largely upon husbands, either because of their inherent gender or because of their traditional role as breadwinners. However, like the Qur'an, Buddhist scriptures expect that wives will obey husbands, and run the household properly. With respect to sexual roles, Islamic legal codes dictate that a wife must always submit to her husband's desires, but the Buddhist precept that requires refraining from sexual misconduct has usually been interpreted to include prohibiting a husband from forcing himself upon his wife.

In both religions, main parental duties include teaching children their own religion, arranging marriages, and providing inheritances. Just as Buddhist parents are called "first teachers" (*pubbācariyas*), Muslim parents must ensure that the first thing their children hear is the call to prayer and the Qur'an's first chapter, and then continue their children's religious education as they grow up. In regard to inheritance, in most Buddhist societies it has gone to the eldest son or all sons, but in Islamic ones, shares of it must go to daughters. Daughters as well as sons must be found suitable spouses by their parents in both religions, although Muslim children, daughters especially, seem to have more choice in the matter.

Buddhist children are taught to see their parents as divine. In Islam, such an association would result in the grave sin of *shirk*. Obedience is an important trait in both Buddhist and Muslim children, but not if it involves doing evil. Otherwise, Buddhist children, like Muslim ones, are taught that they owe their parents respect and care (especially in old age), but not simply because of parental seniority. Kindness or compassion should be the primary motivating force for honoring one's parents. In both religions, such kindness is engendered by children considering the debt of gratitude they owe their parents for all the good that they have done for them.

As for unconventional families, orthodox Islam has nothing equivalent to Buddhism's frequent privileging of monasticism, which requires severing societal and familial ties. However, Buddhist renunciates are comparable to members of some antinomian Sufi orders in Islam, who often leave their families behind and use familial language to express the brotherly nature of a community of mystics.

SUMMARY

Marriage is a contract in Islam, not a sacrament but a solemn agreement that must be properly recited aloud and witnessed. Law pertaining to the details of the contract is extensive and detailed, but the legalistic nature of the marriage contract should not mask the fact that marriage is the most highly respected social institution in Islam. One of the ways Muslims express their "submission" (Arabic: *islam*) to God's will by treating other people with kindness, compassion, and fairness, and marriage is no exception. But belief in human equality in Islam coexists with belief in different roles for different people. The Qur'an recognizes distinctions in the roles of spouses. In traditional interpretations, men are considered to be responsible for women and children, while women are in charge of the household and nurturing the children. In modern interpretations, men and women may share these responsibilities. Despite the range of opinions on these issues, Muslims agree that males and females are equal before God. This ultimate moral equality finds expression in a marriage relationship in which both partners and children flourish, and all are obedient to the laws of God.

GLOSSARY

jahiliyya "ignorance," a term used to describe the era before the revelation of the Qur'an

mutah "temporary marriage," a kind of marriage contract in which the duration of the relationship is stipulated; permissible in Shi'i Islam, but no longer permitted in Sunni Islam

muslim "one who submits" [to the will of God]

shirk "associating" or "giving partners" to God; polytheism; allowing something or someone (such as material wealth, power, a political ruler) besides God to guide one's actions; the gravest sin in Islam because it blinds one to the source of divine guidance

DISCUSSION QUESTIONS

1. Does Islam allow men to marry more than one wife? Under what circumstances?
2. Is divorce permitted in Islam? Under what circumstances?
3. Are parents allowed to force their children to marry people they don't want to marry in Islam?
4. Are women allowed to inherit in Islam?
5. Are Muslim children required to care for their parents when they get old?

 INFOTRAC

If you would like additional information related to the material discussed here, you can visit our Web site: http://www.wadsworth.com

4

Hinduism

BY BRIAN K. SMITH

CONVENTIONAL EXPECTATION VERSUS THIS RELIGIOUS TRADITION: WHAT DO HUSBANDS AND WIVES OWE ONE ANOTHER?

Conventional Expectations Versus This Religious Tradition

In Hinduism, as in most other traditional world religions, a very high premium is placed on the family. It is by forming and maintaining a family that a man and a woman fulfill some of their most important religious duties—to themselves, to one another, to their ancestors, to society, and to posterity. Indeed, while families are obviously regarded as important in many societies (including our own, as is witnessed by the frequent political appeal to "family values"), in the Hindu religious tradition one's very salvation is often said to hinge on a timely and proper marriage and the production of offspring. Despite the fact that Hinduism has had a long tradition of world renunciation, asceticism, and chastity, these other-worldly values and practices are almost always set within a context of the prior fulfilling of one's obligations to the family.

The family in Hinduism is the essential germ of social and even cosmic order, the microcosm of stability, regularity, and propriety. The social and moral order of things and beings (seen and unseen) depend on a correctly structured, hierarchically governed, and well-functioning family. Conversely, as we shall see below, when the family is threatened or ruined, the ramifications are severe and wide-ranging.

Another reason the family plays such a vital role in both society and the cosmos as a whole is because for most strands of Hinduism religious life revolves around the householder stage of life, during which one marries, reproduces, and raises children. It is in this stage of life that one's ritual obligations to the gods, the ancestors, and to one's fellow human beings are discharged. For this reason and others, the householder stage is said to be the best—better even than those stages of life in which one is pursuing the ultimate religious goal of final liberation from rebirth, or *moksha*. Furthermore, all other stages of life (those of the student, forest-dweller, and world renouncer) depend on the householder, in part because it is the householder who feeds and donates to them when they beg from him:

> A householder alone offers sacrifices. A householder afflicts himself with aus-
> terities. Of the four stages of life, therefore, the householder is the best. As all
> rivers and rivulets ultimately end up in the ocean, so people of all stages of
> life ultimately end up with the householder. As all creatures depend on their
> mothers for their survival, so all mendicants depend on householders for their
> survival.[1]

Thus, as another text puts it, when "carried out with zeal" the householder stage of life procures both happiness in this life and heaven in the next:

> Just as all living creatures depend on air in order to live, so do members of
> the other stages of life subsist by depending on householders. Since people in
> the other three stages of life are supported every day by the knowledge and
> food of the householder, therefore the householder stage of life is the best. It
> must be carried out with zeal by the man who wants to win an incorruptible
> heaven (after death) and endless happiness here on earth. . . .[2]

Yet another reason for the emphasis on the family in Hinduism is the traditional importance placed on the begetting of sons to carry on the family name
and lineage. Already in some of the earliest and subsequently most authoritative
sacred texts of the Hindu tradition, the Vedas (composed ca. 1200–400 B.C.E.),
the critical and supreme importance of sons and the value of the wife who produces them is evident. In one such passage, comprised of a discussion between a
king named Hariscandra, who has one hundred wives but no sons, and a priest
named Narada, the king asks, "What does one gain by a son? Tell me that, O
Narada." The priest replies by enumerating the many benefits a son brings to his
father:

> A debt he pays in him,
> And immortality he gains,
> The father who sees the face
> Of his son born and alive.
> Greater than the delights
> That earth, fire, and water
> Bring to living beings
> Is a father's delight in his son.
> By means of sons have fathers ever
> Crossed over the mighty darkness;
> For one is born from oneself,

---

[1]Vasistha Dharma Sutra 10.14–16. Translated in Patrick Olivelle, *The Asrama System: The History and Hermeneutics of a Religious Institution* (New York: Oxford University Press, 1993), 93.

[2]Manusmriti (hereafter abbreviated as Manu) 3.77–79. This and all other quotations from this text are taken from *The Laws of Manu*, translated by Wendy Doniger with Brian K. Smith (London: Penguin Books, 1991).

A ferry laden with food.
What is the use of dirt and deer skin?
What profit in beard and austerity?
Seek a son, O Brahmin,
He is the world free of blame.[3]

Narada, in this glorification of male offspring, begins with an articulation of a very common Hindu theme: it is through the production of sons that a man repays a "debt" he owes to his ancestors and thereby also wins a kind of immortality for himself. By creating a son a father perpetuates himself ("for one is born from oneself") and also "crosses over the mighty darkness." Furthermore, Narada contrasts the life of the family man to that of the ascetic or world-renouncer (covered in "dirt and deer skin" practicing his austerities), and claims that it is through a son that a father wins a "world free of blame," that is, a pleasant and righteous life in both this world and the next.

Narada then goes on to specify yet more of the benefits and joys the birth of a son brings to the father, and expands his discussion to extol also the role the wife plays in a man's life as well:

Food is breath, clothes protect.
Gold is for beauty, cattle for marriage.
The wife is a friend, a daughter brings grief.
But a son is a light in the highest heaven.
The husband enters the wife;
Becoming an embryo he enters the mother.
Becoming in her a new man again,
He is born in the tenth (lunar) month.
A wife is called "wife,"
Because in her he is born again.
He is productive, she is productive,
For the seed is placed in her.
The gods and the seers
Brought to her great luster.
The gods said to men:
"She is your mother again."[4]

Here again we see the idea that one is reproduced in the form of one's son. A man is said to be born again in his wife's womb and thus, as another text puts it, "in your offspring you are born again; that, o mortal, is your immortality" (Satapatha Brahmana 1.5.5.6). If the son is a means of extending his own life into another generation, or, indeed, into a kind of "immortality," a man's wife is thus considered his second mother, "because in her he is born again." As such, as we shall see, both offspring and wife are to be revered by the man as the very agents of his happiness in this life and the next.

---

[3]Aitareya Brahmana 7.13. Translated in Olivelle, *The Asrama System*, 44.

[4]Ibid., 45.

Thus, at all levels—cosmic, social, and individual—the family is at the center of religious life in Hinduism. Because of the prominence of family life in this religion, guidelines are set out for the proper establishment and maintenance of the family and to direct the relationships between husbands and wives and parents and children. These interrelationships are guided by a set of mutually obtaining obligations between the various members of the Hindu family.

What Do Husbands Owe Wives?

While Hindu texts of all sorts maintain that ultimately the supreme goal of religious life is reached through detachment from and renunciation of the world of family, work, and social ties, most also insist that this pursuit of final liberation from karma and rebirth must wait until one's obligations (or "debts") are fulfilled. Chief among these are the debts to the ancestors, paid off, as we have seen above, through the production of a son with one's wife. But other debts are also owed and are repaid by the study of the sacred Veda and by sacrificial rituals, both of which are part and parcel of the householder's ritual routine and all of which are incumbent upon a man before he may renounce the world:

> When a man has paid his three debts, he may set his mind-and-heart on Freedom; but if he seeks Freedom when he has not paid the debts, he sinks down. When a man has studied the Veda in accordance with the rules, and begotten sons in accordance with his duty, and sacrificed with sacrifices according to his ability, he may set his mind-and-heart on Freedom. But if a twice-born man seeks Freedom when he has not studied the Vedas, and has not begotten progeny, and has not sacrificed with sacrifices, he sinks down.
>
> (Manu 6.35–37)

Another text makes a similar point and adds other obligatory duties to the list a man must perform as a householder before he is allowed to renounce: "No one but a man who has studied the Vedas, muttered prayers, fathered sons, given food (to guests and others in various rituals), maintained the sacred fires, and offered sacrifices according to his ability, may set his mind on renunciation."[5]

Thus, Hinduism demands that a man complete himself as a householder—a husband, father, and man-in-the-world—before pursuing final liberation. A man's responsibilities, if they are to be properly fulfilled, require that he, after a period as a student under the guidance of a teacher, select a suitable woman, marry her, and thus begin the stage of life of a householder. A wife not only enables a man to fulfill his spiritual and ritual obligations, playing as she does an indispensable role in those arenas; she also, it is said, completes the very being of a man: "A full half of one's self is one's wife. As long as one does not obtain a wife, therefore, for so long one is not reborn and remains incomplete. As soon as he obtains a wife, however, he is reborn and becomes complete" (Satapatha Brahmana 5.2.1.10). "When he finds a wife, therefore," it is said in another text, "a

---

[5]Yajnavalkya Dharmasmriti 3.56, in ibid., 143.

man considers himself to be, as it were, more complete" (Aitareya Aranyaka 1.2.5). It is as a pair that husband and wife participate in the sacrificial rituals and carry out other of the household's ritual duties. They are, therefore, jointly responsible for both the ritual obligation and for the merit that comes from fulfilling such duties. The wife is thus said in at least one text to be "qualified to perform sacrifices" because she assumes the responsibilities for carrying out the rituals on her own when her husband cannot:

> Together do these two (husband and wife) constitute a couple; together do these two maintain the sacred fires; together do these two procreate and obtain progeny. The eastern world pertains to the husband, the western world to the wife. Since the wife takes upon herself the responsibility of the vow (to maintain the sacrificial rites) of the husband who has gone out on a journey or who has become incapacitated, therefore she is entitled to half (of the ritual's benefits). Women are (thus) qualified to perform sacrifices.
>
> (Manava Srauta Sutra 8.23.10–14)

Because she will be so crucial to his future well-being, selecting a wife is a matter of great concern. She should, of course, come from the right caste and from a good family, but she should also possess good qualities and character: "One should examine the family (of the intended bride), those on the mother's side and on the father's side. . . . One should marry a girl who possesses the characteristics of intelligence, beauty, and good character, and who is free from disease" (Apastamba Grhya Sutra 1.5.1–3). Some texts, like the following, go into some detail about the type of woman one should seek as a wife, and the types one should definitely avoid:

> When he has received his guru's permission and bathed and performed the ritual for homecoming according to the rules (i.e., when he has completed the student stage of life), a twice-born man should marry a wife who is of the same class and has the right marks. A woman who does not come from the same blood line on her mother's side, nor belongs to the same ritual line on her father's side, and who is a virgin, is recommended for marriage to a twice-born man. When a man connects himself with a woman, he should avoid the ten following families, even if they are great or rich in cows, goats, sheep, property, or grain: a family that has abandoned the rites, or does not have male children, or does not chant the Veda; and those families in which they have hairy bodies, piles, consumption, weak digestion, epilepsy, white leprosy, or black leprosy. A man should not marry a girl who is a redhead or has an extra limb or is sickly or has no body hair or too much body hair or talks too much or is sallow; or who is named after a constellation, a tree, or a river, or who has a low-caste name, or is named after a mountain, a bird, a snake, or has a menial or frightening name. He should marry a woman who does not lack any part of her body and who has a pleasant name, who walks like a goose or an elephant, whose body hair and hair on the head is fine, whose teeth are not big, and who has delicate limbs. A wise man will not marry a woman who has no brother or whose father is unknown. . . .
>
> (Manu 3.4–11)

Later on, after a man has married a woman of his own caste, he may wed other women as well. Men "driven by desire" may take additional wives from castes other than their own caste, assuming the first wife has the proper pedigree. But the highest castes are prohibited under any circumstances from forming unions with women of the servant classes, for if they do they drag their own families down the caste ladder:

> A woman of the same class is recommended to twice-born men for the first marriage; but for men who are driven by desire, these are the women, in progressively descending order: According to tradition, only a servant woman can be the wife of a servant; she and one of his own class can be the wife of a commoner; these two and one of his own class for a king; and these three and one of his own class for a priest. Not a single story mentions a servant woman as the wife of a priest or ruler, even in extremity. Twice-born men who are so infatuated as to marry women of low caste quickly reduce their families, including the descendants, to the status of servants.
>
> (Manu 3.12–15)

Having thus selected the right woman to wed, a man should marry her according to the proper rites of marriage laid out in the scriptures. When he has done so, the husband becomes her "master" but he also takes on certain duties vis-à-vis his new wife:

> Benedictory verses are recited and a sacrifice to the Lord of Creatures is performed at weddings to make them auspicious, but it is the act of giving away (the bride by the father) that makes (the groom) her master. A husband who performs the transformative ritual (of marriage) with Vedic verses always makes his woman happy, both when she is in her fertile season and when she is not, both here on earth and in the world beyond.
>
> (Manu 5.152–153)

Note here that the husband has, according to the text, the responsibility to keep his wife happy and sexually fulfilled, even in times when she will not conceive.

In addition, however, and among the most important of all duties that husbands have to wives, is the obligation to impregnate them. In another passage we read of the exact times when a husband may and may not approach his wife for sex, and the type of offspring they will produce out of intercourse at different times of the month:

> A man should have sex with his wife during her fertile season, and always find his satisfaction in his own wife; when he desires sexual pleasure he should go to her to whom he is vowed, except on the days at the (lunar) junctures. The natural fertile season of women is traditionally said to last for sixteen nights, though these include four special days that good people despise. Among these (nights), the first four, the eleventh, and the thirteenth are disapproved; the other ten nights are approved. On the even nights, sons are conceived, and on the uneven nights, daughters; therefore a man who wants sons should unite with his wife during her fertile season on the even nights. A

male child is born when the semen of the man is greater (than the seed of a woman), and a female child when (the seed) of the woman is greater (than the semen of a man); if both are equal, a hermaphrodite is born, or a boy and a girl (i.e., fraternal twins). . . .

(Manu 3.45–49)

A husband also has the obligation to support his wife and family materially; he must provide for their shelter and subsistence and other necessities of life. In the householder stage of life, in fact, one has the religious duty to pursue *artha,* "advantage" or "self-interest" as it pertains to the political and economic spheres of life. Such an obligation to work and provide for the wife continues even if a man is called upon to travel, although it appears that the husband needs to do more than just leave money behind—he should find an occupation to keep his wife busy so as to keep her honest:

A man may go away on a journey on business only after he has established a livelihood for his wife; for even a steady woman could be corrupted if she is starving for lack of livelihood. If he goes away on a journey after providing a livelihood, she should subject herself to restraints in her life; but if he goes away on a journey without providing for her, she may make her living by crafts that are not disapproved of.

(Manu 9.74–75)

Furthermore, if a husband goes on such a journey (with or without making provisions for his wife) a woman need not wait forever for her husband to return before carrying on with her own life: "If the man has gone away on a journey to fulfil some duty, (she) should wait for him for eight years; (if he has gone) for learning or fame, six; for pleasure, three years" (Manu 9.76).

A wife with whom one makes a family and who is and remains virtuous should be revered by her menfolk; she is equated with "the goddesses of good fortune" and becomes worthy of worship by her husband. The virtuous wife and mother becomes the linchpin for the proper performance of a householder's dharma or religious duty, which includes the procreation and care of children, the running of the household, and sexual pleasure (or *kama,* another of the pre-scribed "ends of life" for the Hindu in the householder stage of life), but also the attainment of heaven itself for the male householder and his ancestors:

There is no difference at all between the goddesses of good fortune who live in houses and women who are the lamps of their houses, worthy of reverence and greatly blessed because of their progeny. The wife is the visible form of what holds together the begetting of children, the caring for them when they are born, and the ordinary business of every day. Children, the fulfilment of duties, obedience, and the ultimate sexual pleasure depend upon a wife, and so does heaven, for oneself and one's ancestors. The woman who is not un-faithful to her husband but restrains her mind-and-heart, speech, and body reaches her husband's worlds (after death), and good people call her a virtuous woman.

(Manu 9.26–29)

The good wife and "virtuous woman" is thus crucial to the success of the
family as a whole and to the husband's welfare in particular. In the following text,
it is said that women who fulfil such an ideal should be worshiped and revered,
for through their virtue and the respect paid to them by their male family members the gods are pleased and the family thrives. Conversely, in homes where virtuous women are not so honored and become unhappy, the family is destroyed:

> Fathers, brothers, husbands, and brothers-in-law who wish for great good for-
> tune should revere these women and adorn them. The deities delight in
> places where women are revered, but where women are not revered all rites
> are fruitless. Where the women of the family are miserable, the family is soon
> destroyed, but it always thrives where the women are not miserable. Homes
> that are cursed by women of the family who have not been treated with due
> reverence are completely destroyed, as if struck down by witchcraft. There-
> fore men who wish to prosper should always revere these women with orna-
> ments, clothes, and food at celebrations and festivals. There is unwavering
> good fortune in a family where the husband is always satisfied by the wife,
> and the wife by the husband. If the wife is not radiant she does not stimulate
> the man; and because the man is unstimulated the making of children does
> not happen. If the woman is radiant, the whole family is radiant, but if she is
> not radiant the whole family is not radiant. Through bad marriages, the ne-
> glect of rites, failure to study the Veda, and transgressing against priests, fami-
> lies cease to be families.
>
> (Manu 3.55–63)

Such then, is the supreme importance of the family in general and of the mutual respect between husbands and wives under ideal circumstances. The husband's duty to his wife is to care for her in all ways and to do his best to make
her happy; the wife's duty to her husband, as we shall see shortly, is to please,
honor, and obey him in all things. But certain texts also take into account the
unfortunate possibility that a wife will, for one reason or another, not be satis-
factory and will need to be, as the following passage puts it, "superseded" (i.e.,
replaced by another wife):

> A husband should wait for one year for a wife who hates him; but after a
> year, he should take away her inheritance and not live with her. If she trans-
> gresses against a husband who is infatuated, a drunk, or ill, he may deprive
> her of her jewelry and personal property and desert her for three months. But
> if she hates him because he is insane, fallen, impotent, without semen, or suf-
> fering from a disease caused by his evil, she should not be deserted or de-
> prived of her inheritance. A wife who drinks wine, behaves dishonestly, or is
> rebellious, ill, violent, or wasteful of money may be superseded at any time.
> A barren wife may be superseded in the eighth year; one whose children have
> died, in the tenth; one who bears (only) daughters, in the eleventh; but one
> who says unpleasant things (may be superseded) immediately. But if a woman
> who is kind and well-behaved becomes ill, she should be superseded (only)
> when she has been asked for her consent, and she should never be dishon-

ored. And if a woman who has been superseded should leave the house in
fury, she should be locked up immediately or deserted in the presence of the
family.

(Manu 9.77–83)

The ancient Indian equivalent of divorce (being "superseded"; however, this
need not entail the ex-wife leaving the house, but merely losing her pride of
place to another wife who succeeds her) is justified here on a number of different grounds. A wife may be replaced if she is cruel to her husband (even, it appears, if he deserves it), is herself undisciplined and ruled by vice, or if she cannot
bear sons for the husband.

These reasons for "superseding" a wife point to traditional Hinduism's set of
virtues for the ideal wife, and to what this wife owes her husband.

What Do Wives Owe Husbands?

A girl, a young woman, or even an old woman should not do anything inde-
pendently, even in (her own) house. In childhood a woman should be under
her father's control, in youth under her husband's, and when her husband is
dead, under her sons'. She should not have independence. A woman should
not try to separate herself from her father, her husband, or her sons, for her
separation from them would make both (her own and her husband's) families
contemptible. She should always be cheerful, and clever at household affairs;
she should keep her utensils well polished and not have too free a hand in
spending. When her father, or her brother with her father's permission, gives
her to someone, she should obey that man while he is alive and not violate
her vow to him when he is dead.

(Manu 5.147–151)

Here we have a classic formulation of male dominance: a woman should be
under a man's control and guidance at every stage of life. A girl's father should
supervise her in her childhood, her husband in her youth and middle age, and
if she survives her husband she should be placed under the care of her sons—
such is the way to prevent families from becoming "contemptible." "Men must
make their women dependent day and night," it is said in another passage, "and
keep under their own control those who are attached to sensory objects. Her father guards her in childhood, her husband guards her in youth, and her sons
guard her in old age. A woman is not fit for independence" (Manu 9.2–3).

The wife's duties to her husband are thus to obey him absolutely and to care
for his home diligently; she is not only to be submissive but also wholly occupied with the pursuits of domesticity. She should, as the text cited above puts it,
carefully but "cleverly" run the household affairs (under the supervision of a
male) and keep herself focussed on her chores. Marriage is for life, without the
possibility of divorce for the woman, and remarriage should the husband die first
is strictly forbidden. A wife should be loyal to her husband in this life and "not
violate her vow to him when he is dead." She should "care for his body and perform the obligatory daily chores" (Manu 9.86) and if she remains faithful to him

throughout his life she will join him in heaven. If, however, she is unfaithful an unsavory fate awaits her after death:

> The woman who is not unfaithful to her husband but restrains her mind-and-heart, speech, and body reaches her husband's worlds (after death), and good people call her a virtuous woman. But a woman who is unfaithful to her husband is an object of reproach in this world; (and after death) she is reborn in the womb of a jackal and is tormented by the diseases (born) of (her) evil.
>
> (Manu 9.29–30)

A woman should not leave her husband for another no matter how bad he is, for "A woman who abandons her own inferior husband and lives with a superior man becomes an object of reproach in this world; she is said the be 'previously had by another man'" (Manu 5.163).

This is the traditional (and, need it be said, patriarchal) standard for the Hindu wife: wholly dependent on her male family members and absolutely faithful to her husband (even if he is "inferior"), she is assigned her place in the home where she is charged with the production and proper upbringing of children and the supervision of domestic affairs. She is to remain restrained in mind and body and loyal and obedient to her husband, and, as we have seen, if she does so the husband is to regard her with respect and even veneration. The wife's role is pivotal both to the well-being of the family as a whole and to the fate of her husband, and she in turn should be accorded the good, if paternalistic, treatment she deserves.

In the following, taken from a famous play by the Sanskrit author Kalidas, the dramatist has a young woman's father pass along some advice regarding how she should comport herself with her future royal husband. Later on in the passage, the daughter calls this "an excellent compendium, truly, of every wife's duties":

> Listen, then, my daughter. When thou reachest thy husband's palace, and art admitted into his family,
>> Honour thy betters; ever be respectful
>> To those above thee; and, should others share
>> Thy husband's love, ne'er yield thyself a prey
>> To jealousy; but ever be a friend,
>> A loving friend, to those who rival thee
>> In his affections. Should thy wedded lord
>> Treat thee with harshness, thou must never be
>> Harsh in return, but patient and submissive.
>> Be to thy menials courteous, and to all
>> Placed under thee, considerate and kind:
>> Be never self-indulgent, but avoid
>> Excess in pleasure; and, when fortune smiles,
>> Be not puffed up. Thus to thy husband's house
>> Wilt thou a blessing prove, and not a curse.[6]

---

[6]From Kalidasa's *Sakuntala,* cited and translated in Ainslie T. Embree, editor, *The Hindu Tradition: Readings in Oriental Thought* (New York: Vintage Books, 1966), 167–168.

This outline of the ideally humble, dependent, submissive, and utterly faithful wife is sketched on a background that assumes a rather different notion of the inherent nature of women. Left to her own devices, some texts assert, women will follow their intrinsic and evil proclivities. By nature, women are said to be lustful and unfaithful, unable to control their sexual desires; they must, therefore, be carefully guarded by their husbands. Such natural promiscuity is even said to be wholly indiscriminate:

> Good looks do not matter to them, nor do they care about youth; "A man!" they say, and enjoy sex with him, whether he is good-looking or ugly. By running after men like whores, by their fickle minds, and by their natural lack of affection these women are unfaithful to their husbands even when they are zealously guarded here. Knowing that their very own nature is like this, as it was born at the creation by the Lord of Creatures, a man should make the utmost effort to guard them. The bed and the seat, jewellery, lust, anger, crookedness, a malicious nature, and bad conduct are what Manu assigned to women. There is no ritual with Vedic verses for women; this is a firmly established point of law. For women, who have no virile strength and no Vedic verses, are falsehood; this is well established.
>
> (Manu 9.14–18)

Such an extremely unflattering view of women as "by nature" promiscuous, untrustworthy and evil—the very essence of "falsehood"—is replicated in a variety of ancient texts. "There exist no friendships with women," says the most ancient of Hindu texts, the Rig Veda, for "they have the hearts of hyenas" (Rig Veda 10.95.15). Elsewhere in that work we read that women are ineducable (Rig Veda 8.33.17), an early sanction for the prohibition on teaching women the sacred texts of Hinduism. The somewhat later Mahabharata declares that "women are speakers of untruth," that "fickleness is the norm in women," that "women are the root of faults and have weak understanding," and that "nothing exists that is more wicked than women" (Mahabharata 1.68.72; 5.36.56; 13.38.1; 13.38.12).

These kinds of assumptions about women justify the insistence that a husband must guard and protect his wife from her own inborn proclivities. The following text claims this is in fact the husband's "supreme duty," and suggests the best way to guard one's wife is to keep her busy at home and indoctrinate her so thoroughly that she "guards herself":

> Women should especially be guarded against addictions, even trifling ones, for unguarded (women) would bring sorrow upon both families (her own and her husband's). Regarding this as the supreme duty of all the classes, husbands, even weak ones, try to guard their wives. For by zealously guarding his wife he guards his own descendants, practices, family, and himself, as well as his own duty. . . . No man is able to guard women entirely by force, but they can be entirely guarded by using these means: he should keep her busy amassing and spending money, engaging in purification, attending to her duty, cooking food, and looking after the furniture. Women are not guarded when they are confined in a house by men who can be trusted to do their jobs well; but women who guard themselves are well guarded. Drinking, associating with

bad people, being separated from their husbands, wandering about, sleeping, and living in other peoples' houses are the six things that corrupt women.

(Manu 9.5–7, 10–13)

The "well-guarded" wife will, in addition to tending to the children and household, help her husband carry out the family's ritual and religious ceremonies and duties. Women themselves, however, were specifically precluded from many of these regularly performed religious duties; they were not allowed to study or recite the Veda and therefore did not undergo the initiation ceremony that signified a "second birth" for young men. Those rites of passage that women did undergo were performed without the ritual accompaniment of recited verses from the Veda, for women were traditionally prohibited from even hearing the sound of this sacred text. Nevertheless, in the following passage certain of the important life-cycle rites, stages of life, and subsequent ritual duties of the male householder are equated to their supposed correlates in the woman's life:

> For women, this cycle (of rites of passage) should be performed without Vedic verses, leaving nothing else out, at the proper time and in the proper order, to perfect the body. The ritual of marriage is traditionally known as the Vedic initiation ritual for women; serving her husband is (the equivalent of) living with a guru, and household chores are the sacrificial rites of the fire.
>
> (Manu 2.66–67)

The domestic life of the dependent wife is here valorized by connecting it to the religious life of men: marriage is equated to the initiation ceremony, service to the husband is correlated to the study of the Veda under the tutelage of a guru, and household chores are regarded as the female equivalent of the sacrificial rituals performed by the husband.

The religious duties or dharma of a woman, under this view, revolve entirely around affairs of the home, the family, and the marriage; what she owes her God and what she owes her husband are thus conflated. In a summary of the "duty of the woman" (*stri-dharma*), one author wholly confounds the woman's religious duties with her "service to her husband":

> The husband is thus to be propitiated (by the wife as follows): by observing the rules of purification; by attending to the fire ritual; by paying homage to guests; by taking care of the household duties; by keeping close watch over the household (accounts), both income and expenditure; by attending to her husband's bodily comfort; by serving food to her husband's dependents, etc.; . . . by love-making and so on at night; by avoiding both those things which are forbidden to her and those which her husband does not like; by putting into practice both those things which are prescribed and those which her husband likes; . . . by obedient service to her husband; and by doing what he says. Propitiating him in this way is said to constitute true "service" to one's husband.[7]

---

[7]The *Stridharmapaddhati* of Tryambakayajvan, 86.4–88.1; translated in I. Julia Lessa, *The Perfect Wife: The Orthodox Hindu Woman according to the Stridharmapaddhati of Tryambakayajvan* (Delhi: Oxford University Press, 1989), 314–315.

In this traditional system, should a wife outlive her husband she is not allowed to remarry. A good widow should honor her husband's memory by her ascetic lifestyle, chastity, and loyalty.

> A virtuous wife should never do anything displeasing to the husband who took her hand in marriage, when he is alive or dead, if she longs for her husband's world (i.e., heaven after her death). When her husband is dead she may fast as much as she likes, (living) on auspicious flowers, roots, and fruits, but she should not even mention the name of another man. She should be long-suffering until death, self-restrained, and chaste, striving (to fulfil) the unsurpassed duty of women who have one husband.
>
> (Manu 5.156–158)

Indeed, a widow should not remarry even if she has remained childless; such is the binding force of the marriage vow for her, and such is her obligation to her husband:

> Many thousands of priests who were chaste from their youth have gone to heaven without begetting offspring to continue the family. A virtuous wife who remains chaste when her husband has died goes to heaven just like those chaste men, even if she has no sons. But a woman who violates her (vow to her dead) husband because she is greedy for progeny is the object of reproach here on earth and loses the world beyond. No (legal) progeny are begotten here by another man or in another man's wife; nor is a second husband ever prescribed for virtuous women.
>
> (Manu 5.159–162)

The tradition has presented another alternative for the wife whose husband dies before her. Among the most controversial elements of the traditional Hindu view of a wife's obligations to her husband is the ritual called *sati*. This practice, performed especially among the upper classes (and most especially among women from the warrior castes) from the eighth century C.E. onward, entailed the self-sacrifice of the widow who joined her deceased husband on his funeral pyre. Sati, which literally means the "virtuous woman," was regarded by some Hindu women as both the ultimate act of devotion to the husband and as a preferable alternative to life as a widow. The following depicts a queen's conversation with her son who was trying to prevent her from cremating herself in the fire:

> If at this hour my regard is not towards you, it is that my lord's great condescension comes between us. Furthermore, dear son, I am not ever craving for the sight of another lord. I am the lady of a great house, born of stainless ancestry, one whose virtue is her dower. . . . Daughter, spouse, mother of heroes, how otherwise could such a woman as I, whose price was valour, act? . . . I would die while still unwidowed. I cannot endure, like the widowed Rati, to make unavailing lamentations for a burnt husband. Going before, like the dust of your father's feet, to announce his coming to the heavens, I shall be high esteemed of the hero-loving spouses of the gods. . . . Not to die, but to live at such a time would be unfeeling. Compared with the flame of wifely sorrow, whose fuel is imperishable love, fire itself is chilly

cold. . . . Not in the body, dear son, but in the glory of loyal widows would I abide on earth. Therefore dishonour me no more, I beseech you, beloved son, with opposition to my heart's desire. . . . Having embraced her son and kissed his head, the queen went forth on foot from the women's quarter, and, though the heavens, filled with the citizen's lamentations, seemed to block her path, proceeded to the Sarasvati's banks. Then, having worshiped the fire with the blooming red lotus posies of a woman's timorous glances, she plunged into it, as the moon's form enters the adorable sun.[8]

The practice of sati became a major issue among both the British colonial rulers and Hindu reformers in the beginning of the early nineteenth century, and was officially outlawed in 1829. Nevertheless, satis have occurred occasionally since; one recent case in north India received much media attention and was the cause of great controversy.

WHAT DO PARENTS OWE THEIR CHILDREN?

If one of the great obligations husbands and wives have to one another is to bring children into the world, it is certainly in part because of self-interest that they should be glad to do so. Children, and especially male children, provide all kinds of benefits to their parents—emotional, economic, and spiritual. A son who is "wise and virtuous" and has "good qualities" is capable of bringing good fortune to the entire family; his very existence has a salutary effect on the whole group:

A single son who is wise and virtuous, a lion among men, illuminates the family as the moon illuminates the sky. A single good tree, sweet-smelling and in flower, perfumes the entire wood; so does a single good son perfume the family, a single son who has good qualities.[9]

For a woman, the birth of children (and especially the birth of sons) ensures that she will be supported throughout her life, even if she survives her husband. And for a man, the birth of a son, as we have seen, guarantees not only the continuity of his family and lineage but also confers upon the father immortality, for "in your offspring you are born again; that, o mortal, is your immortality" (Satapatha Brahmana 1.5.5.6). Elsewhere we read that "A man wins worlds through a son, and he gains eternity through a grandson, but he reaches the summit of the chestnut horse (i.e., the sun and the heavenly world associated with it) through the grandson of his son." Thus, this text continues, sons and grandsons (born of either the son or the daughter) are a man's salvation:

---

[8] *The Harsacarita of Bana*, translated by E. B. Cowell and F. W. Thomas (London: Royal Asiatic Society, 1897), 153–155; reprinted in Embree, editor, *The Hindu Tradition*, 98–100.

[9] From the Garuda Purana, translated in Wendy Doniger O'Flaherty, editor and translator, *Textual Sources for the Study of Hinduism* (Manchester: Manchester University Press, 1988), 81.

Because the male child saves his father from the hell called *put,* therefore he was called a "son" (*putra*) by the Self-existent one himself. There is no distinction between a son's son and a daughter's son in worldly matters, for a daughter's son also saves him in the world beyond, just like a son's son.

(Manu 9.137–39)

So it is that the production of sons, among other merit-making activities, is said to prepare a man's body for "ultimate reality" and salvation:

By the study of the Veda, by vows, by offerings into the fire, by acquiring the triple learning, by offering sacrifices, by sons, and by the great sacrifices and the (other) sacrifices, this body is made fit for ultimate reality.

(Manu 2.28)

In return for these benefits a son confers upon his parents, parents are obliged to care for and nurture him the first few years of his life—a parental obligation in Hindu India as in everywhere else where parents bring children into the world. The upbringing of a child involves, among other things, proper discipline, and although in general violence toward others is not condoned in Hindu texts, a man is allowed to beat "his son or pupil . . . for the sake of instruction" (Manu 4.164). Or again,

If a wife, a son, a slave, a menial servant, or a full brother has committed an offence, they may be beaten with a rope or with a split bamboo cane, but only on the back of the body, and never on the head; anyone who beats them anywhere else will incur the guilt of a thief.

(Manu 8.299–300)

Proper upbringing also involves teaching the child how to read, for "The mother is an enemy and the father an opponent to their children if they do not teach them to read; without reading, a man cannot shine in the midst of the assembly, but is like a heron in the midst of swans."[10]

But beyond this, parents also have religious obligations to the son, and these tend to revolve around a series of rituals called the *samskaras*. The term *samskara* literally means "to make whole or perfect," and connotes a set of rites of passage that not only move the child from one status to another but transform or even construct a new and better being for the individual. For according to the Hindu texts, a child is born inherently defective and in a natural state of irresponsibility: "They do not put any restrictions on the acts of (a child) before the initiation, for he is on the level with a servant (no matter what his caste) before his (second) birth through the Veda" (Baudhayana Dharma Sutra 1.2.3.6).

Usually there are twelve of these life-cycle rites enumerated in the text. The first three concern the creation and proper formation of the embryo and begin at conception and continue at intervals through the woman's pregnancy. There are also a birth rite and a naming ritual, and a ritual in which the infant is taken out of the house for the first time, which is performed shortly after birth. During early

---

[10]Ibid., 84.

childhood, rituals also mark the child's first eating of solid food and a ceremonial haircut. Later, one of the most important samskaras is performed for the young boy, the initiation ritual that inaugurates a period of study of the sacred Veda under the tutelage of the teacher. Two different rites of passage mark the end of the time of studentship, and the marriage ceremony (the final samskara) signals the beginning of the second stage of life as a householder.

These samskaras are meant not only as rites of passage but as the ritual means for constructing a strong, viable, and purified self for the boy who undergoes them. Several also act as healing rituals to counteract the impurities of biological birth, as the following indicates:

> The transformative rituals for the bodies of the twice-born, beginning with the rite of the infusion (of semen, at conception), which purify them here on earth and after death, should be performed with excellent Vedic rites. The offerings into the fire (accompanying the *samskaras* performed) for the embryo, the birth rites, the ceremonial haircut (performed on a toddler) and the tying of the belt of rushes (one of the main features of the initiation rite), wipe away from the twice-born the guilt of the seed and the guilt of the womb.
>
> (Manu 2.26–27)

The samskara of initiation is of particular importance because, among other reasons, it is the occasion when the parents turn over their son to the care of a religious teacher, or guru, who becomes the boy's new father, for it is he that will give the boy a "second birth"—a male-produced ritual birth "out of the Veda," which is regarded as superior to the biological birth he received from his mother:

> (The teacher) who fills (the pupil's) two ears with the Veda not in vain is to be known as his mother and his father, and he must not act with malice against him. . . . Between the one who gives him birth and the one who gives him the Veda, the one who gives the Veda is the more important father; for a priest's birth through the Veda is everlasting, both here on earth and after death. That his mother and father produced him through mutual desire, and he was born in the womb, he should regard as his mere coming into existence. But the birth that a teacher who has crossed to the far shore of the Veda produces for him through the verse to the sun-god, in accordance with the rules, is real, free from old age and free from death. . . . The priest who brings about the Vedic birth of an older person and who teaches him his own duties becomes his father, according to law, even if he is himself a child.
>
> (Manu 2.144, 146–148, 150)

According to the traditional law books, parents turn over their sons to the teacher at the age of eight or ten, and the boy lives with his new "father" until graduation in his late teens. At that point he is eligible for marriage, and his parents also have a duty to make sure he finds a suitable wife and has success starting up a new household. As for the daughter, however, the making of a good marriage is the parents' supreme obligation to her. (We will recall here that marriage is said to be the female equivalent of the male's initiation.) The father's responsibility is to give his daughter away in marriage, and if he does not do so "at the proper time" (i.e., when she has reached puberty) he is as blameworthy as other men who do not fulfill their obligations to their women: "A father who does not give her away at the proper time should be blamed, and a husband who does not have sex with her at the proper time should be blamed; and the son who does not guard his mother when her husband is dead should be blamed." (Manu 9.40)

Elsewhere we read that it is critical for a father to give his daughter to a man with good qualities, and should such a potential husband appear she could be married even before puberty. But if the father does not fulfil this obligation to her, the young woman is allowed to make her own match:

A man should give his daughter, in accordance with the rules, to a distinguished, handsome suitor who is like her, even if she has not reached (the right age). But it would be better for a daughter, even after she has reached puberty, to stay in the house until she dies than for him to give her to a man who has no good qualities. When a girl has reached puberty she should wait for three years, but after that period she should find a husband like her. If she herself approaches a husband when she has not been given one, she commits no error, nor does the man whom she approaches.

(Manu 9.88–91)

But it is better if the marriage is arranged properly, that is, with the father playing his role to the fullest. The offspring of unions formed in this way purifies the family for many generations:

The father may give away his daughter after decking her with ornaments and having first offered a libation of water: This is the *Brahma* form of marriage. A son born to her after such a marriage purifies twelve descendants and twelve ancestors on both her husband's and her own sides. The father may give her away after decking her with ornaments to an officiating priest while a Vedic sacrifice is being performed: that is the *Daiva* form of marriage. A son born of such a marriage purifies ten descendants and ten ancestors on both sides.[11]

WHAT DO CHILDREN OWE
THEIR PARENTS?

Children, first and foremost, owe their parents respect and obedience, for as the text below states, what they have gone through by having and raising children "cannot be redeemed even in a hundred years." Note also how the teacher is put on a par with the mother and father in the following passage, for as we have seen he becomes the boy's new father after initiation. These three figures—father, mother, and teacher—are to be revered and obeyed; they are the very form of

---

[11]From the Asvalayana Grhya Sutra, cited and translated in Ainslie T. Embree, editor, *Sources of Indian Tradition, Volume One: From the Beginning to 1800,* 2nd ed. (New York: Columbia University Press, 1988), 226.

cosmic powers and deities. By "loving devotion" to them, a son wins all three of the "worlds" of ancient Indian cosmology; no other duty is higher than revering and obeying them, and no other duties should be assumed by a man without first asking the permission of his parents and teacher. Such treatment of these three, it is said, is a man's "ultimate duty," and all other duties are subordinate to this one:

> A teacher, a father, mother, and older brother should not be treated with contempt, especially by a priest, not even by someone who has been provoked. The teacher is the physical form of ultimate reality, the father the physical form of the Lord of Creatures, the mother the physical form of the earth. . . . The trouble that a mother and father endure in giving birth to human beings cannot be redeemed even in a hundred years. He should constantly do what pleases the two of them, and always what pleases his teacher. . . . Obedience to these three is said to be the supreme generation of inner heat; he should not assume any other duties without their permission. For they alone are the three worlds, they alone are the three stages of life, they alone are the three Vedas, and they alone are said to be the three sacrificial fires. . . . The householder who does not neglect these three conquers the three worlds; illuminated by his own body, like a god, he rejoices in heaven. By loving devotion to his mother he wins this world; by loving devotion to his father, the middle world; and by obedience to his guru the world of ultimate reality. A man who has deeply respected these has deeply respected all duties; but all rites are fruitless for the man who has not deeply respected these. As long as these three should live, he should not undertake any other (duties); he should constantly give them his obedience, taking pleasure in what pleases them and is good for them. . . . For by treating these three in this way a man accomplishes what ought to be done; this is the ultimate duty right before one's eyes, and any other is said to be a subordinate duty.
>
> (Manu 2.225–230; 232–235; 237)

A child should in particular treat his mother with respect and solicitation: "The teacher is more important than ten instructors, and the father more than a hundred teachers, but the mother more than a thousand fathers" (Manu 2.144). While all other elder female relations should be treated as a mother, the mother herself is the most important: "He should treat his father's sister, his mother's sister, and his own older sister like a mother; but his mother is more important than they are" (Manu 2.133).

The only or eldest son has a special responsibility at the time of the death of a parent, for it is he who with the help of specialized priests oversees the rituals designed to transform the deceased parent into an ancestor. Such rites begin with cremation at which time the skull is cracked in order to free the soul. Rituals involving the offering of rice balls, food, and gifts continue at intervals for a year; it is through these gifts and sacrifices that the spirit of the deceased parent becomes an ancestor. Death rites are thus conceived of as both a kind of last sacrifice to the gods (in which the body is the offering) and as a rebirth or transformation of the dead into a new life. But they also serve to ease the pain and discomfort of the recently departed and nourish the disembodied spirit; this, then, is the final duty of the son to his parents:

> When his corpse is being burnt, he experiences terrible burning; and when it is beaten he suffers too, and when it is cut he suffers intense agony. When a man('s body) stays wet for a very long time he suffers miserably, even if by the ripening of his own karma he has gone to another body. But whatever water, together with sesamum seeds, his relatives offer (in the rites for dead relatives), and whatever balls of rice they offer, he eats that as he is being led along. When his relatives rub his (dead) body with oil and massage his limbs, that nourishes and strengthens a man, and so does whatever his relatives eat. A dead man who does not (take the form of a ghost) and bother his relatives on earth too much when they are asleep and dreaming is nourished and strengthened by them as they give him gifts (in the form of offerings to his departed soul).[12]

WHEN THE FAMILY BREAKS DOWN: WHAT HAPPENS THEN?

The critical role played by the family within Hinduism is gauged also by depictions of what happens when the family breaks down. Such, indeed, is the premise of one of the most important texts of the Hindu tradition, the Bhagavad Gita. This classic is drawn from one of the great epics of Indian literature, the Mahabharata, which concerns a war between two sides of the same family for the rule of India. The Gita opens with the warrior Arjuna and his divine charioteer, Krishna, looking across the battlefield at the erstwhile "enemy"—their own kinsmen!

> Arjuna saw them standing there:
> fathers, grandfathers, teachers,
> uncles, brothers, sons,
> grandsons, and friends.
> He surveyed his elders
> and companions in both armies,
> all his kinsmen
> assembled together.
> Dejected, filled with strange pity,
> he said this:
> > "Krishna, I see my kinsmen
> > gathered here, wanting war.
> > My limbs sink,
> > my mouth is parched,
> > my body trembles,

---

[12]Markandeya Purana 10.47–87, translated in O'Flaherty, *Textual Sources,* 117.

the hair bristles on my flesh.
The magic bow slips
from my hand, my skin burns,
I cannot stand still,
my mind reels.
I see omens of chaos
Krishna; I see no good
in killing my kinsmen
in battle."[13]

Arjuna's dilemma turns on the apparent conflict he faces between doing his duty as a warrior, on the one hand, and the demands of loyalty to his family on the other. The warrior's paralysis is well justified, for as Arjuna observes a bit later in the text, a man who kills members of his own family sets into motion a process that spirals downward quickly. Like falling dominoes, the destruction of the family inevitably leads to the corruption of women, social disorder, and the annihilation of the ancestors. It is no wonder, then, that a punishment in hell awaits anyone who dares to undermine the sanctity of the family:

When the family is ruined,
the timeless laws of family duty
perish; and when duty is lost,
chaos overwhelms the family.
In overwhelming chaos, Krishna,
women of the family are corrupted;
and when women are corrupted,
disorder is born in society.
Thus discord drags the violators
and the family itself to hell;
for ancestors fall when rites
of offering rice and water lapse.
The sins of men who violate
the family create disorder in society
that undermines the constant laws
of caste and family duty.
Krishna, we have heard
that a place in hell
is reserved for men
who undermine family duties.

(Bhagavad Gita 1.40–44)

While Krishna does eventually reveal to Arjuna a way out of his dilemma, the fact remains that Hindu texts often do manifest a kind of horror at the

---

[13]Bhagavad Gita 1.26–31. This and all subsequent translations from this text are taken from *The Bhagavad Gita: Krishna's Counsel in Time of War,* translated by Barbara Stoler Miller (New York: Bantam Books, 1986).

prospect of the breakdown of families, a state of affairs regarded as chaotic and dangerous and even a harbinger of the end of the world. Whereas in the Gita the danger to the family is posed by fratricidal violence, more often the threat stems from intermarriage among castes or, as one text put it, the "confusion of classes, by means of which irreligion, that cuts away the roots, works for the destruction of everything" (Manu 8.353). The offspring born out of such unholy unions are, it is said, inherently inferior and kingdoms where such practices prevail are doomed:

> An unknown man, of no (visible) class but born of a defiled womb and no Aryan, may seem to have the form of an Aryan, but he can be discovered by his own innate activities. Un-Aryan behavior, harshness, cruelty, and habitual failure to perform the rituals are the manifestations in this world indicating that a man is born of a defiled womb. A man born of a bad womb shares his father's character, or his mother's, or both; but he can never suppress his own nature. A man born of the confusion of wombs, even if he comes from a leading family, will inherit that very character, to a great or lesser degree. But the kingdom in which these degraded bastards are born, defiling the classes, quickly perishes, together with the people who live there.
>
> (Manu 10.57–61)

In some descriptions of the last and "dark" age (the so-called Kali Yuga) before God ends the world, this intermixture of castes and the resulting degeneracy of the family feature as signs of the utter corruption of things characteristic of that bleak period. In the following two passages describing the outrages and signs of chaos that will occur in the dark age, the intermingling and intermarriage between members of high and low castes is listed together with other markers of the breakdown of all order:

> In the Kali (Yuga) the twice-born are ignorant of the Vedas. Nor do they perform sacrifice; others of inferior intellect do the sacrifice, and they recite the Vedas incorrectly. In this Kali age there will occur the association of servants with Brahmins through . . . marriages and the practice of sleeping and sitting together. Kings who are mostly of the servant class will have Brahmins killed; abortion and hero-murder will prevail in this age.[14]

> In the Dark Age, there is always carelessness, passion, hunger, and fear; the terrible fear of drought pits one country against another. Scripture has no authority, and men take to the violation of sacred duty. . . . When sacred duty is destroyed, and people attack one another, they will become stunted and live only twenty-five years; their senses will become confused with arguing, and they will abandon their sons and wives. . . . They will fall away from the system of classes and stages of life and fall prey to the terrible mingling of classes.[15]

---

[14]From the Kurma Purana, translated in Cornelia Dimmitt and J. A. B. van Buitenen, *Classical Hindu Mythology: A Reader in the Sanskrit Puranas* (Philadelphia: Temple University Press, 1978), 40.

[15]From the Linga Purana, translated in O'Flaherty, *Textual Sources,* 71.

UNCONVENTIONAL FAMILIES,
SUPERNATURAL FAMILIES

The ideal structure of the Hindu family and the ideal roles played by husbands and wives within it have been projected into the heavenly realm by Hindu mythologists and theologians. Gods and goddesses of certain sorts are meant, in part at least, to serve as divine models for human imitation. For example, the epitome of the ideal Hindu wife—utterly devoted and loyal to her husband—is found in the figure of the goddess Sita, wife of god-king Rama. At one point in the narrative of the great epic called the Ramayana, Rama is banished from his kingdom and exiled to the wilderness. Rama proposes to leave Sita in the city because he thinks she could not bear the discomforts of the forest. Sita insists on following her husband, threatening even to kill herself if forced to separate from him; the husband's fate is that of the wife, and devotion to him is the "single goal for a woman":

> A wife wins the fate of her husband, and not her own, O bull of a man. Knowing this, I shall live in the forest from now on. Here and hereafter there is only a single goal for a woman: her lord, and not her father, her child, herself, her mother nor her friends. . . . O take me with you, noble husband! Do as I ask, for my heart is devoted only to you. If you leave without me, I shall die![16]

Later in the story, Sita is abducted by the wicked Ravana and taken to the island of Lanka where she is held hostage. Throughout her abduction, however, Sita remains unswervingly loyal to Rama—and to her religious duty:

> I cannot be seduced by wealth or glory. I belong only to Raghava (i.e., Rama) as light belongs to the sun. After having leaned on the honored arm of that world-protector, how could I ever turn to anyone else? I am the proper wife of the lord of the earth; I belong to him as the law belongs to a self-aware Brahmin (priest) who has faithfully kept his vows.[17]

But Sita's loyalty to her husband (a kind of metaphor for the human being's devotion to God, even under trying circumstances) is tested to even a greater extent when, after being rescued by Rama, the latter doubts her fidelity during the period of captivity. Distraught by Rama's false accusations, Sita no longer wishes to live and enters the fire of her own funereal pyre. But because of her innocence, the god of fire refuses to harm her; Rama, finally convinced of her purity, takes her back.

On a symbolic level, Sita's faithfulness to Rama even when he apparently abandons her serves as a cautionary tale about the need for devotion to God under the most trying of circumstances, that is, even when God appears to have

---

[16]Ramayana 2.24.3,4,18; cited and translated in Cornelia Dimmitt, "Sita: Fertility Goddess and *Sakti*," in John Stratton Hawley and Donna Marie Wulff, editors, *The Divine Consort: Radha and the Goddesses of India* (Boston: Beacon Press, 1982), 210.

[17]Ramayana 5.19.14–16; in ibid., 221.

abandoned the devotee. But the figure of Sita also carries with her more particular and gendered messages concerning the social ideal of the Hindu woman and wife. "The husband is as a God to the woman," says Sita; "he is her family, and her *guru*. Therefore, even at the price of her life, she must seek to please her lord."[18]

In the traditions within Hinduism that emphasize devotionalism and faith, the paradigmatic relationships and accompanying emotions within the family are called up and redirected toward God as a means of heightening and strengthening the love of the devotee for his or her deity. One can imagine the deity as a father and oneself as a son or daughter, with all the attendant emotions of such a relationship, or as a brother and friend. Among the most powerful and emotion-laden of family relations is that between parents and their children, and in certain traditions of Hinduism this special bond is exploited for religious purposes. In the following myth, Krishna is represented as a mischievous toddler who, while playing outside, eats dirt. His mother, Yasodha, scolds him and demands that he open his mouth, at this point still unaware that her little child was also the Lord of the Universe:

> She then saw in his mouth the whole eternal universe, and heaven, and the regions of the sky, and the orb of the earth with its mountains, islands, and oceans; she saw the wind, and lightning, and the moon and stars, and the zodiac. . . . She saw within the body of her son, in his gaping mouth, the whole universe in all its variety. . . . Then she became afraid and confused.[19]

Having had such a disturbing vision of the true nature of her son, Yasoda is subsequently deceived again as Krishna casts a magical spell over her "in the form of maternal affection." For God knows that it is impossible for humans to love God in his cosmic form as they do when he takes the form of a son:

> When the cow-herd's wife had come to understand the true essence in this way, the lord spread his magic illusion in the form of maternal affection. Instantly the cow-herd's wife lost her memory of what had occurred and took her son on her lap. She was as she had been before, her heart flooded with even greater love. She considered Hari (i.e., Krishna) . . . to be her son.[20]

Indeed, in some cases the love of God, regarded in such familiar and familial fashion, can come to replace human objects of love. In the devotional tradition one encounters women poet-saints whose overwhelming and all-encompassing love for God supersedes their duties as wives and mothers. For such devotees, God becomes one's true husband. One such case is that of Mahadevi, the twelfth-century poet-saint and devotee of the god Siva, who in the

---

[18]Ramayana 7.48; cited and translated in David Kinsley, *Hindu Goddesses: Visions of the Divine Feminine in the Hindu Religious Tradition* (Berkeley and Los Angeles: University of California Press, 1986), 74.

[19]From the Bhagavata Purana, translated in Wendy Doniger O'Flaherty, *Hindu Myths: A Sourcebook Translated from the Sanskrit* (Harmondsworth, Middlesex, England: Penguin Books, 1975), 220.

[20]Ibid., 221.

following claims Siva as her true husband in contrast to human and mortal husbands who "die, decay":

> I love the Beautiful One
> > with no bond nor fear
> > no clan no land
> > no landmarks
> > for his beauty.
> So my lord, white as jasmine, is my husband.
> Take these husbands who die,
> > decay, and feed them
> > to your kitchen fires!
> Better than meeting
> > and mating all the time
> > is the pleasure of mating once
> > after being far apart.
> When he's away
> > I cannot wait
> > to get a glimpse of him.[21]

Here is another example, taken from the poems of the same female poet-saint, of devotion overriding and superseding ordinary family life but also appropriating the language of familial relationships:

> I have Maya ("illusion") for mother-in-law;
> > the world for father-in-law
> > three brothers-in-law, like tigers;
> > and the husband's thoughts
> > are full of laughing women;
> > no god, this man.
> And I cannot cross the sister-in-law.
> But I will
> give this wench the slip
> and go cuckold my husband with Hara, my Lord.
> > My mind is my maid:
> > by her kindness, I join
> > my Lord,
> > > my utterly beautiful Lord
> > > from the mountain-peaks,
> > > my lord white as jasmine,
> > and I will make Him
> > my good husband.[22]

In such cases of extreme devotion, one leaves behind one's earthly family, with its roles, duties, obligations, and mutual dependencies, and imaginatively

---

[21]From the *Mahadeviyakka*, translated by A. K. Ramanujan in his *Speaking of Siva* (Baltimore: Penguin Books, 1973), 134, 141.

[22]Ibid., 141.

joins a kind of spiritual family. Mahadevi has replaced her human husband with a divine one, and has redirected her love and obedience from a mundane personage to a heavenly one. But she is still the good wife, just as Yasodha, God's mother, replicates the virtues of the human mother and Rama enacts the role of the ideal husband. Whether projected into the divine realm or lived out in the realities of the human world, families and the relations between family members are regarded as the bedrock of religious life in Hinduism.

COMMENTARIES

Judaism on Hinduism

by JACOB NEUSNER

Judaism concurs on the centrality of the householder in the family structure. Not only so, but the priority of caste relationships in the Hindu social order finds its counterpart on the Judaic side. In the classical, formative age, holy Israel was divided by the criterion of status in the Temple of Jerusalem. The divisions involved priests, the highest caste, who actually offered the sacrifices; Levites, who assisted and also sang Psalms in the Temple; Israelites; and lesser castes:

> Ten castes came up from Babylonia: (1) priests, (2) Levites, (3) Israelites, (4) impaired priests, (5) converts, and (6) freed slaves, (7) mamzers, (8) Netins, (9) "silenced ones" [shetuqi], and (10) foundlings. Priests, Levites, and Israelites are permitted to marry among one another. Levites, Israelites, impaired priests, converts, and freed slaves are permitted to marry among one another. Converts, freed slaves, mamzers, Netins, "silenced ones," and foundlings are permitted to marry among one another.
>
> And what are "silenced ones"? Any who knows the identity of his mother but does not know the identity of his father. And foundlings? Any who was discovered in the market and knows neither his father nor his mother.
>
> All those who are forbidden from entering into the congregation are permitted to marry one another.
>
> Mishnah-tractate Qiddushin 4:1–3

These considerations compare with those important in the Hindu caste system. But while in the formative law that is the case, in modern times the differences between priests, Levites, and Israelites have lost importance.

The conception that a woman should be under a man's control and guidance at every stage of life fits well with Scripture's account of matters. But the rabbis of Late Antiquity, founders of Judaism as we know it, in the normative law liberated Israelite women by according to them what Scripture had denied: the standing and powers of sentient beings, possessed of a role that was, if not entirely equal, then corresponding, to that of men in critical transactions of their existence. They made them active, responsible beings; they legislated to take account of their intentionality. Women were not only chattel, talking cows, animate sofas, as some have maintained. The rabbis endowed women with the power of intentionality and the concomitant responsibility for their own actions and condition that Scripture denied them.

Above all, Judaism will differ from Hinduism in the latter's treatment of the widow. The Hindu widow is not to remarry. The Judaic widow is expected to. Her life goes on. She has accomplished her obligation to the deceased. There is a proviso, beginning in Scripture (Deuteronomy 25:2–5), that if the husband dies childless, his wife is expected to marry his surviving brother and produce children with him. If she has had children with the husband, she has no further obligations that survive the grave. Death serves to deconsecrate the conjugal bed. But that is for a different reason. Now the governing intentionality has accomplished its purpose. That is to say, if the husband dies having produced offspring, the wife automatically proceeds to the next marriage if she wishes. The act of consecration by that man of that woman has completely fulfilled its goal. The wife was consecrated for the purpose of procreation of that man in his household, that purpose has been realized by the man who has sanctified her for his purpose, and therefore the intentionality that has brought about the relationship has been fully realized in action: the transaction is sealed. But what happens if the husband's goal in consecrating the woman—engendering children in his name ("name" standing for household, extended family)—has not come to fruition? Then, Scripture maintains, the original act of consecration has not accomplished its goal. Then desacralization of the original intention, confirmed by action, of sanctification, does not take place. The woman therefore remains consecrated for the as-yet-unrealized purpose embodied in the intention of betrothal and the action of consummation of the union. Then, so far as is possible, the widow bears the obligation to accomplish the intention that effected the original act of consecration. Here circumstance intervenes. Since at issue is the household, the Torah holds, if brothers survive the deceased, then a surviving brother of the childless deceased may take his place as husband of the widow. The law of levirate marriage—marriage of the widow to a brother of the childless deceased husband for purpose of procreation—aims at bringing about the realization of that original act of consecration. This is a far cry from the ongoing link of the widow to the deceased in Hinduism.

Christianity on Hinduism
by BRUCE CHILTON

The exposition of Hinduism's evaluation of family life both intersects and departs from Christianity's. The embeddedness of salvation within timely and proper marriage and the production of offspring is comparable in a way to Paul's incentive for married Christians to seek to save their unbelieving spouses (1 Corinthians 7:16, discussed in Christianity's response to Judaism's address of this topic). But at key points, just where it concerns what is "timely and proper," and how salvation can be promoted, Hinduism and Christianity go quite separate ways.

The cosmic order of which family relations are the germ is for Christianity a form that is passing away in any case, so that the same imperative for marriage and procreation cannot be discovered in Christianity. Christian teachers have indeed urged them quite vehemently in certain periods, but the reason for their vehemence is precisely that the timeliness and propriety of marriage are—in the Scriptures—vanishing categories. Similarly, the householder is not the ordinary integer of sacrifice, as in Hinduism, because the self-giving of the believer in baptism and one's practice of that dynamic in the Eucharistic repetition of Christ's sacrifice eventually subsumed any literally sacrificial act within Jerusalem's Temple.

In somewhat the same way, the concept of a debt owed to one's ancestors, dischargable by the production of a son, is interestingly comparable to the construction of sin as debt, an Aramaism that is preserved in the Gospels, and whose meaning is exploited there (Matthew 6:12; 18:23–35). But then, the payment of such a "debt" is more to the other debtors than to the only ultimate creditor, who is God. Indeed, the parable in Matthew 18 sets up a scenario in which a king is willing to forgive debts on an outlandish scale, provided only that his subjects forgive one another in their ordinary relations. Christianity's terms of reference are not the logical constructions of this world, wonderful though they may be, but the challenge of the world that is coming.

In the world of normal human relations, you pay back what you owe to the person you owe. In the world of divine sovereignty, you pay what you owe God to other people who owe God. In this world, you can be saved from a condition of slavery only by exploiting the prevailing conditions—including marriage and procreation—in just the right way; in the world that is coming and already influencing us, you can pass salvation on by the means of marriage, procreation, and other social relations.

But Christianity knows of no necessity to marry or have children, and in this Hinduism's insistence seems to involve a greater degree of responsibility, more widely distributed among practitioners. That sense of incompleteness that awaits the unmarried is indeed referred to among Christian families, anxious to see their names carried on, but their anxiety is exacerbated by the knowledge that religious imperative is really not on their side.

A man's being driven by his desire so as to take additional wives, a permission rather than a duty in Hinduism (and far from universal) has more in common with Paul's idiom of exhortation. When Paul admits that it is "better to marry than to burn" (1 Corinthians 7:9), that is scarcely a ringing endorsement of marriage (and, of course, no departure from the practice of monogamy), but it does represent a comparable adjustment of ideals to the exigencies of the human condition.

But as in Hinduism, so in Christianity, adjustments to the so-called facts of human nature can be quite peculiar. Although the language of the allegedly uncontrollable character of women may be more pronounced in some of the Hindu sources cited than in the *Shepherd of Hermas,* the common features of their negative evaluation are quite stunning. In this regard, we have a vivid reminder that men were overwhelmingly dominant in the production of the texts, and were talking at least as much about their own fears and hopes as about the impetus of their religious systems. At the same time, the systemic privilege of sons over daughters in the exposition of Hinduism is evident, and simply contrasts with Paul's announcement, never perfectly put into practice by him or by any known Christian, that in Christ "there is neither Jew nor Greek, there is neither slave nor free, there is not male and female" (Galatians 3:28). Jesus' principle of how resurrected life is a disruption, impinging even now in our temporal state, stands in relief to the ordered cosmos Hinduism here represents.

Perhaps it sums up such strong differences over what is real and what is not, when we see that knowing one's teacher as "father" is commended in Hinduism, while Jesus in Matthew 23:9 says that only God is to be known as "father." Of course, much Christian tradition has ignored that injunction, and controversy persists over how much Jesus in the Gospels speaks of ideals not yet achieved, but the binding authority of the present world is, as a matter of consensus, not acknowledged by Christianity.

Islam on Hinduism
by TAMARA SONN

A primary difference between Islam and Hinduism can be seen in the attitudes of each regarding females. Islamic scripture, the Qur'an, levels direct criticism at those who favor sons over daughters, chastising those who consider it a matter of shame to have daughters (Qur'an 16:59–60). Furthermore, among the Qur'an's relatively scant prohibitions is the absolute prohibition of female infanticide, apparently a widespread practice in pre-Islamic Arabia (Qur'an 81:9–10). Reflecting its overall teaching of human equality, the Qur'an insists that male and female children are to be equally cherished. Islam also rejects the complete control of women, insisting that women be given inheritance shares and that their dowries be given to them, rather than to their families. Women's wealth is theirs to do with as they will; although wives are required to be obedient to their husbands in Islam, husbands have no right to interfere with their wives' private wealth. Nor is there a stigma attached to remarriage for a woman in Islam, as there is in Hinduism. Women are expected to choose their spouses with family approval (just as men are), and traditionally some Muslim cultures allow arranged marriages in which women are given no say in the choice of a spouse. Nevertheless, the Qur'anic ideal is one that respects the individuality of all people, so that marriage is seen as a mutually nurturing institution for both partners. Similarly, oral tradition in Islam does contain some unflattering descriptions of women as the source of social chaos, lacking in intelligence, excessively emotional, and needing the firm discipline of a man. However, such descriptions are balanced by those that more closely reflect the Qur'an's presentation of women. In the Qur'an there is no hint of women as the source of evil. On the contrary, the Qur'an presents numerous women as role models for all Muslims—males as well as females. Hindu thought concerning mothers, at least as expressed in the Code of Manu, comes closer to the Islamic attitude. Indeed, the claim that "the mother [is more important] than a thousand fathers" is very similar to the popular Islamic tradition that "paradise lies at the foot of the mother."

Buddhism on Hinduism
by BRAD CLOUGH

Because Buddhism developed in the same culture (ancient India) as Hinduism, when both traditions present injunctions regarding family life that concur with conventional expectations, the two religions tend to agree. For example, while both religions accord the wife and mother great respect and authority as the caregiver within the household, they also place women in roles of submissive subservience to the men of the family. Buddhist literature, which has been most often composed by monks, also does often depict women as beings with more natural sexuality than men, although it still sees men, who are more exposed to the outside world, as more susceptible to temptations that could bring about the ruin of the family. Negative views about women, though hardly absent in Buddhism, tend not to be as extreme in Buddhism as they are in Hinduism. Buddhists also found the practice of *satī* abhorrent. Still, Buddhism and Hinduism agree on many other family matters, such as the parental arrangement of suitable marriages for their progeny (although class/caste has been less important within Buddhist communities), the role of husband and father as the source of material support for the family, the general unacceptability of divorce, and children's obligations to honor and obey parents.

On the other hand, Buddhism often saw its value system as strongly opposing many of the Brahmanical voices and compositions that are at Hinduism's foundations, and this led to some significant points of departure between the two religions. One difference is that despite the Buddha's legendary initial reluctance to ordain women as nuns, his doing so meant that early Buddhism gave women greater opportunities to participate in the religious life than early Hinduism did, until the rise of the vastly popular *bhakti* ("devotionalism") movement in Hinduism.

Furthermore, as Professor Smith states, Hinduism's traditions of world renunciation have almost always been set in the context of worldly values. In Hinduism, it has often been the case that, despite theoretical models like the four stages and four aims of life (which place renunciation and liberation at the top), worldly values, especially those relating to *dharma* or "duty" to one's family and caste, have superseded other-worldly ones, to the extent that people's salvation has depended on fulfilling certain familial obligations. Again, as Professor Smith shows, family life in Hinduism is the basis for stability, order, and propriety (in other words, for dharma). In Buddhism, renunciation can sometimes also be seen as set within the context of family duties, but not nearly to the extent that it is in Hinduism. On one hand, one must receive permission from one's parents before one becomes a monk or nun, which implies that one's family and home must be in order before one leaves it. And in Buddhism, as in Hinduism, the renunciates depend on householders' generosity, in the form of food and clothing (robes), in order to survive and be able to pursue the goal of spiritual emancipation. On the other hand, there are examples like the episode in the *Buddhacarita,* the most well-known version of the Buddha's life, in which the Buddha's father insists that he must fulfill his familial duty (*dharma*) as a ruler, instead of becoming a renunciate. The Buddha-to-be, Siddhārtha Gautama, then asks his father if, by following his familial duty, he could discover a way to overcome suffering and death. When his father replies that this is impossible, Siddhārtha then tells his father that he must not stop him from escaping a burning house. So, here we see not only that Buddhism sometimes uses the home as a metaphor for *saṁsāra,* the vicious cycle of repeated birth, suffering, and death from which Buddhists (and Hindus) seek liberation, but that the dharma of Hinduism, in the sense of social and familial duty, is subordinated to what Buddhism sees as a higher *dharma,* the teaching of the Buddha that will set people free from suffering.

SUMMARY

The properly constituted family is the centerpiece of Hinduism, the pillar of the social and moral order, and even the pivot on which the cosmic order as a whole turns. Marriage provides the opportunity for both husband and wife to fulfill essential religious duties, including the procreation and religious upbringing of offspring. Hindu texts offer detailed advice about who to marry, the religious importance of children, and the obligations each member of the family has to the others. The family is so crucial to the order of things that deviations from the ideal are depicted in Hindu texts as having dire consequences. On the other hand, idealized relationships within the family are often used as metaphors for the ultimate relationship: that between human beings and God.

GLOSSARY

Adharma   "unrighteousness" or "evil"; the opposite of dharma

Adhikara   "predilection," "competency," "inherent ability," or "predisposition." People born into different castes are said in Hinduism to be endowed by birth with differing adhikaras.

Arjuna   a warrior who is one of the two main protagonists in the *Bhagavad Gita*

Atman   the true, changeless, and eternal "Self," distinct from the ego

Artha   "private gain" or "material or political advantage," "self-interest," "getting ahead in the world." One of the "ends of life" in Hinduism, especially appropriate to the householder.

Aryan   literally "noble one," the name the early Indo-European invaders of India gave to themselves

Bhagavad Gita   a key text of Hinduism that synthesizes some of the strands of the tradition around the concept of bhakti

Bhakti   literally "participation" in the divine being, or more commonly translated as "devotion" to God

Brahman the macrocosmic principle of unity in the Hindu philosophy of monism; often equated to the atman or "Self"

Brahmins "priests" or religious specialists, the highest of the classes or castes in the traditional Hindu social order

Dharma a multivalent word that in Hinduism usually refers to "religious duty," determined by one's caste and stage of life

Gopis "cowherder women" who figure prominently in the mythology of Krishna

Gunas the three elemental "constituents," "qualities," or "strands" that alone or in combination underlie all things and beings in the universe: "goodness," "activity," and "inertia"

Guru religious teacher

Jiva "self" or "subtle body" of a person, sometimes used as a synonym for atman

Jivan mukta "one who is liberated while living," a living human being who has attained liberation or freedom (*moksha*)

Kali Yuga the "dark age" in which we presently live, according to Hindu theory, characterized by degeneracy and corruption. At the end of this "dark" era, the world will be destroyed and re-created anew.

Kama "sensual pleasure," one of the "ends of life" in Hinduism

Karma "work," originally in the sense of "ritual activity" and later generalized to include all acts. In all senses of the word, karma refers also to actions that create the causes for experiences (pleasant and unpleasant) in the future.

Krishna one of the chief deities of the Hindu pantheon and the central figure in the *Bhagavad Gita*

Kshatriyas the warrior class of the traditional Hindu social order

Mahabharata one of the two great epics of the Hindu tradition (cf. *Ramayana*)

Mirabai sixteenth-century Hindu poet-saint, renowned for her devotion to Krishna

Moksha "freedom" or "liberation" from samsara, the ultimate goal of Hinduism

Prajapati "Lord of Creatures," a name for the creator god in Vedism

Purusa "Cosmic Man," one name for the creator god of the Vedic pantheon

Putana "The Stinking One," name of a demoness in Hindu mythology

Radha One of the gopis or cowherder women in the mythology of Krishna, often portrayed as Krishna's consort

Raksasa a demon

Rama one of the principal deities of Hinduism, depicted in mythology as a righteous warrior-king

Ramayana one of the two great epics of the Hindu tradition (cf. *Mahabharata*)

Rig Veda the oldest text of the ancient Indian Vedas, which are regarded as sacred scripture by most Hindus

Samsara the wheel of continual birth, life, death, and rebirth. Samsara in Hinduism and Buddhism is also characterized in general by suffering.

Samskaras   the term for the rites of passage in Hinduism

Sati   literally "a virtuous woman," also the name for a controversial historical practice in Hinduism (now illegal) in which a widow joins her deceased husband on his funereal pyre in an act of self-sacrifice

Shudras   "servants," the lowest class or caste in the traditional Hindu social order

Sita   the wife of the god Rama, depicted in Hindu texts as the ideal Hindu wife

Stri-dharma   the religious duties of a woman

Svadha   a ritual utterance in some Hindu ceremonies

Svadharma   one's "own duty"; dharma particularized to one's class or caste and stage of life

Tantricism   an esoteric tradition within Hinduism characterized by use of radical and unconventional methods to obtain liberation quickly

Upanayana   the most important of the Hindu rites of passage, during which a young boy is initiated into the study of the Veda and receives the sacred thread symbolizing his "second birth"

Upanishads   ancient texts in Hinduism that deal with philosophy and metaphysics

Vaishyas   The commoners (merchants, agriculturalists, traders, etc.) of the traditional Hindu social order

Veda   collective term for a group of ancient Indian texts regarded by most Hindus as sacred scripture

Vedism   the earliest form of the Hindu tradition in India. The religion centered on the performance and ideology surrounding the fire sacrifice.

Yajnavalkya   a religious teacher who figures prominently in some of the Upanishads

Yoga   "discipline" of the mind and body, entailing detachment from the world of the senses

DISCUSSION QUESTIONS

1. Describe several reasons why the family is so important in Hinduism. What is the religious value of procreating a son in traditional Hinduism?

2. What are the obligations a husband has towards his wife in Hinduism?

3. What is the religious importance of the wife in traditional Hinduism, and what kind of woman is regarded as the ideal wife? What are her obligations to her husband?

4. Why do parents have the religious duty to see that their children undergo the "samskaras" or rites of passage? What do these rituals accomplish?

5. How are parents to be treated by their children according to Hinduism?

6. What kinds of consequences are depicted in Hindu texts when the family "breaks down"?

7. Describe the ways in which relationships within the human family are used metaphorically to depict the relationship between human beings and God.

 **INFOTRAC**

If you would like additional information related to the material discussed here, you can visit our Web site: http://www.wadsworth.com

5

Buddhism

BY BRAD CLOUGH

Hardest of all is to practice the Way of the Buddha at home, second in the market, and third in the pagoda.[1]

INTRODUCTION

Of the five major world religions whose views on family life are examined in this volume, Buddhism is often perceived as the tradition least concerned with worldly affairs. This perception is by no means an unfounded one. One of the basic principles that practically all Buddhists hold to be true is that *upādāna,* "attachment" or "clinging" to the things of this world—even to loved ones such as members of one's own family—can consequently cause a profound sense of *dukkha* or "suffering," especially when one expects the objects of one's affection to provide everlasting happiness, but then inevitably becomes separated from them or loses them to death. This principle is expressed in a text—in its third verse in particular—from the Pāli canon that is part of an evening liturgy communally chanted (and ideally, taken to heart as well) by Buddhist monastics and laypeople at many temples in South and Southeast Asia. This text is known as the *Mettā Sutta* or "Discourse on Loving-kindness," and it goes as follows:

> He who is skilled in good and who wishes to attain the
> state of tranquility should act in this way:
>
> He should be capable, upright, perfectly upright,
> noble in speech, gentle, and humble.
>
> Contented, easily supported, with few duties,
> of simple livelihood, restrained in senses,
> discreet, not impudent, he should not be
> attached to families.
>
> He should not commit the slightest wrong,
> such that other wise men might censure him.

---

[1]This is a line from a Vietnamese Buddhist folk song. Quoted in Thich Nhat Hanh, *The Miracle of Mindfulness: A Manual of Meditation* (Boston: Beacon Press, 1975), 12.

May all beings be happy and secure!
May their minds be contented!

Whatever living beings there may be,
feeble or strong, tall, stout, medium,
short, small or large, without exception,
seen or unseen, dwelling near or far,
those who are born and those yet to be born,
may all beings be happy!

One should not deceive another,
nor despise any person whatsoever in any place.
One should not wish any harm to another,
out of anger or ill-will.

Just as a mother would protect her only child,
at the risk of her own life,
one should cultivate a boundless heart towards all beings.

Let one's thoughts of boundless love pervade the whole world,
above, below, and across, without any obstruction,
without any hatred, without any enmity.

Whether one stands, walks, sits, or lies down,
as long as one is awake, one should develop mindfulness.
This, they say, is the divine abode in this world.

Not falling into wrong opinions,
virtuous and endowed with insight,
one lets go of attachment to the desires of the senses,
and truly never enters a womb again.

So, while Buddhism does indeed emphasize to a great extent the importance of cultivating deep loving-kindness (*mettā*) and compassion (*karunā*) for others, it also insists that these qualities ultimately are to be extended even-mindedly, dispassionately, and universally to all beings. Exclusive love for particular beings over others is generally seen as a form of attachment that must ultimately be overcome. Indeed, the highest goal for Buddhists is to achieve liberation from *duḥkha* by attaining *bodhi* ("enlightenment") or *nirvāṇa*, the "extinguishing" of what Buddhists call the "three poisons" of desire, hatred, and ignorance. The tremendous value that Buddhist traditions place on the path of moral and mental cultivation aimed at liberation in relation to the ultimate worth stemming from family life is succinctly captured in this verse from one of the few texts that occupies an important place in all Buddhist canons, the *Dhammapada* ("Sayings of Truth"):

What neither a father, mother, nor other relative can do,
so much better does a rightly-directed mind do.[2]

---

[2]*Dhammapada*, v. 43.

Along similar lines, there is the instance told of a laywoman, a wife and a mother who, upon hearing the Buddha's words, proclaims:

> Dear unto us is our children, and dear is our husband;
> Even more dear to me than those is the Dharma,
> Which sets forth the path of liberation.
> Neither child nor husband, though they be dear to us,
> Can free us from this mass of suffering,
> Such as the hearing of the auspicious Dharma can.[3]

While Buddhist traditions theoretically have allowed for the possibility that laypeople with work and family lives can achieve *nirvāṇa* or *bodhi,* in practice one finds that in general, Buddhist traditions historically have held to the conviction that it is through eventual renunciation of societal and familial life, usually for the monastic life, that conditions most conducive to liberation from suffering are created.

Similarly, when one looks to the stories about the life of the Buddha himself in his final and previous existences,[4] stories that serve as inspirational and exemplary models for Buddhists of how to best live the religious life, one finds that the *bodhisattva* or "Buddha-to-be" is portrayed performing acts which show that family life was far from his central concern. In recalling his penultimate life, when he was reborn as a wealthy prince named Vessantara, the Buddha tells how he not only gave away his entire kingdom, but also his wife and two children, when he was asked to do so by a Brahmin priest. In accounting for the *bodhisattva*'s actions in this *Jātaka* or "Birth Story," another Buddhist text, *The Questions of King Milinda,* explains that "It is not that he disliked his wife and children, but that he loved omniscience more." According to tradition, it was by perfecting virtues such as the selfless generosity displayed in the *Vessantara Jātaka* that the *bodhisattva* merited a final rebirth in which he could become a Buddha or "Enlightened One," and thus help others to transcend their suffering in this world.

In Buddhist tellings of this final lifetime, in which the *bodhisattva,* again reborn as a prince, this time by the name of Siddhārtha Gautama, finally becomes a Buddha, the *bodhisattva* shows great disenchantment with family life at a crucial point in his spiritual development. Witnessing for the first time the sorrows of the world and recognizing the futility of human efforts to ignore those sorrows by indulging in fleeting pleasures, the *bodhisattva* comes to long to live the life of the religious renunciate who devotes his entire life to the pursuit of spiritual liberation from suffering. By naming his newborn son Rāhula, which, according to popular Buddhist etymology, means "fetter" or "bond," the *bodhisattva* shows that he had come to see family life as a hindrance to the religious life. And indeed, it is only a short time later that he abandons his wife and child, to take up the life of the forest-dwelling mendicant, which eventuates in his attaining *bodhi* and becoming a Buddha. Even when he later returns home, sup-

---

[3]Saṁyutta Nikāya I, 210.

[4]As a religion that originally developed in India, Buddhism, like Hinduism, accepts the idea that beings are subject to repeated rebirth, according to the nature of their *karmas* or "acts."

posedly to make amends with his family, the Buddha ends up convincing several members of his family to "go forth from the householder's life," as it is traditionally put, and join his *saṅgha* or religious community.

So, what does such a world-renouncing religious figure and the religious tradition that developed in his mold—a tradition that oftentimes, as the passages and stories referred to above indicate, equates the householder's existence with *saṁsāra,* the repeated round of birth, suffering, and death—have to say constructively and positively about issues concerning family life? A great deal, as it turns out. From Buddhism's earliest times, its traditions have recognized that while living the life of a monk or nun provides the best conditions for achieving liberation from suffering, most people in their present circumstances do not have the inclination or, perhaps more important, the opportunity, to pursue such a life, as they must remain householders and providers for their family's welfare. Therefore, the question of how a person can best meet familial responsibilities, while also remaining true to the fundamental moral principles of Buddhism, has been a very important one for Buddhist traditions throughout history, one that lay Buddhists have continuously sought answers for, by turning to their scriptures and teachers for guidance.

With respect to scriptures, we need be reminded that, as the appendix points out, there has long been a significant amount of disagreement among Buddhists who follow different forms of Buddhism, about which canon or dispensation of scriptures holds the Buddha's highest teachings. However, Buddhists, whether followers of Theravāda, Mahāyāna, or Vajrayāna, have generally agreed that the earliest-appearing dispensation, the only fully surviving version of which is the Pāli canon preserved by Theravāda Buddhists, contains the Buddha's most basic, foundational teachings. For this reason, we will refer most often to texts contained in the Pāli canon and to the Buddhist tradition that holds those texts to be of the highest authority—the Theravāda tradition—in our ensuing discussion of family life in Buddhism.

CONVENTIONAL EXPECTATION VERSUS THIS RELIGIOUS TRADITION: WHAT DO HUSBANDS AND WIVES OWE ONE ANOTHER?

Many of the Buddha's discourses in the Pali canon address issues pertaining to ethical responsibility in family life. One discourse, however, stands above the rest as being the one that Buddhists refer to most frequently for advice on proper familial morals, and that is the *Sigālovāda Sutta* or "Discourse on Advice to Sigāla." The high place that this text occupies is seen in the fact that Theravada Buddhists have come to call it the *Gihi Vinaya* or "Householder's Vinaya." The *Vinaya* is the collection of teachings found in all Buddhist canons that contain the codes of ethical discipline for monks and nuns, and its contents are vital to the lives of communities throughout the Buddhist world. So, the *Sigālovāda Sutta* is regarded as having the status equivalent to that of the *Vinaya,* only its advice pertains directly to those who have not renounced family life, who are the majority of Buddhists. In the *Sigālovāda Sutta,* the Buddha, while on alms-begging rounds, sees a young man named Sigāla, who is referred to as a "householder's son," paying homage to the dieties of the six directions: north, east, west, south, zenith, and nadir. The Buddha approaches Sigāla and asks him why he is performing this kind of worship. When Sigāla tells the Buddha that he is doing so to honor a deathbed request made by his father, a wealthy and powerful man, the Buddha responds by informing him that in the "noble discipline" (*ariyassa vinaye*) of his teaching, the worship of the six directions is regarded in a different way. According to his "noble discipline," the most appropriate way to worship the six directions is as follows:

> Mother and father are the east,
> Teachers are the south,
> Wife and children are the west,
> Friends and relatives are the north.
>
> Servants and workers are the nadir,
> Ascetics and brahmins are the zenith.
> One fit to lead the household life,
> Should worship these six directions.
>
> The wise and virtuous person,
> Kind and of deep understanding,
> Humble and free from pride,
> Such a one may gain honor.
>
> Rising early and scorning laziness,
> Unperturbed by misfortune,
> Faultless in conduct and ready in mind,
> Such a one may gain honor.
>
> Making friends and hosting them,
> Welcoming and generous,
> A guide, teacher, and leader,
> Such a one may gain honor.
>
> Giving of gifts and nice in speech,
> Spending life well for the good of others,
> Even-handed towards all,
> And impartial as each circumstance demands.
>
> These four ways of living make the world go round,
> Like the axle-pin that keeps a chariot rolling.
> If these ways did not exist in the world,
> Neither mother nor father would receive respect from their children.
>
> Since these four ways of living,
> Are esteemed by the wise in every way,
> They are given prominence,
> And are rightly praised by all.[5]

---

[5]Dīgha Nikāya III, 192–193.

Besides the third through sixth verses, which establish a lofty set of moral expectations for laypersons to meet (each of those four verses is one of the "four ways of living" referred to in the final two verses), what is also most significant here is that the Buddha replaces the gods of the six directions with familial and social groups, and that he designates them as the truly worthy objects of worship. In the Brahmanic (early Hindu) tradition of the Buddha's day, which clearly is being challenged here, it was a common ritual act to worship the gods of the six directions, in exchange for their protection. What Buddhist tradition is saying here is that it is really humans, the ones that a person is closely related to in various ways, who will provide one with protection in this life. So, family and social groups are established as sacred in a profound sense here, in that they are deemed worthy of a degree of respect and veneration that was higher than even that which was due to the gods.[6] But what exactly did the Buddha mean when he said that these people were to be worshiped? The core of the *Sigālovāda Sutta* concerns itself with answering that question.

The Buddha's general answer to this question in this discourse is that one can best worship the people in one's life by performing particular duties toward them, duties that each personal relation is deserving of receiving. With respect to the duties that husbands and wives owe one another, the *Sigālovāda Sutta* says the following:

> There are five ways in which a husband should worship his wife as the western direction: by honoring her, by not disparaging her, by not being unfaithful to her, by giving authority to her, and by providing her with adornments. And there are five ways in which a wife, thus worshipped by her husband as the western direction, loves him: by properly organizing her work, by being kind to servants, by not being unfaithful, by protecting what he provides, and by doing her duties well and with diligence.[7]

As in most human societies over the course of history, the conventional expectations of the societies into which Buddhism has been introduced, based on patriarchal domination of male over female family members, have dictated that wives be subordinate to their husbands, and that the wives' main if not only domain of influence be in the home. In the injunctions from the *Sigālovāda Sutta* quoted above, we see Buddhist tradition providing religious sanction for those conventional expectations on some points, and challenging them with the authority of the Buddha's word on other points.

With respect to the sanctioning of conventional expectations, we see that the views that women should remain largely in the home, and that they should do most of the household work, are perpetuated here. We see that three out of the

---

[6]Despite modernist claims that Buddhism is an atheist or nontheistic religion, in Buddhist societies gods, as powerful beings capable of great benevolence or malevolence, especially with respect to worldly concerns such as health, food, and fortune, are the objects of much reverence and fear, and the recipients of much in the way of ritual offerings. However, they are still seen as subject to the law of *karma* and continued rebirth in realms of suffering, and are thus regarded as lesser than enlightened beings like Buddhas, who have transcended suffering completely.

[7]Dīgha Nikāya III, 190.

five injunctions—to properly organize work, to do duties well and with dili-
gence, and to protect what the husband has brought home as a product of his
work in the fields or elsewhere outside of the home—keep women in their place
in the household, where their role has often been basically that of a servant. One
of the other two injunctions to wives does refer to servants who would work
under the wife's authority and help her in many of her chores. In many traditional Asian societies in which Buddhism has become the major religious influence, servants have indeed been part of the household division of labor, although
it would be mistaken to assume that all families have had servants, although it is
probably safe to say that most households have had at least a few servants from
lower classes, living at subsistence level and taking on some of the more difficult
and unpleasant forms of labor. Here we must also take into consideration the
context of the Buddha's time and of this discourse in particular. Many of the
Buddha's first lay disciples, like Sigāla himself, were from wealthy families of a
merchant class that was on the rise during the Buddha's lifetime, in the region
of northeastern India where he preached. Buddhist traditions have strongly
maintained that the Buddha always skillfully adjusted his teachings so that they
would speak most directly to the person or audience he was addressing. In this
case, the Buddha was giving advice to a well-to-do young man who could have
afforded servants and adornments to give to his wife. So, while the injunctions
of the *Sigālovāda Sutta* have indeed been generalized and broadly applied in Asian
Buddhist societies, some of them have not applied to all Buddhists in these societies, especially the illiterate poor.

One very revealing and typical discourse, which simultaneously promotes
high ethical standards for wives while holding to conventional expectations of
wives' main duties as housekeepers, is the *Bhariyā Sutta* or "Discourse on Wives."
In this episode from the Buddha's teaching career, the Buddha approaches the
home of Anāthapiṇḍika, a wealthy merchant and his most consistent and generous patron, on his alms-begging rounds. As he nears the home, he hears much
noise, and upon seeing Anāthapiṇḍika, he asks him why the people in his house
are causing such an uproar. Anāthapiṇḍika replies that it is due to his new
daughter-in-law Sujātā who, coming from a wealthy family, is spoiled and arro-
gant, and thus refuses to pay any attention to her mother-in-law, father-in-law,
and husband. The Buddha then calls for her, and proceeds to offer her the following words:

> She who is without compassion, defiled in mind,
> Neglectful of her husband and unfriendly,
> Impassioned by other men, a prostitute, bent on murder,
> Let her be called a killer and a wife!

> She who would steal her husband's wealth,
> Although he makes little profit,
> By carpentry, trade, or the plough,
> Let her be called a robber and a wife!

> She who is lazy, gluttonous, and bent on doing nothing,
> Who gossips and speaks with sharp temper,

Who belittles her husband's energy and effort,
Let her be called a shrew and a wife!

She who cares for her husband and his accumulated gains,
Who watches over and protects him with loving-kindness,
Like a mother cares for her only son,
Let her be called a mother and a wife!

She who holds her husband in the same regard,
As a younger sister regards the older,
She who is tender in heart and serves her husband's every wish,
Let her be called a sister and a wife!

She who is as happy to see her lord,
As a friend is to meet her separated companion,
A kind character, gentle, and an adoring helper,
Let her be called friend and wife!

If fearless of the whip and stick, even-minded,
Enduring in all things, calm and pure in heart,
She obeys her husband's word without anger,
Let her be called a servant and a wife!

Now, she who is called a killer, robber, and shrew,
Who is harsh, immoral, and lacking in respect,
When death arrives,
She will wander in the miseries of hell.

But mother, sister, friend, servant,
Restrained and long established in the moral precepts,
When death arrives,
She will wander in a blissful divine abode.[8]

This "Discourse on Wives" concludes with the Buddha asking Sujātā which kind of wife she would like to be, and Sujātā replying that the Buddha should think of her as a servant and a wife.

The "Discourse on Wives" provides us with a very telling example of the powerful role that religion can play in the sanctioning, if not the creation or construction, of gender roles. While the Buddha, a male figure of considerable religious authority (Sujātā addresses him as "venerable one," and positions herself in a seated posture of reverence below him, when called by him to receive his words), does not directly tell Sujātā which wifely role to adopt, he greatly influences her decision by warning her of the dire consequences that will result from her present conduct (*karma*), and by promising the joyful consequences of the roles of mother, sister, friend, and servant. He also powerfully directs her, as well as generations of Buddhist women following her who regard this discourse as authoritative scripture, into a subordinate role, by setting up a hierarchy in which it is the servant wife, not the motherly, sisterly, or friendly wife, who occupies the highest position. However, it is important to note that many contemporary

---

[8]Aṅguttara Nikāya IV, 91–93.

Buddhist women, especially those from higher class families who live in urban environments, who have educated themselves and have careers of their own, would reject the role of the servant wife and still consider themselves good Buddhists, in spite of this scripture's privileging of the servant wife.

At the same time, by grouping the servant wife—who is said to be enduring, calm, pure in heart[9]—with the motherly, sisterly, and friendly wives—who are said to be loving, caring, and gentle—and by opposing that group with the group of the killer, robber, and shrew wives—who are described as pitiless, corrupt, lazy, and unsupportive—the "Discourse on Wives" positively encourages the cultivation of noble social and moral qualities in Buddhist wives. These positive qualities have been accepted by Buddhist women over the course of time, whether they be small village–dwelling women in premodern, agrarian Buddhist societies who most likely had little choice but to take on these qualities, or modern, urban-dwelling Buddhist women, many of whom in recent decades have been able to gain more personal independence and control over their lives, and thus have provided themselves with greater opportunities for choice in the roles they adopt.

Besides the *Sigālovāda* and *Bhariyā Suttas,* there are other standards established in the Pali canon for the ideal wife. In keeping with some conventional expectations, but in also offering practical advice that would create harmonious relations among family members, the Buddha enjoins a newly married wife to pay every respect to her mother-in-law and father-in-law, and to serve them lovingly as if they were her own parents. Furthermore, he continues, she should honor and respect her husband's relatives and friends, thus creating a congenial and joyous atmosphere in her new home. The Buddha also advises her to study and ascertain her husband's nature, so as to learn how best to get along with him.[10] At another point, he advises a group of laywomen that they should always be polite and kind in the home. Echoing the *Sigālovāda* and *Bhariyā Suttas,* they are further advised to keep a watchful eye over whatever food or earnings a husband brings home, and they are told that it is they who are responsible for seeing that all household expenditures are administered properly.[11] As the Venerable Sri Dhammānanda, one of the leading voices in the Theravada Buddhist world, whose writings are popular from Sri Lanka to Malaysia, observes, this advice is followed by Buddhist women to this day.[12]

One of the main Buddhist perspectives on family life that emerges from the scriptural advice just described is that responsibility for the well-being of the family lies almost entirely with the wife. That this is the case is further evidenced

---

[9]The reference to the servant wife as "fearless of whip and stick," while possibly being a most ugly threat of violence aimed at forcing a woman to comply with a subservient role, seems to this reader at least to be presented as a praiseworthy attribute of a person who will remain fearless, enduring, calm, and so on, even when faced with a frightening situation.

[10]Aṅguttara Nikāya II, 103–104.

[11]Aṅguttara Nikāya IV, 20.

[12]Venerable Sri Dhammānanda, *A Happy Married Life: A Buddhist Perspective* (Kuala Lumpur: Buddhist Missionary Society, 1987), 18.

by the fact that one of the few Pali phrases that most lay Theravada Buddhists know is, *mātā mittaṁ sake ghare,* "the mother is (your) friend in the home."

On the one hand, while the mother or wife is seen as the friend in the home who ensures internal familial harmony and welfare, the husband, on the other hand, while also being important to the family as the working provider of food and money from outside the home, is frequently portrayed as the one more likely to bring the family to ruin. In contemporary Buddhist books on family life, one of the most frequently quoted discourses is the *Parābhava Sutta* ("Discourse on Ruin") of the Sutta Nipāta. In this discourse, the Buddha responds to a god, who asks how a man brings his family to ruin:

> Easily known is the one who progresses,
> Easily known is the one who causes ruin.
> He who loves the Buddha's teaching progresses,
> He who hates it causes ruin.

> He who loves the company of the vicious,
> Finds no delight in the virtuous.
> He who prefers the teaching of the vicious,
> He is the cause of ruin.

> Being fond of sleep,
> Talkative and lethargic,
> Lazy and irritable,
> He is the cause of ruin.

> He who is sufficiently wealthy,
> But does not support his mother and father,
> Who are old and infirm,
> He is the cause of ruin.

> He who deceives,
> By lying to a brahmin priest,
> Monk, or other virtuous teacher,
> He is the cause of ruin.

> He who has ample wealth,
> Assets and property,
> But enjoys them alone,
> He is the cause of ruin.

> He who is arrogant,
> Because of birth, wealth, or community,
> And looks down on his own family,
> He is the cause of ruin.

> He who consorts with other women,
> And squanders all that is earned,
> By drinking and gambling,
> He is the cause of ruin.

> He who is not content with his wife,
> But is seen with prostitutes,

Or other men's wives,
He is the cause of ruin.

He who is past his youth,
But takes a young wife,
Only to go sleepless out of jealousy,
He is the cause of ruin.

He who gives responsibility to a woman,
Who is given to drinking and squandering,
Or to give it to a man of like behavior,
He is the cause of ruin.

He who is the member of an influential family,
Of great ambition but little means,
Who seeks power or control over others,
He is the cause of ruin.[13]

Given this perspective, it is not so surprising to find Buddhist tradition most strongly issuing a challenge to conventional expectations and most forcefully insisting on a higher standard of ethical conduct, in its injunctions (given in the *Sigālovāda Sutta*) on how a husband should treat his wife. As is well known today, some of the most unfortunate and tragic consequences of the historical domination of males over females in human societies, including Buddhist ones, have been the all-too-common forms of physical, verbal, and psychological abuse that women have suffered at the hands of men. According to the ideals presented in the *Sigālovāda Sutta*, especially those that insist that the husband honor his wife and not disparage her, it is clear that such conduct is intolerable. The admonitions to treat one's wife with due respect and kind support are given even greater weight by the Buddhist belief in the law of karma, which teaches that harmful deeds will inevitably result in equally bad results for the doer of the deed in the future. Buddhist teachings on the nature of karma, however, go further than simply reminding individuals of the future personal consequences of their actions, by also emphasizing the immediate harm done to those who are the objects of one's physical, verbal, or mental violence. So, here we see how the most fundamental principle of Buddhist morality, *ahimsā* or nonviolence in body, speech, and mind, finds its way into the religion's teachings about marital relations.

Another significant challenge to conventional expectations is the *Sigālovāda Sutta*'s instruction to give the wife authority. While one has to allow for the possibility that some or even many have taken this to refer to authority only with respect to servants, it appears rather likely that this was not the intent of this injunction, since servants are explicitly mentioned elsewhere in the very same passage, but not so here. At the very least, then, the tradition's intent was that a wife should have authority along with her husband in familial decision making. If we again take historical context into account, in this case the larger context of India

---

[13]*Sutta Nipāta*, vv. 92–114 (the repeated questioning verses—93, 95, 97, 99, 101, 103, 105, 107, 109, 111, and 113—have been omitted).

in the middle of the first millenium B.C.E., this is truly a challenge to conventional expectations, in which the husband was quite literally his wife's lord, as is indicated by the common word for husband being *pati,* or "lord."[14] When Buddhism spread from India, to become a major religious force on practically the whole Asian continent, conventional expectations about a wife's subservient role did not typically change much from those of India, although it has been clear to those Buddhists who endeavor to follow the teachings of the *Sigālovāda Sutta* that those expectations have to be left behind in pursuit of a higher ideal.

Finally, the wording of the *Sigālovāda Sutta* makes it clear by its order and wording that the primary obligation in the marriage relationship rests with the husband, who is *first* commanded to treat his wife respectfully and kindly (the section on worshipping the western direction begins with, "There are five ways in which the husband *should* [my emphasis] worship his wife . . ."). Only after providing such treatment is he deserving of her love ("And there are five ways in which a wife, thus worshipped by her husband as the western direction, loves him"), without any obligatory injunctions directed toward her (the text never explicitly says that she should worship him). While the wife clearly has certain duties to perform, it is revealing and interesting to see that the main obligatory responsibility lies in the husband's half of the relationship, at least as far as the *Sigālovāda Sutta* is concerned.

The one injunction in the *Sigālovāda Sutta* that is common to both husband and wife is to not be unfaithful to one another. Walpola Rāhula reminds us that Pāli scriptures also see this particular relationship as sacred, as they frequently refer to the husband's relationship with his marriage partner as *sadāra-brahmacariya* or "divine living together with (one's) wife."[15] Otherwise, while this injunction does reinforce conventional expectations, which advocate marital loyalty, it also opposes the majority of human societies over the course of history, in which one finds that women often have paid a much more severe price for infidelity than men, and that men have been forgiven, if taken to task at all, for having one or more mistresses. As with the just-discussed case of equal authority in familial decisions, in this case Buddhist tradition, in the form of the *Sigālovāda Sutta,* once again differs from conventional expectations and calls for mutual responsibility, respect, and loving care on the part of both husbands and wives. In interviews with contemporary Theravāda monks in Sri Lanka about how they counsel married couples, the most frequent response was first to point to the *Sigālovāda Sutta*'s advice, which in their eyes calls for them to admonish men not to betray their wives. Echoing the verses quoted above from the *Parābhava Sutta,* most monks said that husbands were much more apt to commit adultery than wives. One monk, after condemning such unfaithful men as "scoundrels," related their proclivity to infidelity to a basic Buddhist teaching about the insidious nature of

---

[14]This Sanskrit word *pati* continues in many modern Indian languages to be the word for husband, and the corresponding relationship between husband and wife also continues to this day in many Indian marriages. It probably goes without saying, but still bears reminding, that the notion of the husband as the "king of the house" is hardly unique to Indian or even Asian settings; it still prevails today in much of the West as well.

[15]Walpola Rāhula, *What the Buddha Taught* (New York: Grove Press, 1959), 79.

sensual desire: "Succumbing to the temptation, they accrue the poison of lust, which becomes ingrained as a tendency that is hard to eradicate. Belief in the law of *karma* can be a powerful deterrent, but not an absolute one, because of the powerful hold of habitualized passionate dispositions."[16]

The Buddhist ideal of what a husband and wife owe each other, which captures well the Buddhist insistence on mutual reciprocity and equality in marital relations, is perhaps best captured in the *Samajīvano Sutta* or "Discourse on the Well-Matched." In this discourse, an elderly couple, who had been married since they were children,[17] and whose love had clearly flowered and endured, ask the Buddha how they can stay together not only for the remainder of their present lives, but in the next life as well. The Buddha responds to their question in the following manner:

> If both wife and husband desire to behold each other in this very life and in the life to come, and both are matched in faith, matched in virtuous conduct, matched in generosity, matched in wisdom, then they will behold each other in this very life and in the life to come.
> If both are faithful, self-controlled, kind in speech,
> Live as the Dharma teaches, and use loving words,
> One to the other, manifold are the blessings,
> That will come to a wife and husband,
> And to them the blessing of a pleasant life come.
> Dejected are their enemies, for both are good.
> So, in this world, living as the Dharma teaches,
> The couple is matched in goodness.
> And in the realm of the gods, rejoicing,
> They will win the bliss that they desire.[18]

WHAT DO PARENTS OWE THEIR CHILDREN?

The *Sigālovāda Sutta* speaks in the following manner about the duties of parents, with respect to their children:

> There are five ways in which parents, worshipped by their child as the eastern direction, show their compassion: they will restrain him from doing evil, they will support him in doing good, they will teach him a skill, they will find him a suitable wife and, in due time, they will hand over their inheritance to

[16]Interview with Professor Bhikkhu Dhammavihārī at the International Buddhist Research and Information Centre, in Colombo, Sri Lanka, on 1/8/00.

[17]The practice of arranged marriages, in which the couple is married at a very young age, was common in ancient India, and continues to be so in South Asia to this day.

[18]Aṅguttara Nikāya II, 61. For most Buddhist laypeople, from ancient times to today, rebirth in a divine realm has been a common religious goal. Still, *nirvāṇa* or *bodhi* remain the ultimate goals for practically all Buddhists.

him. In this way, the eastern direction is covered, making it peaceful and free from fear.[19]

There are two aspects of this passage that are immediately striking. The first is the emphasis on the male child, the son. The word *putta,* translated here in the first sentence as "child," is also a common Pāli word for "son." When one also considers that most parents in traditional Buddhist societies have given most if not all of their inheritance to their sons (or to their eldest son),[20] that the passage says that parents must find the child a wife (but a husband is not explicitly mentioned), and that the pronoun "him" is used throughout the passage, one could argue that these parental duties are mostly if not entirely directed toward male offspring. But this is not how Buddhists—especially Buddhists in modern times—have interpreted this passage and correspondingly carried out its injunctions. As we will show in more definitive fashion in a moment, the first two injunctions—to discourage evil and encourage good—are clearly intended for all Buddhists, regardless of gender. As for the third injunction, while it is certainly true that the duty of teaching a specific craft (usually the same craft that the father knew and did) for the essential purpose of making a living to support a family has been applied almost exclusively to sons, it is also true that daughters, who have been expected in traditional Buddhist cultures to remain in the home until they are married, must learn the skills that are necessary to maintain the household, such as cooking, mending clothes, and so forth. Furthermore, in village agrarian cultures, which have made up the greater part of Buddhist Asia, young women are also often called upon, *in addition to* their household work, to help the men in tending livestock and tilling fields, and thus they must be familiar with those skills as well. So, the third injunction certainly applies to children of both genders. As for the fourth injunction, although it does explicitly say that parents have the responsibility to "find him a suitable wife," parents in Buddhist cultures usually have been equally concerned with arranging a marriage for their daughters in which her spouse will treat her well, and so they also interpret this injunction in a way that applies to children of both sexes. Again, in Asian Buddhist societies, we are looking mostly at village agrarian cultures, and it must be acknowledged that sometimes families will be reluctant to marry off their daughter or daughters to other families, because the daughters do such much of the necessary work, both in the household and in the fields.

The second striking feature is its emphasis on ethical conduct (*śīla*), which is the foundation of all Buddhist paths of religious practice. Along with meditation (*samādhi*) and liberative insight into the true nature of reality (*prajñā*), ethical conduct is one of the "three trainings" that all Buddhists must endeavor to follow to the best of their abilities. The attitude that the *Sigālovāda Sutta* encourages parents to have toward their children is that of showing compassion. The

---

[19]Dīgha Nikāya III, 190.

[20]This has usually but not always been the case in traditional Buddhist cultures. In Tibetan cultural areas for example, a daughter is given a considerable portion of her parents' wealth, which is then considered hers and hers alone, when she gets married and leaves her family to live with her husband's family.

current Dalai Lama—who, like his predecessors in their position as the secular and spiritual leaders of the Tibetan people, is considered by Tibetan Buddhists to be an emanation or incarnation of the *bodhisattva* epitomizing compassion, Avalokiteśvara (Tibetan: Chenrezig)—has famously said on many occasions that although Buddhism believes in no absolutes, if he were pressed to identify one, it undoubtedly would be compassion. That compassionate caring for children is the primary responsibility of parents is further brought out in the two brief definitions of the father and mother found in the Pāli canon. The father is defined as *puttaṁ pāletiti pitā*, or "he who protects (his) child is called father," and the mother is defined as *mamāyati ti mātā*, or "she who cares is called mother."

The injunction that parents look after their children with care hardly makes Buddhism unusual in the history of the world's religions and civilizations. But one dimension that Buddhists have distinctively contributed to this universal human concern is their identification and application of what they call the four "divine or sublime states (of mind)" (*brahma-vihāra*). These four so-called divine or sublime states are loving-kindness (*maitrī*), compassion (*karuṇā*), sympathetic joy (*muditā*), and equanimity (*upekṣā*). On the path to spiritual liberation, it is important for the Buddhist to transform herself or himself by learning how to apply these "sublime" emotional and ethical attitudes to all beings. But Buddhist parents are also taught that the sublime states can be a very helpful way of dealing with their children. While it is taught that demonstrating any of these attitudes in any situation can be useful in raising children, there is also a more directed and specific teaching, which says that each of the four sublime states is particularly appropriate for dealing with children at four main stages of their lives. To quote the Venerable Sri Dhammānanda, whose writings have enjoyed great popularity and influence in the Theravāda Buddhist world of South and Southeast Asia:

> Perhaps the greatest challenge that a married couple has to face is the proper upbringing of a child. This is another aspect which distinguishes us from animals. While an animal does care for its offspring with great devotion, a human parent has a greater responsibility, which is the nurturing of the mind. The Buddha has said that the greatest challenge a man faces is to tame the mind. Ever since the child is born, from infancy through adolescence to maturity, a parent is primarily responsible for the development of a child's mind. Whether a person becomes a useful citizen or not depends mainly on the extent to which its mind has been developed. In Buddhism, a good parent can practice four great virtues to sustain his or her child and to overcome the great frustrations which are so closely related with parenthood.
>
> When a child is yet a toddler, unable to express its needs, it is quite prone to indulge in tantrums and crying. A parent who practices the first virtue of loving kindness can maintain peace within himself or herself to continue to love the child while it is being so difficult. A child who enjoys the effects of this loving kindness will himself learn to radiate it spontaneously.
>
> As the child becomes more mature as an adolescent, parents should practice *karuṇā* or compassion towards him. Adolescence is a very difficult time

for children. They are coming to terms with adulthood and therefore are rebellious, with a great deal of their anger and frustrations directed at their parents. With the practice of compassion, parents will understand that this rebelliousness is a natural part of growing up and that children do not mean to hurt their parents willfully. A child who has enjoyed loving kindness and compassion will himself become a better person. Having not had hate directed at him, he will only radiate love and compassion towards others.

Just before he becomes an adult, a child will probably meet with some success in examinations and other activities outside the home. This is the time for parents to practice sympathetic joy. Too many parents in modern society use their children to compete with their associates. They want their children to do well for selfish reasons; it is all because they want others to think well of them. By practicing sympathetic joy, a parent will rejoice in the success and happiness of his or her child with no ulterior motive. He is happy simply because his child is happy! A child who has been exposed to the effects of sympathetic joy will himself become a person who does not envy others and who is not overly competitive. Such a person will have no room in his heart for selfishness, greed, or, hatred.

When a child has reached adulthood and has a career and a family of his own, his parents should practice the last great virtue of equanimity. This is one of the most difficult things for Asian parents to practice. It is hard for them to allow their children to become independent in their own right. When parents practice equanimity, they will not interfere with the affairs of their children and not be selfish in demanding more time and attention than the children can give. Young adults in the modern society have many problems. An understanding parent of a young couple should not impose extra burdens by making unnecessary demands on them. Most importantly, elderly parents should not try to make their married children feel guilty by making them feel that they have neglected their filial obligations. If parents practice equanimity, they will remain serene in their old age and thereby earn the respect of the younger generation.

When parents practice these four virtues towards their children, the children will respond favorably and a pleasant atmosphere will prevail at home. A home where there is loving kindness, compassion, sympathetic joy and equanimity will be a happy home. Children who grow up under such an environment will grow up to be understanding, compassionate, willing workers and considerate employers. This is the greatest legacy any parent can give to his child.[21]

Dhammānanda's straightforward advice is an excellent example of why the world's great religions have had and continue to exert such a profound influence on humanity. It exemplifies the dynamism of religion, its ability to reformulate and reapply its most foundational teachings in response to changing historical circumstances. At several points in his writing, Dhammānanda refers to changes

---

[21]Venerable Sri Dhammānanda, *A Happy Married Life: A Buddhist Perspective*, 39–41.

and new problems that have arisen in modern Asian societies, and then shows ways in which important, fundamental Buddhist principles can help one to deal with change and solve problems. This kind of adaptability, as well as the immediate, if difficult, practicality of the teachings expressed here, show us some of the reasons why a great religious tradition like Buddhism can continue to speak to people's most pressing concerns about life. To paraphrase the Buddhist folk song quoted at the very beginning of this chapter, it is indeed most difficult to bring religion—in this case the Buddha's way of loving-kindness, compassion, sympathetic joy, and equanimity—into the home, but here Sri Dhammānanda has pointed his fellow Buddhists to a way in which it is possible in practice. And echoing the conviction that comes at the end of the passage of the *Sigālovāda Sutta* quoted at the beginning of this section, he is sure that the results will be a family environment that is "peaceful and free from fear." Furthermore, in Sri Dhammānanda's statements at the outset of the passage quoted above, in which he identified the parents' primary responsibility as "development of a child's mind," and in the *Sigālovāda Sutta*'s first two injunctions to parents, which were to restrain a child from doing evil and support a child in doing good, we find that another responsibility of Buddhist parents is, not surprisingly, to teach their children the Dharma. Modern Buddhist books on family life encourage parents to read religious stories to their children, and to establish a religious fervor in them. Throughout the Pali canon, parents are referred to as *pubbācariyas* or "first teachers." In those particular statements from Dhammānanda and the *Sigālovāda Sutta,* one can see the attempt to foster the Dharma according to its basic definition, found in a verse from the *Dhammapada,* a verse that so many Buddhists regard as expressing the essence of their religion:

> To refrain from all evils, to cultivate good, to purify one's mind: this is the teaching of all the Buddhas.[22]

At other times when householders asked the Buddha about which qualities parents should cultivate most in caring for their children, he responded by praising what are called the "four qualities of togetherness" (*cattāri saṅgaha-vatthūni*), which are generosity (*dāna*), loving speech (*peyyavajja*), productive livelihood (*atthacariyā*), and impartiality (*samānattatā*). The first and third qualities seem to be ones that in traditional Buddhist societies have rested more with fathers, who go outside of the home and work to provide food and clothing for their children. Indeed, there is a discourse from the Pāli canon where a layman named Dīghajanu asks the Buddha how he can best support his wife and children and make them happy. The Buddha responds by telling him that there are four ways to ensure his family's happiness. The first is that the father should be skilled, efficient, earnest, and energetic in whatever profession he is engaged in, and that he should know it well. Second, he should protect the income that he has earned righteously, with the sweat of his brow. Third, he should keep company only with good friends who are faithful, learned, virtuous, generous, and intelligent. Finally, he should spend reasonably in proportion to his income, neither too

---

[22]*Dhammapada*, v. 183.

much nor too little.[23] So, it seems that the duties that a father in particular owes to his children are specifically economic. He should earn enough and then protect his earnings well enough so that his children can be fed and clothed comfortably.

Just as the Buddha is well known by Buddhists for having taught a practical middle way between self-indulgence and severe asceticism, and a philosophical middle way between what he regarded as the two extreme perspectives of nihilist worldviews and eternalist beliefs in a soul or creator God, here he seems, especially in the fourth piece of advice, to be preaching an economic middle way, in which one spends enough to keep one's children happy, but does not spend too much, thus leaving them wanting for more. Once again, we are shown here another source of religion's great appeal and influence over the ages. Here in the case of Buddhism, as with the world's other great religions, we have a tradition that simultaneously addresses issues concerning the highest spiritual life and philosophical intricacies, as well as the nitty-gritty financial concerns of the average householder.

Whereas the duties specifically assigned to the father in Buddhism typically have to do with living a productive life and providing economic support, the duties specifically associated with the mother in Buddhism are usually associated with emotional support, such as loving speech and impartiality, which were the second and fourth qualities frequently praised by the Buddha, on the subject of parental care for children. As the reader will recall from the Buddha's discourse on the seven kinds of wives, it was the motherly, sisterly, and friendly wives who embodied and provided the family with such positive emotional qualities as kindness, gentleness, affectionate caring, and love. Perhaps the best summation of what Buddhism has regarded as the ideal mother in relation to her child, are the following verses from a *Jātaka* story, where the bodhisattva sings the virtues of his mother:

> Kind, sympathetic, my refuge, she fed me at her breast.
> A mother is the way to the divine states, and she loves you the most.
>
> She nursed and fostered us with care; graced with good gifts is she.
> A mother is the way to the divine states, and she loves you the most.[24]

WHAT DO CHILDREN OWE THEIR PARENTS?

On the subject of what children owe their parents, the *Sigālovāda Sutta* says:

> There are five ways in which a child should worship his mother and father as the eastern direction. Having been supported by them, I will support them. I will perform their duties for them. I will keep up the tradition. I will be

[23]Aṅguttara Nikāya II, 106.

[24]Sonadanda Jātaka.

worthy of my heritage. After my parents' deaths, I will distribute gifts on their behalf.[25]

With the exception of the final injunction, which refers to a common ancient Indian funerary practice, the *Sigālovāda Sutta* is surprisingly quite general here in its instructions to children, given the very specific nature of the advice on familial relations given in the rest of the *sutta*. So, to learn more about children's obligations to their parents in Buddhism, we will have to turn to other sources.

Along with the *Sigālovāda Sutta,* by far the most well-known discourse on family life among Buddhists—Theravāda Buddhists in particular—is the following one from the Aṅguttara Nikāya. In this passage, the theme of parental kindness, caring, and love continues, but the context is what children owe their parents in return:

> O monks, those families in which mother and father are worshipped in the home are comparable to Brahma. Those families in which mother and father are worshipped in the home are ranked alongside the first teachers of old. Those families in which the mother and father are worshipped in the home are ranked alongside the gods of old. Worthy of offerings, o monks, are those families in which mother and father are worshipped in the home.
>
> "Brahma," o monks, is a term for mother and father. "First teachers," o monks, is a term for mother and father. "Gods of old," o monks, is a term for mother and father. "Worthy of offerings," o monks, is a term for mothers and fathers. Why so? Because mother and father do much for children, they bring them up, they nourish them, and they introduce them to the world.
>
>> Parents are called "Brahmā" and "first teachers."
>> Compassionate to their flock of children,
>> They are worthy of offerings.
>> Thus the wise should worship them, pay them due honor,
>> Serve them with food and drink, clothing and beds,
>> Anoint their bodies, and bathe and wash their feet.
>
>> For giving such service to their parents,
>> In this life sages will praise that man,
>> And in the next life he will attain the bliss in a divine realm.[26]

The phrase *brahmā ti mātāpitaro,* "mother and father are (called) '*brahmā,*'" is one that is frequently repeated by Buddhists to this day. We have already discussed the significance of the term *brahmā,* so here it will suffice to remind the reader that it refers to the highest divine reality. As we have also said, the goals of *nirvāṇa* or *bodhi* are regarded by Buddhists as the truly ultimate attainments, higher than any godly realm. However, to say that parents are *brahmā* is enormously high praise indeed, for it is similar to saying that one's parents are like the highest gods. This is reinforced by the statement that follows in the passage above, which says that parents are like the gods of old. Especially for lay Buddhists, rebirth in a

---

[25]Dīgha Nikāya III, 190.

[26]Aṅguttara Nikāya II, 69.

brahmā-loka or "divine world" is a high spiritual achievement, the fruition of a great store of the most virtuous past action (*karma*), and is thus second only to *nirvāṇa* and *bodhi* as a spiritual accomplishment.

Another way in which this *sutta* establishes the extremely high status of parents in the eyes of Buddhist children is through calling the parent *āhuneyya* or "worthy of offerings." Being worthy of gifts or offerings is an honor otherwise reserved in Buddhism for what is called the "noble and great community" (*ariya mahāsaṅgha*) of monks and nuns, who are regarded as even higher than divine beings or gods, because they are devoting their lives fully to the ultimate goal of the religion, liberation from suffering. Indeed, in the Theravada tradition, the term for a person who has attained *nirvāṇa,* an *arahant,* means "worthy," in just this sense of one who is worthy of veneration and offerings because of his or her supreme realization. So, in an important sense, children are being told to honor their parents as they would honor the most highly accomplished figure in the religious life.

The offerings that parents are worthy of receiving are explicitly laid out in a popular modern pamphlet for young Buddhists entitled *Love Your Parents:*

> The looking after the welfare of one's parents should be done, not merely in its outward form of reverential worshipping of one's parents . . . , but by also providing them with various kinds of food and drink, clothes to wear, to protect them from the heat and cold, and comfortable beds and chairs. This attention and loving care that parents are entitled to can come only from good and loving children. . . . By doing their duty in this manner, the children are not only praised by the wise, but, on their deaths will, it is said, be born in a divine realm.[27]

In comparing the contents of this popular pamphlet with the *sutta* quoted at the outset of this section, one can see how ancient teachings have been brought into modernity, and how they are seen as still relevant. The very concrete contents about what material comforts children should provide to care for their parents are almost identical in both passages, as is the promise of a divine future rebirth for the child who so attends to his parents. Indeed, future rewards for *karma* done well toward one's parents (and others), and future punishments for *karma* done badly, still loom large for Buddhists. Later in the *Love Your Parents* pamphlet, the reader is reminded that those children who have been properly cared for and taught by their parents, but who do not look after their own parents' welfare, and instead become disobedient and troublesome toward them, are said in the sacred texts to be destined for rebirth in one of the hell realms. By way of contrast, the pamphlet also reminds the reader of scriptural passages which say that children who constantly care for their parents are blessings (*maṅgala*) not only to their parents, but to their whole village, country, and race.[28]

Ideally in Buddhism, desire and fear are two aspects of human experience that can and should be overcome by the diligent and sustained practice of virtue

---

[27]Egerton C. Baptist, *Love Your Parents* (Singapore Buddhist Meditation Centre, 1982), 12.

[28]Ibid., 14.

(*śīla*), meditation (*samādhi*), and insight (*prajñā*),[29] and so desire for a divine rebirth and fear of a hellish rebirth should not be the primary motivating factors
for treating others, especially one's parents, well. It should be clear by now that
the primary motivating force should be a genuine and deep sense of compassion.
For children, Buddhism teaches that sense of compassion, accompanied by gratitude, can be engendered by reflecting on all of the emotional and material support that one's parents have provided. The importance in Buddhism of realizing
the enormous generosity of one's parents and wanting to reciprocate in kind was
made clear to this author recently, in hearing a teaching given by a highly regarded *lama* or "teacher" in the Vajrayāna tradition. After guiding his students
through an esoteric, advanced visualization exercise, the lama rather dramatically
changed the topic of his teaching, and began to speak to his audience, which was
comprised mostly of American college students from upper-middle-class families, about how important it was to recognize the great debt of gratitude that
they owed their parents, and how extremely fortunate they were to have the opportunity to be in an environment of inquiry and learning—an opportunity, he
emphasized once more, that was largely made possible by the love and generosity of their parents.[30] Along very similar lines, the Theravada tradition teaches
that even if children were to carry one's mother on their shoulders for one hundred years, they would not come close to repaying their parents for all that they
have done for their children.

In most Buddhist cultures to this day, it is also emphasized that the time when
children can best try to compassionately repay the debt of gratitude they owe
their parents is when they are aging and infirm. In marked contrast with American culture, in most Buddhist cultures it is regarded as the height of ingratitude
and selfishness to neglect one's elderly parents or send them out of the home.[31]
Those who look after the parents only long enough to ensure reception of an
inheritance or the like are seen as the worst kind of children.

Buddhist expectations of what children owe their parents are by no means
reserved for older or adult children. Children at a very young age are instilled
with lessons that teach them to have the greatest respect for their parents. One
way to understand what the most important lessons are for young children, concerning their obligations to their parents, is to look at what is taught in school
primers or textbooks about the Dharma. At a young age, children are not ready
to absorb the teachings as they are expressed in canonical literature, and so these
primers give us the best perspective on what Buddhist teachings are selected as
most important for small children, and how those teachings are imparted. In
most societies that are predominantly Buddhist, there is often no marked separation between religious and secular education. There are also other institutional

---

[29]*Śīla, samādhi,* and *prajñā* are known in Buddhism as the "three trainings," and are
regarded as the main components of its paths to liberation.

[30]Public teaching given by Lama Norlha at the Kagyu Pende Kunchab, Annandale-on-
Hudson, New York, 3/27/00.

[31]One notable exception here is Tibetan culture, in which elderly parents are sent out of
the main house to reside in smaller quarters on a family's property, and are mostly
expected to fend for themselves.

structures set up to establish Buddhist values in young people. For example, in Sri Lanka, there are special "Dhamma schools" where children can be sent to receive their education and, in an interesting adaptation of Christian practice that became well known during the centuries when Western colonial powers ruled the country, there are also what are known as "Buddhist Sunday schools."

As early as step two in a popular Dhamma school primer entitled *Buddhism: A Graduated Course,* there is a section called "My Precious Parents." The section reads as follows:

> The Buddha has said:
>
> Noble and holy are the parents. They are the first teachers of children. Therefore, all children should love them, respect them, honour them, and be obedient to them. When the parents are sick, children should help them and nurse them. When the parents are old they should be affectionately looked after by the children, remembering all the good things they have done to make the children happy.
>
> Following the Buddha's advice I worship them daily:
>
> You brought me up with loving care,
> Introducing me to important people everywhere.
> You have wonderful qualities, which are so rare.
> To me, you have always been very fair.
> So, my dear father, I kiss your feet and say:
> "To displease you, I'll never dare."
>
> For ten long months you bore me,
> Risking your own life;
> Fed me, nursed me, showered me with love,
> Throughout the day and night.
> You were always behind me,
> Never letting me out of your sight.
> You taught me more than anyone else,
> What is really proper and right.
> So, my dear mother, I lovingly kiss your feet and say:
> "As before, please show me the way."[32]

This poem, which in its simple language and rhyming format is almost surely meant to be memorized and thus taken to mind and heart by Buddhist children, clearly directs them to many of the same lessons that are found in the scriptural passages already discussed in this section—the lessons of the divine status of parents and of the debt of gratitude and reciprocal compassion that is owed to parents, especially in their waning years, for their caring support and teaching, which are never to be forgotten.

The authority of seniority is also something that is extremely important in Buddhist cultures, from the hierarchy of monastic organizations to that of lay

---

[32]Sanath Nanayakkara et al., *Buddhism: A Graduated Course (Step Two)* (Colombo: Buddhist Cultural Center, 1993), 52–53.

families. The lesson that parents also deserve respect and obedience because of their seniority is also brought out in the Dhamma school primer series referred to above. In step three of this series, this is taught through the retelling of a popular Buddhist tale from the *Jātakas,* a genre of stories about the Buddha's previous lives that have always enjoyed immense popularity and moral influence among Buddhists of all traditions. The tale tells of an elephant, a monkey, and a partridge, all of whom live in the vicinity of the same tall banyan tree, but who cannot seem to get along with one another. When the three animals could no longer bear the unpleasant situation, they entered into a discussion about who had lived for the longest time. The elephant said that he had known the banyan tree since it was a small bush, and the monkey said that when he was young, he could pick leaves from its highest branches. When the partridge said he had once dropped some dung that contained the seed that became the banyan tree, they all agreed that the partridge was the most senior among them, and thus was worthy of the elephant's and monkey's highest respect and obedience. The story closes by saying that ever since then, the three lived happily together.[33]

WHEN THE FAMILY BREAKS DOWN: WHAT HAPPENS THEN?

Of course, not everyone can coexist as happily as the elephant, monkey, and partridge eventually did, and one of the major roles of religious teachers and texts over history has been to help families solve the problem of internal conflict. Obviously, conflict causes suffering for all involved in it. The central doctrine of Buddhism, known as the Four Noble Truths, teaches that in order to transcend suffering, one needs to become aware of the cause or causes of suffering, so that one knows what to eradicate in the course of one's spiritual practice. In the case of family conflict or dissolution, the *Kalahavivāda Sutta* or "Discourse on Disputes and Contention" identifies some of the major causes, and begins to point toward a way to overcome them:

> "Sir," said a questioner, "whenever there are arguments and quarrels, there are tears and anguish, and arrogance, pride, grudges, and insults to go with them. Can you explain how these things come about? Where do they all come from?"

> "The tears and anguish that follow arguments and quarrels," said the Buddha, "and the arrogance, pride, grudges and insults that go with them are all the result of one thing. They come from having preferences, from holding things precious and dear. Insults are born out of arguments and grudges are inseparable from quarrels."

> "But why, venerable sir, do we have these preferences, these special things? Why do we have so much greed? And all the aspirations and achievements that we base our lives on, where do we get them from?"

---

[33]Ibid. (Step Three), 10–14.

"The preferences, the precious things," said the Buddha, "come from the impulse of desire. So too does the greed and so too do the aspirations and achievements that make up people's lives."

"From where, venerable sir, comes the impulse of desire? From where do we derive our theories and opinions? And what about all the other things that you, the Wanderer, have named—such as anger, dishonesty, and confusion?"

"The impulse from desire arises when people think of one thing as pleasant and another as unpleasant. That is the source of desire. It is when people see that material things are subject to both arising and passing away that they gain insight about the world.

"Anger, confusion, and dishonesty arise when things are set in pairs of opposites. The person who is deluded must train himself in the path of knowledge. After realization, this is the truth that this renunciate has declared."[34]

This passage presents the Buddhist philosophy of the Four Noble Truths, in the particular context of interpersonal conflict, in a nutshell. The reason we have suffering (the First Noble Truth: *duḥkha*), or in this case why we enter into disputes, which cause hurtful arrogance, pride, grudges, insults, anger, and dishonesty, is because of our desire (the Second Noble Truth: *tṛṣṇā* or desire is the cause of suffering), our passion, our greed for things that we believe (in our "theories and opinions") will provide lasting satisfaction for us, and so we crave them and become inordinately attached to them ("holding things precious and dear"). From the Buddhist perspective, the problem is that we desire permanence from things in a world in which all things are characterized by their impermanence (*anitya*) and insubstantiality (*anātman* or *śūnyatā*).[35] In particular, it is our preferentiality, our passion-based tendency to label certain things as pleasant and other things as unpleasant that causes our dissatisfaction (another way to render the concept of *duḥkha*). Because we have this preferential tendency, we desire and expect lasting satisfaction out of the things we label as pleasant, and we desire to avoid or become averse to the things we label as unpleasant. It is only when we stop thinking in terms of preference, of like and dislike, and dispassionately and even-mindedly recognize that everything is impermanent ("It is when people see that material things are subject to both arising and passing away that they gain insight into this world") that we will find true happiness both within ourselves, in terms of a peaceful, even blissful, acceptance of the nature of reality, and in our interactions with others. This is the Third Noble Truth: there is an end to suffering. To find that happiness which puts an end to the "anger, dishonesty and confusion" that come with conflict, the Buddha finally recommends that one embark upon a path that will provide that liberating knowledge about the nature of things ("the person who is deluded must train himself in the path of

---

[34] *Sutta Nipāta*, vv. 862–868.

[35] The concept *anātman* means that things are "without self," in the sense that they lack a permanent, unchanging essence, and the concept of *śūnyatā* means that all things lack or are empty of inherent, independent existence.

knowledge"). This is a reference to the Fourth Noble Truth, which is that of the path that leads to an understanding of reality that puts an end to suffering.

The idea that our passion for personal preferences is a main cause of discord within the family is underscored in another scripture from the Pāli canon, the *Dhammacetiya Sutta* or "Discourse on Monuments to the Dhamma." Here the Buddha says that the basis for "mother quarreling with child, child with mother, father with child, child with father, brother quarreling with brother, brother with sister, sister with brother, and friend with friend," are occasions when competing aims and objectives are raised.[36]

So, when the unity of the family is threatened by competing desires and preferences, what solutions has Buddhism offered to restore that unity? One frequently expressed solution by both Buddhist scriptures and teachers is that family members strive to live according to the aforementioned *cāttari saṅgaha-vatthūni* or the "four qualities of togetherness," which are generosity (*dāna*), loving speech (*peyyavajja*), useful living (*atthacariyā*), and equanimity (*samānattatā*). If, Buddhism maintains, instead of stubbornly and selfishly arguing for their own individual opinions and preferences, family members endeavored to be more generous toward each other, compassionate when speaking with one another, concerned about reaching a productive solution to conflicts of interest, and impartial instead of self-centered, there would be much greater harmony within the family. One way that is taught throughout the Buddhist world to overcome selfishness and become sympathetic to others' wants and needs is to imagine putting yourself in another person's position, or as we would say today, putting yourself in someone else's shoes. For example, all Mahāyāna and Vajarayāna Buddhists who want to take up the path of the *bodhisattva,* which is based on the compassionate vow to achieve Buddhahood not only for oneself but for the benefit and eventual enlightenment of all beings, must engage in an important meditative exercise called the "exchange of self and other," which was developed by the great master Śāntideva in his classic work on Buddhist ethics and meditation, the *Bodhicaryāvatāra* or "Guide to the Way of Enlightenment."[37]

Another solution, quite similar in spirit to that expressed by the teaching of the four qualities of togetherness, is found in the *Kosambiya Sutta* or "Discourse to the Kosambians." Although the context of this discourse is a group of quarreling monks, the six measures that the Buddha gives them to solve their troubles are often recommended as solutions to family problems in modern Buddhist treatises and by contemporary Buddhist teachers. The six ways that this *sutta* says pave the way for social harmony are (1) physical acts of loving-kindness (*mettaṁ kāya-kammaṁ*); (2) verbal acts of loving-kindness (*mettaṁ vacī-kammaṁ*); (3) thoughts of loving-kindness (*mettaṁ mano-kammā*); (4) sharing all things with others (*sādhārana-bhogi*); (5) living a life of complete virtue (*sīlesu sīla-samannāgato viharati*); and (6) living according to understanding the truth (*diṭṭhi samannāgato vi-*

---

[36]Majjhima Nikāya II, 121.

[37]See especially Chapter 8, vv. 90–154. There are many fine translations of this Buddhist classic. One recommended version is Kate Crosby and Andrew Skilton, *The Bodhicaryāvatāra* (Oxford: Oxford University Press), 1995.

harati). After declaring these six principles, the Buddha declares, "These are the six memorable qualities that create love and respect, and conduce to happiness, the absence of disputes, to concord, and to unity."[38] As for the first three injunctions here, we see once again that the principle of loving-kindness is absolutely central to the Buddhist way of social harmony, within and without the family. With respect to performing physical, verbal, and mental acts of loving-kindness, in the *Ambalaṭṭhikārāhulavāda Sutta* or "Discourse to Rāhula at Ambalaṭṭhikā," the Buddha tells his son (Rāhula) that before he commits any act, he should first very consciously reflect on its potential harm or benefit to both himself *and* (my emphasis) to others.[39]

Finally, any discussion of family ethics in Buddhism must at least refer to the five moral precepts that all family members, as lay Buddhists, must abide by to the best of their abilities. As one Buddhist monk and teacher put it to me, "The five precepts of refraining from taking life, refraining from taking what is not given, refraining from sexual misconduct—which includes all forms of sexual abuse—refraining from speaking falsely, and refraining from intoxicants that lead to heedlessness, are the heart of Buddhism. Their main concern is social harmony in this world and in the home. The last three precepts in particular are of the greatest importance for maintaining harmony in the home. So for these reasons, one must say that Buddhism begins in the home."[40]

UNCONVENTIONAL FAMILIES, SUPERNATURAL FAMILIES

While it would be absurd to suggest that most lay Buddhists, or even Buddhist monks and nuns who have renounced family life, do not have great love for their families, only an incomplete picture of Buddhism would be given if it was not added here, at the conclusion of our discussion of the ethics of family life in Buddhism, that most Buddhists at least implicitly accept the idea that there is another significant family in their religion, membership in which is of greater ultimate importance than membership in one's own immediate family. This family is the monastic community of monks and, in many Buddhist cultures, nuns. While the possibility of a person leading the family life of a householder attaining *nirvāṇa* or *bodhi* has been recognized by Buddhist traditions in theory, in practice, it is typically assumed that only the monastic life creates conditions that are conducive to achieving the goal of liberation from suffering. Still, there are several familial dimensions to the monastic life. According to the Vinaya Piṭaka, which is the canonical collection of monastic regulations, to be ordained as a monk or a nun, prospective initiates, no matter what age, must have their parents' permission.

---

[38]Majjhima Nikāya I, 322.

[39]Majjhima Nikāya I, 416–417.

[40]Interview with Professor Bhikkhu Dhammavihārī at the International Buddhist Research and Information Centre in Colombo, Sri Lamka, on 1/8/00.

This is an indication of deference to parents and recognition of their high status in Buddhist cultures. Furthermore, it implies that before one can be ordained, it must be clear that one's parents and their household are in good order. Once ordained, the new monk or nun must live in apprenticeship to a mentor, under whose tutelage the monk or nun must live for a period of at least five years. In the case of a monk, he is to regard his mentor as his father and treat him accordingly, acting as his personal attendant and applying himself diligently to what the mentor is teaching—the path of moral conduct (*śīla*), meditation (*samādhi*), and wisdom (*prajñā*). However, in an interesting contrast with family life outside the monastery, the new monk is not obliged to always obey his senior teacher. If he feels that his mentor does not have his best interests at heart, he is free to search for another senior monk to be his mentor. Only when his knowledge of the Dharma is confirmed as sufficiently extensive, and his ethical behavior, according to the high standards of renunciatory discipline of the Vinaya codes, is deemed appropriately reliable, is he freed from his apprenticeship as a "son" to his mentor and allowed to set out on his own.[41] Male and female members of the monastic community, in their renunciation of society and family, in their lives of great simplicity and chastity, and in being exempt from military service and tax paying, are surely members of a most unconventional human family.

Familial terminology is also used to recognize the spiritual progress of those who, through meditation, have attained liberating insights into the nature of reality. In the Theravada tradition, when one gains insight (known as the "Dharma eye") into the impermanent and insubstantial nature of things, and has thus gained entry into the stream of realizations that will inevitably eventuate in the attainment of *nirvāṇa,* one becomes known as a *gotrabhū* or "family member" of the extraordinary lineage of so-called noble persons (*ariya puggala*) who have previously attained such high levels of realization. The *gotrabhū* is regarded as having transcended the existence of those who have a *puthujjana-gotra* or "ordinary person's family." Similarly, in Mahāyāna traditions, those who are progressing along the path of the *bodhisattva* are referred to as "sons and daughters of good family" or "sons and daughters of Buddha."

There are also supernatural families in the more devotionally oriented forms of Buddhism, which subscribe to belief in the existence of savior Buddhas and kinds of *bodhisattvas* known as *bodhisattva-mahāsattvas* or "great beings whose essence is enlightenment." For example, in the most popular form of Buddhism in East Asian Mahāyāna countries, a form known as Pure Land Buddhism, the Buddha Amitābha ("Endless Light") is regarded as the father of the retinue of *bodhisattva-mahāsattvas* who also reside in his heavenly pure land, a retinue that includes the extremely popular figure Avalokiteśvara ("Lord Who Gazes Down"), the *bodhisattva-mahāsattva* who epitomizes compassion. Pure Land Buddhists are devoted to attaining rebirth in Amitābha's pure land or Buddha field, known as the "Land of Bliss" (*sukhāvatī*), where they can learn the Dharma from him and his retinue under optimal conditions and eventually become

---

[41]Richard Robinson and Willard Johnson, *The Buddhist Religion* (Belmont, CA: Wadsworth, 1997), 71.

members of his Buddha family themselves. In the Vajrayāna Buddhism of Tibet and the Himalayan regions, the female *bodhisattva-mahāsattvas* Prajñāparamitā ("Perfection of Wisdom") and Tārā ("Savioress") are regarded as the "mother of all Buddhas," and the compassionate "mother of all beings of the past, present, and future," respectively. Finally, in Vajrayāna Buddhism, there is also belief in what are called the "Five Buddha Families," which are fathered by the Buddhas Amitābha ("Endless Light"), Akṣobhya ("Imperturbable"), Vairocana ("Illuminator"), Ratnasambhava ("Jewel Born"), and Amoghasiddhi ("Unobstructed Accomplishment"). By meditating on these fathers of the five Buddha families, Vajrayāna Buddhists believe that they can transform certain unwholesome states of mind into particular kinds of liberating wisdom.

COMMENTARIES

Judaism on Buddhism

by JACOB NEUSNER

Judaism parts company from Buddhism in its affirmation of marriage and family as the norm: the divine imperative, not a mere concession to a less-than-perfect reality. Man and Woman, Adam and Eve, are created to complete one another: "therefore a man leaves his father and his mother and cleaves to his wife and they become one flesh" (Genesis 2:24). Marriage and family take an integral part in God's design for humanity, and in that context, merely conceding that a superior existence to marriage and family cannot be attained hardly compares. The chapter on Judaism contains numerous statements that affirm marriage as the highest form of social life for man and woman. Not only so, but the Halakhah (law) of Judaism, presupposes that a woman always relates to a man, first the father, then the husband or, in the case of death or divorce, a second husband. And a man without a wife is regarded as incomplete.

If the basic view of Judaism, invoking as it does the creation of the world, treats marriage as an absolute good, in practical terms, Buddhism and Judaism say much the same thing about marriage and family. For when we come to the practical counsel of the Buddhist texts, we should be hard put to find important points of difference from that of the Judaic classical writings. The same advice about mutual respect and dignity takes an important place in both religious traditions. That fact emerges when we turn, for example, to the five ways in which parents show compassion for their children. The parents are to teach upright conduct, support him, teach him a skill, find a wife, and hand over an inheritance to him. Judaism concurs, but adds a critical consideration: the parents also see to the children's education in the Torah. And that will always form a unique, systemically critical focus for Judaism, differentiating that religion from all others at its mythic foundations.

What about the unconventional family? Where the two religions concur is on the possibility of forming a family on other than natural grounds, that is, a supernatural family: the master-disciple circle of Judaism, the monastic community of monks and nuns. These represent comparable social entities: families formed by like-minded persons sharing a common task and commitment. Not surprisingly for Judaism, the generative force for the supernatural family is Torah, in this case, study of the Torah by a disciple with a master, in the manner in which Moses studied Torah as God's disciple, and Joshua as Moses'.

That is why the master of Torah and the father and mother have to be set into hierarchical relationship with one another, as we have seen in the chapter on Judaism. Not only so, but when the master dies, he is mourned in the way in which a parent is mourned, as is stated explicitly in the following:

> *Our rabbis have taught on Tannaite authority:*
>
> These tears on the garments are not to be sewn up again: he who makes a tear for his father or his mother, his master who taught him wisdom, a patriarch, a principal of the court, for having bad news, for having heard blasphemy, when a scroll of the Torah has been burned, for seeing the ruined cities of Judea, the holy house, or Jerusalem. One makes a tear first for the Temple and then enlarges it for Jerusalem.
>
> "he who makes a tear for his father or his mother, his master who taught him wisdom": how on the basis of Scripture do we know this fact?
>
> As it is written, "And Elisha saw it and cried, My father, my father, the chariots of Israel and the horsemen thereof" (2 Kings 2:12)—
>
> "My father, my father": this means to tear one's garment on the death of a father or mother.
>
> "the chariots of Israel and the horsemen thereof": this means that one tears one's garment on the death of his master who taught him wisdom.
>
> *And what is the sense?*
>
> *It is in line with the Aramaic version given by R. Joseph, "My master, my master, who protected Israel with his prayer better than chariots and horsemen could."*
>
> Bavli Moed Qatan 3:7 I.16–17/25A

Still, when we approach the details of the supernatural family—what exactly defines the Buddhist monk or nun as against what defines the disciple of the master of Torah—the two religions part company in a dramatic way. So the resemblances are formal and superficial, the differences substantive. What looks alike turns out not to be alike.

Christianity on Buddhism

by Bruce Chilton

Many Christians in the period since the Enlightenment have found in Buddhist texts and theology a sustaining resource within their own spiritual and practical lives. To a large extent, that is because both religious systems address a similar paradox about how we are to conduct ourselves in families. In a radical sense, both religions portray families as ancillary to the aim of salvation or enlightenment, and yet they normally make familial obligations the field within which those aims are to be worked out.

By putting some of the key texts Brad Clough has cited alongside pivotal Christian Scriptures, we can see this paradox spelled out in a way that enables us to hear their resonance. So, the assertion in *Dhammapada* (v. 43) that "What neither a father, mother, nor other relative can do, so much better does a rightly-directed mind do," invites comparison with the claim that "Whoever does the will of God, he is my brother and sister and mother" (Mark 3:35). On the side of categorical imperatives about family life, the warning to Hermas' wife (*Shepherd of Hermas* II.2.3), "For she does not refrain her tongue, with which she sins; but when she has heard these words she will refrain it, and will obtain mercy," is as pointed in its own way as the advice that "She who is without compassion, defiled in mind, neglectful of her husband and unfriendly, impassioned by other men, a prostitute, bent on murder, let her be called a killer and a wife!" (*Aṅguttara Nikāya* IV, 91, within the *Bhariya Sutta* or "Discourse on Wives").

The treatment of women as subordinate, together with the qualification of that treatment with an emphasis upon the duties that husbands owe their wives, is also a common factor between the two religions, and the exposition of Buddhism here, with its historical clarity, invites comparison with how Christianity adapted the conventions of its world, both accepting and subverting them. The study of these historical and systemic questions, of how people and their genders are seen both as obligated and freed from their familial ties, has been pursued with vigor in recent years. It has become increasingly apparent that there is no "essential" perspective of Buddhism or Christianity (or Hinduism or Islam or Judaism) that wraps up the teaching of the religion into a neat generalization. Rather, a dialectical relationship, between the perceived aim of human life and the ambient demands of a changing social order, plays out within the histories of the great systems we study. The observation and analysis of that dialectic tells us a great deal about the grounding orientations that are involved, without actually resolving into easily packaged insights about how children, men, and women are to behave.

At the level of defining the aim of human life, however, whatever the variations that changing conventions involve, Buddhism and Christianity do manifest distinctive (and comparable) views. Throughout the exposition of Buddhism, the focus on *bodhi* ("enlightenment") is insistent. That insistence is not only a matter of the word that is used, but involves persistent attention to the cognitive issue of how one's behavior contributes to the extinction of desire or to increasing attachment. In contrast, Christianity's emphasis on cognition is targeted, not on the aim of life, but on the related issue of the discernment of God's Spirit. Such discernment is indeed a virtue, but not an end in itself from the point of view of the human being involved. Discerning Spirit opens the possibility that Spirit will transform one's life—and that transformation is the goal of existence. This is what Christianity most typically calls "salvation" (*soteria*).

Salvation, as we have seen, comes at the cost of the self in Christianity, but the self that is lost is changed, rather than extinguished, just as the world is promised a transfiguration beyond its impermanence. Insofar as the discernment of Spirit cooperates in that divine activity, Christians have actively pursued spiritual disciplines, some of them comparable to those of Buddhism. Yet however helpful and even pleasurable knowing God's Spirit can be, Spirit itself transcends human knowing, and can operate without people's awareness. As a result, monastic life has often been prized in the history of the Church, but skepticism as to its ultimate value is also a deep part of Christian tradition.

Confronting as we do a similar paradox of obligation to and freedom from families, Buddhists and Christians have found ways to learn from one another, beyond the politesse of benign tolerance. And it is no coincidence that this mutual learning has chiefly been conducted, not among scholars or religious leaders, but among contemplative writers. The best example is the fruitful collaboration between Thomas Merton and D. T. Suzuki,[42] where Christianity's desire to learn from the discernment of Buddhism comes to rich expression.

Islam on Buddhism
by TAMARA SONN

Like Buddhism, Islam stresses a mother's love as a paradigm. One of the most popular sayings in Islam is "Paradise lies at the foot of the mother." And like Buddhism, Islam stresses that the mother's role is to manage the household and nurture the children. The parents are the children's first teachers, and the mother's aptitude for this task is particularly stressed in traditional Islamic teaching. The parents are responsible for training the children in religion, and are expected to secure for them proper education and training sufficient to ensure their success in life. By law, all children are entitled to inherit a share of their parents' wealth, further assuring their well-being in their parents' absence. This nurturing, guidance, and training are to be carried out with kindness balanced by firmness of purpose. That purpose, of course, is to fulfill the will of God as revealed in the Qur'an.

Therefore, unlike Buddhism, Islam does not allow family relationships to overshadow the believers' relationship to God. As important as family relationships are in Islam, they are subordinated to the divine will. Children are to respect and obey their parents, and care for them when they are old. And traditional Islam teaches that wives are to obey their husbands, while more modern interpretations generally stress spouses' mutual respect and concern for each others' wishes. Nevertheless, no one is above the revealed law in Islam, and no one can take the place of God. No human being is to be worshipped or even obeyed if she or he enjoins what is unlawful. Indeed, as the Qur'an stresses repeatedly, all believers are supposed to prescribe what is lawful and proscribe what is unlawful or evil. If someone insists on doing evil, even if that person is a member of one's family, the evil must be resisted.

Yet in Islam the pursuit of religious fulfillment is rarely seen as in conflict with family responsibilities. (There are some historic cases of Muslim mystics [Sufis] who felt it necessary to leave their families in order to pursue enlightenment, but these cases are noteworthy primarily for their deviation from the norm.) Islamic practices are highly practical and carefully geared to promote a strong, healthy, and

---

[42]See Robert E. Daggy, editor, *Encounter: Thomas Merton and D. T. Suzuki* (Monterey, CA: Larkspur, 1988).

stable society, which in Islamic view is a moral society, at the center of which is the family. Therefore, Islam does not see the family as a "fetter" or "bond"; rather, fulfilling family responsibilities is in fact essential to Islamic religious practice.

Furthermore, Islam does not promote a model of celibacy and, in general, rejects the practice. Again, there are rare instances of Muslim mystics who have remained celibate, but the Qur'anic norm is for Muslims to participate in fulfilling the divine will by marrying, procreating, and nurturing the next generation of believers.

Hinduism on Buddhism

by BRIAN K. SMITH

The principal differences between Hinduism and Buddhism on the question of the ethics of family life might be generalized in this way: From the time of its inception in India as a religious path put forward by a world-renouncer, the main (although certainly not the only) emphasis of Buddhism has tended to be on a renunciatory and monastic way of life and the values stemming from that way of life. These values have "trickled down," so to speak, into the Buddhist vision of the moral life of the householder, which is conceived as a kind of worldly version of the monastic life it is meant to emulate. The Hindu tradition, while not without its own renunciatory component, has since the time of the *dharma sutras* (ca. fourth century B.C.E.) tended toward centering religious life on the figure of the householder, the hierarchically governed social order, and the values associated with one's personal and social duties performed within the world. The development of classical, Brahmanical Hinduism was in fact in part a response to the challenges of the world-renunciatory movements in ancient India, Buddhism being the most popular and threatening among them. In response to Professor Clough's representation of Buddhism, I would suggest two areas in which this generalized distinction between the two religions is manifest in terms of the ethics of family life.

First, the spiritual egalitarianism of Buddhism—a feature of many religious movements that emphasize the renunciatory dimension of religious life—has stamped its imprint on the texts and teachings dealing with the family. While Buddhism, no less than the other world religions, has outlined an ideal family structure that strikes us today as being both hierarchical and patriarchal, it has, in comparison to Hinduism, been more prone to delineate family members as at least spiritual equals, all of whom should be the recipient of typically Buddhist virtues such as loving-kindness, generosity, patience, and so forth. In comparison, the emphasis in Hinduism on hierarchy and the refraction of the concept of dharma or duty according to one's place in the structure has resulted in a view of the ideal family in which religiously ordained roles are separated and given different values. Interrelationships between husband and wife and parents and children cannot usually be guided by a universally applicable set of ethical templates; rather, there will be different guidelines for different players and their different relations to others in the family drama.

Second, and also deriving out of the fundamentally renunciatory and spiritually egalitarian nature of Buddhism, among the highest virtues of that religion is compassion—a virtue stressed as more or less supreme in the Mahāyāna traditions, but also of great importance in the Theravāda strands Professor Clough has concentrated upon above. As Professor Clough has written, in Buddhism the "primary motivating force" for living an ethical life in relations with others "should be a genuine and deep sense of compassion." True compassion for others, including those in one's family, requires at least some sense of their basic similarity to one's self. While compassion is certainly not absent in the Hindu view of ethics, and while the renunciatory strand of Hinduism in particular can move in this direction, in what we might call "this-worldly" Hinduism the dictates of one's "own duty" (*svadharma*) include also knowing what that duty is in relation to your place and the place of others within the hierarchical structure of fundamentally different beings. "Compassion," in this system, tends to be replaced with either "service" to one's superiors, or a sense of obligation and duty toward one's inferiors.

SUMMARY

While Buddhism, probably more than any other major world religion, has consistently placed a premium on renunciation of societal and familial life as a necessity for significant spiritual progress to be made, it also has consistently acknowledged that most members of its communities have been unable to take up the life of a monk or nun, and consequently it has developed ways for people to live according to some of this religion's highest ideals, while following the life of the lay householder. This perhaps can be seen most clearly in Buddhism's teachings on family life, in which the virtues of compassion, loving kindness, sympathetic joy, equanimity, mutual support, and moderation are repeatedly espoused.

Sometimes, Buddhism, like other institutionalized religious systems which have become deeply embedded in the cultures in which they flourish, can function as a sanctifier for cultural beliefs which stray from the noble principles noted just above, and which have brought oppression upon certain individuals and groups (such as women) in a society. Perpetuation of socially oppressive beliefs may have a directly detrimental effect on the harmony and well-being of families.

At other times, Buddhism has radically challenged and profoundly altered oppressive cultural beliefs, with the result being greater social and spiritual freedom for families and their members. Ultimately, Buddhism honors most of those individuals who devote their entire lives to the pursuit of liberation from suffering for both themselves and others, yet it still provides many opportunities for the religious growth of those who cannot pursue the monastic way, because of the responsibilities and affection they have for their families.

GLOSSARY

ahiṁsā   "non-violence" towards all living beings

anātman   "not self." The doctrine that teaches that there is no real, permanent essence (such as a Self or Soul) within persons.

anitya "impermanent," transient, changing. The doctrine of impermanence which, along with *anātman* and *duḥkha,* is one of the three characteristics of existence.

arhat/arahant a "worthy one," who has attained nirvana and who is destined to never be reborn in *saṃsāra* again. Aspiring *arhats,* like *bodhisattvas,* also devote much of their religious life to compassionately helping others to spiritually progress.

Avalokiteśvara/Chenrezig the *bodhisattva* considered to be the epitome of compassion

bodhi the "awakening" or enlightenment achieved by a Buddha, in which liberating insight into the true nature of reality, boundless compassion, and abilities to skillfully guide others along the path are fully realized

bodhisattva "enlightenment being," one who has taken the vow to become a Buddha for the sake of liberating oneself and others, who will attain that goal but continue to take rebirths in *saṃsāra* until all beings are liberated from suffering, and who compassionately helps others along the way. The term sometimes is used to refer to the Buddha before he attained *bodhi.*

brahma–vihāra "the divine abodes," the four moral and contemplative virtues of compassion, loving kindness, sympathetic joy, and equanimity

Buddha "Awakened/Enlightened One," any being who realizes *bodhi,* often applied specifically to Śākyamuni Buddha (born Siddhārtha Gautama, probably around the mid-sixth century B.C.E.), who is regarded as the Buddha of this world age

Dharma the teaching of the Buddha

duḥkha/dukkha "dis-ease," suffering, unsatisfactoriness, angst

Jātaka "Birth Stories," attributed to the Buddha about his previous lives, during which he perfected the virtues necessary to produce, through the law of karma, his rebirth as the persons who would become the Buddha

karma "action," any intentional deed performed by body, speech, or mind, that will result in corresponding effects of happiness or *duḥkha* in this life or a future lifetime. Also, the term refers to the law or principle governing these moral cause and effect relations.

mettā "loving kindness"

nirvāṇa the goal of Buddhism in which desire, hatred, and ignorance are completely extinguished, and freedom from *saṃsāra* and its suffering is attained

Pāli canon the oldest extant collection of scriptures, whose contents are mostly said to be the words of the Buddha

prajñā liberating "wisdom" or insight into the true nature of reality

samādhi "meditation." Often the term has the more specific meaning of meditative concentration or one-pointedness of mind.

saṃsāra "that which flows around," the cycle of death, rebirth, and suffering, into which beings driven by craving and delusion are repeatedly born

Saṅgha the fourfold community of monks, nuns, laymen, and laywomen (often refers exclusively to the monastic part of the community)

śīla   ethics, morality, virtue

śūnyatā   "emptiness." A corollary of the *anātman* doctrine, this teaching maintains that no phenomena have inherent self-existence.

tṛṣṇā/taṅhā   "thirst," craving, lust, desire

upādāna   "attachment" to the phenomena of this world—objects, ideas, opinions, ourselves, etc.

Vinaya   the section of Buddhist canons that contains the rules of discipline for proper monastic behavior

DISCUSSION QUESTIONS

1. What family value do you think is most important for Buddhists? Why do you identify this value as being the most significant Buddhist one?

2. In comparison with other religious traditions covered in this volume, what distinctively Buddhist perspectives on family life do you think would contribute most positively to a family living harmoniously together? Are there ways in which Buddhist teachings could be seen as lacking, in comparison with the other religions' views on how to live a harmonious family life?

3. On one hand, Buddhism often stresses the necessity of renouncing society and family life, in order for significant spiritual progress to be made. On the other hand, it has explicit guidelines for how families can best remain together as integrated units within society, while living up to some of the religion's highest ideals. How can these two seemingly opposing tendencies be reconciled, from a Buddhist perspective?

4. In what ways has Buddhism broken with traditional beliefs of cultures which it has flourished in, with respect to gender roles within family life? In what ways has Buddhism reinforced or given the sanction of religious authority to traditional beliefs about gender roles?

5. In reading this chapter, what Buddhist teachings on family life did you find yourself being most sympathetic to? Why? What Buddhist teachings on family life did you find yourself being least sympathetic to? Why?

 **INFOTRAC**

If you would like additional information related to the material discussed here, you can visit our Web site: http://www.wadsworth.com

APPENDIX

Where Do We Find the Authoritative Statements of the Religious Traditions?

When we represent the views of the religions treated here, we rely upon and cite at some length the classical and authoritative sources of those traditions. The writings on which we base our accounts are the ones that the generality of the faithful of the respective traditions acknowledge as authoritative. That is to say, whatever other writings groups of the faithful of those religious traditions may value, the ones on which we draw exercise authority for all of the faithful within the large and diverse religious tradition at hand.

We recognize that many diverse writings and viewpoints are encompassed by each tradition treated here. For all of them trace long histories, played out over vast spaces and many centuries. Surely over time people formed conflicting opinions on the basis of diverse experience. And in today's world, the faithful of Judaism, Christianity, Islam, Buddhism, and Hinduism divide into competing, often conflicting groups. Reform and Orthodox Jews differ on important religious questions, as do Protestant, Catholic, Orthodox, and Mormon Christians, Sunni and Shi'ite Muslims, Theravāda and Mahāyāna Buddhists, and Vaishnava and Shaivite Hindus. Not only so, but individual practitioners of the great religious traditions accept the faith but also pick and choose and form their own ideals in dialogue with the received ones. But all those who practice (a) Judaism refer to the Torah, all who practice (a) Christianity build upon the Bible, all Muslims base themselves on the Qur'an and the Sunna of Prophet Muhammed, all Hindus acknowledge the authority of the Vedas, and all Buddhists see their authoritative texts as "Buddha-speech." So in portraying the Judaic, Christian, Muslim, Hindu, and Buddhist views on the issues we address, we refer specifically to documents or doctrines to which all of the faithful of Judaism, Christianity, Islam, Hinduism, and Buddhism, respectively, will refer and affirm. Whatever writings may find a hearing in the diverse systems of the families of

Judaism, Christianity, Islam, Hinduism, and Buddhism, the sources cited here will enjoy authoritative standing in their respective traditions. That is what we mean when we call them "classical."

JUDAISM

Like Christianity, Judaism begins in the writings of ancient Israel and appeals to the Hebrew Scriptures that the world knows as "the Old Testament" and Judaism calls "the Written Torah." But Judaism appeals also to oral traditions called "the Oral Torah." So, like Christianity, Judaism values additional writings. To state the matter in simple language: the New Testament is to the Old Testament as the Oral Torah is to the Written Torah. What is the meaning of this key word, "Torah"?

The word covers a number of matters. "The Torah" refers first of all to the Pentateuch, the Five Books of Moses, Genesis, Exodus, Leviticus, Numbers, and Deuteronomy. These are inscribed in a scroll, read aloud in synagogue worship, carefully protected as a holy object: "the Torah." So by "the Torah" Judaism means, the object, the holy scroll that sets forth the Pentateuch. But the Torah is comprised, further, by the remainder of the Hebrew Scriptures, the prophets and the writings. The prophets are the books of Joshua, Judges, Samuel, Kings, Isaiah, Jeremiah, and Ezekiel, as well as the twelve smaller collections. The writings encompass Psalms, Proverbs, Chronicles, Job, the Five Scrolls (Lamentations, Esther, Ruth, Song of Songs, a.k.a. Song of Solomon, and Qoheleth, a.k.a. Ecclesiastes). All together, if we take the first letters of the three words—Torah, Nebi'im, and Ketubim—the Torah (Pentateuch), Prophets (Hebrew: Nebi'im), and Writings (Hebrew: Ketubim) yield the Hebrew neologism for the Old Testament, TaNaKH.

But since Judaism, like Christianity, values further traditions as divinely revealed at Sinai, by "the Torah," more writings are encompassed. Specifically, classical Judaism, which took shape in the first seven centuries of the common era (= A.D.), by "the Oral Torah" means traditions revealed by God to Moses at Sinai—oral traditions right along with the Written Torah (Genesis through Deuteronomy). These other traditions were preserved orally, in a process of oral formulation and oral transmission, from Sinai through prophets and elders, masters and disciples, until they were finally reduced to written form in a set of documents that reached closure from ca. 200 to ca. 600 C.E. (= A.D.). All together, these documents are classified as "the Oral Torah," meaning the repositories of the oral tradition of Sinai.

What are the documents that initially comprise "the Oral Torah"? The first and most important of them is the Mishnah, a law code of a deeply philosophical character, closed at 200. The code quickly attracted commentators, who analyzed its contents and clarified and applied its rules. The work of the commentators was put together and written down. It reaches us in two Talmuds, that is, two distinct traditions of explanation of the Mishnah, the Talmud of the Land of Israel, which reached a conclusion at ca. 400 C.E. in what was then Roman-ruled Palestine, and the Talmud of Babylonia, finished at ca. 600 C.E. in Iranian-ruled Babylonia (approximately the area of central Iraq today).

Once the work of explaining the Mishnah got under way, the same approaches to the reading of the received tradition led the Judaic sages to provide the Hebrew Scriptures with compilations setting forth extensive explanation and amplification. This work of rereading Scripture in light of contemporary questions was called "Midrash," from the Hebrew word *darash*, meaning search. In the formative age of the Judaism based on the written and the oral traditions of Sinai, a number of compilations of readings of scriptural books were completed. In particular, books of the Written Torah that are read in synagogue services received systematic exposition. To the book of Genesis was attached Genesis Rabbah (the amplification of Genesis); so too to Leviticus, Leviticus Rabbah; to Exodus came a work amplifying the normative rules of Exodus, called Mekhilta Attributed to R. Ishmael; to Leviticus another legal commentary, Sifra; to Numbers and Deuteronomy legal commentaries called Sifré to Numbers and Sifré to Deuteronomy. Four of the Five Scrolls—Ruth, Esther, Song of Songs, and Lamentations—were systematically reread. In medieval times, other compilations addressed the books of the Written Torah neglected in the formative age.

These are the sources utilized in the account of Judaism's positions on the practical issues addressed in these pages. Most Judaic religious systems we know today—Reform, Orthodox, Conservative, Reconstructionist, New Age, and the like—value other writings in addition, but all share in common the Torah, oral and written, that took shape in ancient times, differing on its authority and its meaning. And, needless to say, other writings, authoritative for one Judaism or another, take up the same topics. But most Judaisms would concur on the pertinence of the sources cited here, even though each Judaic religious system will assign its own weight to the classical sources and will, further, add to the list of authoritative writings further documents of its own choosing. So "Judaism" here is represented by its formative and normative writings.

CHRISTIANITY

The Scriptures of Israel have always been valued within the Church, both in Hebrew and in the Greek translation used in the Mediterranean world. (The Greek rendering is called the "Septuagint," after the seventy translators who were said to have produced it.) Those were the only Scriptures of the Church in its primitive phase, when the New Testament was being composed. In their meetings of prayer and worship, followers of Jesus saw the Scriptures of Israel "fulfilled" by their faith: their conviction was that the same Spirit of God that was active in the prophets was, through Christ, available to them.

The New Testament was produced in primitive communities of Christians to prepare people for baptism, to order worship, to resolve disputes, to encourage faith, and like purposes. As a whole, it is a collective document of primitive

Christianity. Its purpose is to call out and order true Israel in response to the triumphant news of Jesus' preaching, activity, death, and resurrection. The New Testament provides the means of accessing the Spirit spoken of in the Scriptures of Israel. Once the New Testament was formed, it was natural to refer to the Scriptures of Israel as the "Old Testament."

The Old Testament is classic for Christians, because it represents the ways in which God's Spirit might be known. At the same time, the New Testament is normative: it sets out how we actually appropriate the Spirit of God, which is also the spirit of Christ. That is why the Bible as a whole is accorded a place of absolute privilege in the Christian tradition: it is the literary source from which we know both how the Spirit of God has been known and how we can appropriate it.

Early Christianity (between the second and the fourth centuries C.E.) designates the period during which the Church founded theology on the basis of the Scriptures. Although Christians were under extreme—sometimes violent—pressure from the Roman Empire, Early Christianity was a time of unique creativity. From thinkers as different from one another as Bishop Irenaeus in France and Origen, the speculative teacher active first in Egypt and then in Palestine, a common Christian philosophy began to emerge. Early Christianity might also be called a "Catholic" phase, in the sense that it was a quest for a "general" or "universal" account of the phase, but that designation may lead to confusion with Roman Catholicism at a later stage, and is avoided here.

After the Roman Empire itself embraced Christianity in the fourth century, the Church was in a position to articulate its understanding of the faith formally by means of common standards. During this period of Orthodox Christianity, correct norms of worship, baptism, creeds, biblical texts, and doctrines were established. From Augustine in the West to Gregory of Nyssa in the East, Christianity for the first and only time in its history approached being truly ecumenical.

The collapse of Rome under the barbarian invasions in the West broke the unity of the Church. Although the East remained wedded to the forms of Orthodoxy (and does so to this day), the West developed its own structure of governance and its own theology, especially after Charlemagne was crowned as emperor of the Romans by Pope Leo III on Christmas day in 800 C.E.

To severe arguments regarding political jurisdiction, East and West added doctrinal divisions. The pope was condemned by a synod in Constantinople in 876 for failing to prevent a change in the wording of the Nicene Creed that had become accepted in the West. A papal legate in 1054 excommunicated the patriarch of Constantinople. But even those acts pale in comparison with what happened in 1204: European Crusaders on their way to Jerusalem sacked and pillaged Constantinople itself.

European Christianity flourished during the Middle Ages, and Scholastic theology was a result of that success. The Scholastics were organized on the basis of educational centers, Thomas Aquinas at the University of Paris during the thirteenth century being the best example. During the periods of Early Christianity and Orthodoxy, theologies as well as forms of discipline of worship were developed for the first time. Scholastic theology was rather in the position of systematizing these developments for the usage of the West. At the same time, Scholastic theologians also rose to the challenge of explaining Christian faith in the terms of the new philosophical movements they came into contact with.

The Reformation, between the sixteenth and the eighteenth centuries, challenged the very idea of a single system of Christianity. Martin Luther imagined that each region might settle on its own form of religion, while in England the settlement was on a national basis and in Jean Calvin's Geneva the elders of the city made that determination. But in all its variety, the Reformation insisted that the Bible and worship should be put into the language of the people, and that their governance should be consistent with their faith.

From the eighteenth century until the present, Christianity in its modern form has been wrestling with the consequences of the rise of rationalism and science. The results have been diverse and surprising. They include Protestant Fundamentalism, a claim that the Bible articulates certain "fundamentals" that govern human existence, and the Roman Catholic idea of papal infallibility, the claim that the pope may speak the truth of the Church without error. In both cases, the attempt is made to establish an axiom of reason that reason itself may not challenge. But modern Christianity also includes a vigorous acceptance of the primacy of individual judgment in the life of communities: examples include the Confessing Church in Germany, which opposed the Third Reich, and the current movement of Liberation Theology in Central and South America.

Today, Christians may use many combinations of the sort of sources named here to articulate their beliefs, and the resulting pattern is likely to be as distinctive as what has been produced in the past.

ISLAM

The absolute foundation of Islam is the Qur'an (which used to be spelled phonetically as "Koran"), Islam's sacred Scripture. The Qur'an is believed to be the literal word of God, revealed through Prophet Muhammad, in the early seventh century C.E. in Arabia. (The Arabic word *qur'an* means "recitation.") Muhammad is called the prophet of Islam, but he is not considered its founder. In fact, he is called the last prophet of Islam, the "seal of the prophets" (Qur'an, Sura [chapter] 33:40). He is believed to be the one chosen by God to deliver the full and final message of God to humanity. Islam's beginnings are believed to be primordial; the Qur'an tells of a sacred trust assumed by humanity that guided their very creation. God created human beings specifically to carry out the divine will of creating a just society. (The Arabic word *islam* means "submission"—to the will of God.) The Qur'an then names a number of prophets, beginning with Adam and including many known to Jews and Christians, though not necessarily as prophets (Noah, Abraham, Moses, and Jesus, for example). It also includes others unknown to the earlier scriptural traditions, such as Shu'aib, Salih, and Hud. All the prophets have brought essentially the same message, although some communities have allowed their scriptures to be corrupted. The scripture revealed through Prophet Muhammad is considered the most complete. It provides the necessary correctives to misinterpretations of earlier messages, and the guidance required for effectively carrying out the will of God on earth.

But the Qur'an is not a law book. Of its 114 verses, only a few deal with specific legislation, such as those prohibiting female infanticide, prostitution, usury, and gambling; those imposing dietary restrictions (the prohibition of alcohol and pork); and those specifying family law on issues such as inheritance, dower, and arbitration in divorce. The majority of the Qur'an's verses deal with theological teachings, such as the oneness of God, and moral themes, establishing general standards for virtue and justice. What is more, they were revealed gradually, over some twenty-two years. Over that period, many of the themes developed, some made more specific, some exemplified by the Prophet's words and example.

Those words and examples, though not part of the Qur'an itself, are considered essential to full understanding of Scripture, since the Qur'an itself said repeatedly that Prophet Muhammad set the best example of how to follow its teachings. Collectively known as the Sunna ("way" or normative practice; also spelled Sunnah) of the Prophet, reports (*ahadith*; sing.: *hadith*) of these examples were originally transmitted orally from one generation to another. But by the second century after the Prophet's death in 632 C.E., scholars began to recognize the need to record these reports. They collected as many individual reports as possible, then carefully screened them for authenticity, organized, and codified them. By the third century after the Prophet (late ninth/early tenth century C.E.), there were six major collections of hadith reports for Sunni Muslims. (Shi'i or Shi'ite Muslims, a minority who differ with the Sunni Muslims on issues of community leadership, compiled other collections of hadith reports, and by the eleventh century C.E. had identified three major books of Sunna.) Two of the Sunni collections (those of ninth-century scholars Muhammad al-Bukhari and Muslim ibn Hajjaj al-Nisabur) were designated by the majority of scholars at the time as most authoritative.

The hadith collections, and especially those of al-Bukhari and Muslim, are the basis of commentaries purporting to amplify the meaning of Qur'anic verses (*tafsir*), and provide essential precedents in Islamic legislation (*fiqh*). Islamic law (collectively known as Shari'a; also spelled Shari'ah) is the basis of Islamic life—personal and collective. There are four major schools of Islamic law for Sunni Muslims, and another for Shi'i Muslims. Other, smaller groups of Muslims rely on other formulations of normative behavior. But all Muslims agree that the sources for knowledge of normative behavior are the Qur'an and the Sunna of the Prophet. They are, therefore, the sources used in the treatment of issues presented in this volume.

HINDUISM

The principal texts of Hinduism in which ethics in general, and the ethics of practical matters such as family life, work, and personal virtue, in particular, are covered are those that deal with *dharma,* meaning "duty" or "law." Some references to this topic already appear in the various texts collectively known as the Vedas (ca. 1200 B.C.E.–400 B.C.E.), especially in the philosophical and mystical treatises known as the Upanishads. The works that concentrate on dharma, however, are the somewhat later Dharmashastras and Dharmasutras, some of which have been collected and translated by Georg Buhler under the title *The Sacred Laws of the Aryas* (reprint ed., Delhi: Motilal Banarsidass, 1975). Among these dharma texts, the most important and comprehensive is the Manusmriti; this work has recently been translated by Wendy Doniger with Brian K. Smith as *The Laws of Manu* (Harmondsworth, Middlesex, England: Penguin Books, 1991). These texts on dharma have been regarded and used by Hindus for many centuries as the authoritative guidelines for personal and social duties of an ethical nature.

References to ethics may also be drawn from texts called the Puranas, encyclopedic and sectarian compilations composed during a long period between 200 C.E. and 1700 C.E. Another source for ethical instruction is two epics of the Hindu tradition, the Mahabharata and the Ramayana, both of them compiled between 300 B.C.E. and 300 C.E. The two epics serve as the foundations for Hindu culture and religion; their characters, stories, and plotlines are familiar to nearly everyone in India and are extremely important popular sources for ethical guidance.

Of especial importance is a text enfolded within the Mahabharata and preserved separately: the Bhagavad Gita. The Gita consists of a dialogue between a warrior named Arjuna and his charioteer, the Lord Krishna. In the course of the work, Krishna instructs Arjuna as to how to best perform his duty, or dharma, especially in circumstances where the right thing to do is not always obvious. The Gita has been translated into English many times, most recently by Barbara Stoler Miller as *The Bhagavad-Gita: Krishna's Counsel in Time of War* (New York, Bantam Books, 1986).

BUDDHISM

Buddhism begins with Gautama, the Awakened One (*buddha*), who lived and taught in India in about the fifth century before the common era; scholars frequently give 563–483 B.C.E. as the dates of his life, but they are not certain. Buddhism spread subsequently to many lands in Asia, from India to Sri Lanka and Southeast Asia, and from India to Central Asia and then to China, Korea, and Japan, always developing and adapting as it spread; more recently, it has been embraced and transformed in Europe and the Americas. In this process, its authoritative ideas, practices, experiences, and values have been multiplied in almost every way imaginable, and the modern historian sees Buddhist authoritative literature as a record of that grand process. The resulting diversity of Buddhist life has been so exuberant that we do well to speak of Buddhism in the plural—Buddhist traditions—for this helps us to remember that the basic premise of this series applies to Buddhism alone; the point can be made by altering just slightly the statement made by Jacob Neusner in the preface, "even where [different parts of a religion] appear to resemble one another, they turn out to be different" and thus we have to be careful against being misled by failing to recognize that "what looks alike . . . may upon closer examination prove quite different, and difference may well obscure the meaning of points of concurrence."

When approached with the yardstick of the relatively simple canons of authoritative literature in Islam, Judaism, and Christianity, Buddhists may appear to accept an extraordinarily wide variety of texts as containing authoritative statements. All Buddhists do not accept the same texts, however, and there is no single canon on which all Buddhist religious systems build. In fact, there are very few individual texts that can be found in every Buddhist tradition, not even those statements that a modern historian would take as the record of the teaching of Gautama Buddha, the founder of Buddhism. Moreover, the size of individual canons accepted by particular traditions—whether these are defined on sectarian grounds (for example, Zen Buddhism) or cultural grounds (for example, Tibetan Buddhism)—can be huge in their own right, and we might think of them more as a library than as a "canon" or "scripture." The Chinese Buddhist canon, to take one impressive example, is almost one hundred thousand pages long. It goes without saying that the contents of these many texts are varied, and frequently contradictory.

To give an account of the literature that has been authoritative for Buddhists would be to give an account only of difference, and this would obscure some important points of concurrence among Buddhists. We still need to generalize about *Buddhism* out of the study of many *Buddhisms*. One generalization we should keep in mind is that Buddhists have not seen their own history as simply as the modern historian portrays it. Even as all Buddhists have acknowledged the importance of Gautama Buddha, in their honor and devotion to him especially, no Buddhists have seen the Truth that he taught as beginning with him as an individual. He taught Truth, to be sure, but he only rediscovered it. Truth has been known and taught by others too. Consequently, the record of Gautama's teachings is not the only place where one should expect statements of Truth. There have been other awakened persons, other Buddhas, and there will be more in the future; indeed, Truth is directly available to us now.

This observation is key for understanding where the contemporary Buddhist and the academic student of religion both can look for authoritative statements on the topics addressed by this series. We turn to *buddhavacana*—"Buddha-speech"—but it is important to remember that this does not name the record of the teachings of Gautama Buddha, nor was it ever only that in the eyes of Buddhists. The basic point we should keep in mind is best expressed in an old Buddhist aphorism: "what Buddha taught is well-said," but it is equally true to say that "what is well-said Buddha taught."

Buddha-speech comes in a number of genres, some concerned with monastic life, others with philosophy, but for the purposes of this series the most important genre will be *sutra*. This is a generic name given to an account of an occasion on which a Buddha taught. Most *sutras* are attributed to Gautama Buddha, although a modern historian would be skeptical about any claims that the *historical* Gautama Buddha actually taught some of the most influential ones, such as the *Lotus Sutra* (Saddharmapundarika) and the *Sutra on the Land of Bliss* (Sukhavativyuha), to name two texts that have been very important in East Asian Buddhism.

Another generalization about Buddha-speech draws our attention to another source of authoritative statements. Buddha-speech contains two kinds of sentences: some that have obvious meanings that do not require interpretation or elaboration in order to be understood, and others, that do require their meaning "to be drawn out." The latter kind of sentence thus requires commentary for proper understanding, and the commentaries by learned or spiritually accomplished teachers on Buddha-speech are as authoritative as sources of valid and useful knowledge as Buddha-speech itself. Buddhist sectarian differences can stem from disagreements over what counts as Buddha-speech as well as from disagreements over how to understand a text or statement about which there is concurrence that it is Buddha-speech. In this series, we will turn then both to Buddha-speech and to commentaries to find authoritative statements that address the practical issues of everyday life taken up by each volume.